THIRD EDITION

Objectives, Methods, and Evaluation for Secondary Teaching

MICHAEL A. LORBER
and
WALTER D. PIERCE
Illinois State University

ALLYN AND BACON
Boston London Toronto Sydney Tokyo Singapore

Library of Congress Cataloging-in-Publication Data

Lorber, Michael A.
    Objectives, methods, and evaluation for secondary teaching /
  Michael A. Lorber and Walter D. Pierce.—3rd ed.
        p.   cm.
    ISBN 0-13-629163-5
    1. High school teaching.   I. Pierce, Walter D.
  II. Title.
  LB1737.A3L65   1990
  373.11'02—dc20   89-35978
                                               CIP

Dedicated to Ellen Jane

This title is the third edition of a book formerly titled
Objectives and Methods for Secondary Teaching

 Copyright © 1990, 1983, 1977 by Allyn and Bacon
A Division of Simon & Schuster, Inc.
160 Gould Street
Needham Heights, MA 02194

Printed in the United States of America

10 9 8 7 6 5 4 3   96 95 94 93 92

ISBN 0-13-629163-5

Figure 1, page 13, from James Popham and Eva Baker, *Systematic Instruction* (Englewood Cliffs,
N.J.: Prentice-Hall, 1970), p. 19. Reprinted by permission.
Figure 2, page 14, from Robert J. Kibler, Larry L. Barker, and David T. Miles, *Behavioral Ob-
jectives and Instruction* (Boston: Allyn & Bacon, 1970), p. 13. Reprinted by permission.
The knowledge structure "Forming the Earth's Surface" and associated objectives, rationale, and
unit plan are used with the permission of Kenneth D. Lovett, R.R. 4, Box 336, Clinton, IL 61727.

Contents

Preface   x

Note to Instructors   xii

1 _ The Goals of Education   1

INTRODUCTION 1

SAMPLE OBJECTIVES 2

FIVE GENERAL GOALS 2

To Educate All the Children of All the People 2 __ To Provide for Individual Differences 3 __ Teaching the Basics 3 __ The Integration of Knowledge 3 __ Learning How to Learn 6

FORMAL STATEMENTS OF EDUCATIONAL GOALS 6

Morrill Act (1862) 7 __ The Committee of Ten (1893) 7 The Committee on College Entrance Requirements (1899) 8 The Commission on the Reorganization of Secondary Education (1913) 8 __ The American Youth Commission (1937) 9 __ The Educational Policies Commission (1938) __ 10 __ The National Association of Secondary School Principals (1947) 10 __ The National Defense Education Act (1958) 10 __ The Elementary and Secondary Education Act (1965) 11 __ The National Commission on Excellence in Education (1981) 11

THE EFFECT OF BROAD GOALS 13

SUMMARY 15

STUDY QUESTIONS 16

NOTES 16

2—Writing Precise Instructional Objectives   18

INTRODUCTION   18

SAMPLE OBJECTIVES   19

FIELD LEARNING THEORY VERSUS BEHAVIORISM LEARNING THEORY   19
> *Gestalt, Cognitive-Field, and Perceptual-Field Psychology 19 — Behaviorism 20 — Points to Consider 20*

FOUR-STAGE MODELS OF INSTRUCTION   21

PRECISE INSTRUCTIONAL OBJECTIVES   22
> *Sources of Instructional Intent 23*

THE BASIC PARTS OF PRECISE INSTRUCTIONAL OBJECTIVES   25
> *Observable Terminal Behavior 25 — Conditions 26 Minimum Acceptable Standard 28*

PRACTICE IN WORKING WITH OBJECTIVES   30
> *Practice Exercise 1: Characteristics of Objectives 30 Self-Test: Rewriting Poorly Stated Objectives 32 Self-Test: Characteristics of Objectives 32*

SUMMARY   34

STUDY QUESTIONS   35

NOTES   35

3—Classifying and Using Precise Instructional Objectives   36

INTRODUCTION   36

SAMPLE OBJECTIVES   37

THE TAXONOMY AND ITS USE   37

THE COGNITIVE DOMAIN   38
> *Knowledge 38 — Comprehension 38 — Application 39 Analysis 39 — Synthesis 40 — Evaluation 41*

THE AFFECTIVE DOMAIN   41
> *Receiving 43 — Responding 43 — Valuing 43 Organization 43 — Characterization 44*

THE PSYCHOMOTOR DOMAIN   44
> *Reflex Movements 44 — Basic-Fundamental Movements 45 — Perceptual Abilities 45 — Physical Abilities 46 — Skilled Movements 47 — Nondiscursive Communication 48*

TESTING OBJECTIVES FOR CLARITY   49

USING PRECISE INSTRUCTIONAL OBJECTIVES   49

AN OVERVIEW OF COGNITIVE LEVELS   51

PRACTICE IN CLASSIFYING OBJECTIVES   53
  *Practice Exercise 1: The Domains 53 — Practice Exercise
  2: Cognitive Levels 54 — Practice Exercise 3: Psychomotor
  Levels 55*

SUMMARY   56

STUDY QUESTIONS   58

NOTES   58

4—Selecting Instructional Procedures   **59**

INTRODUCTION   59

SAMPLE OBJECTIVES   59

PREASSESSING ACADEMIC STATUS   60

ADDITIONAL SOURCES OF INFORMATION   61

PREASSESSING MAINSTREAMED STUDENTS   62

THE STANFORD SKILLS   62
  *Set Induction 63 — Communicating the Objective 63 —
  Stimulus Variation 64 — Closure 64*

TEACHER-DIRECTED INSTRUCTIONAL
PROCEDURES   65
  *Formal and Informal Lectures 65 — Questioning 70
  Demonstrations 72 — Guest Speakers 73*

STUDENT-DIRECTED ACTIVITIES   75
  *Discussions 75 — Brainstorming 81 — Panel
  Discussions 82 — Sociodramas 82 — Field Trips 82*

SMALL-GROUP ACTIVITIES   85

OUT-OF-CLASS ASSIGNMENTS   86

SUMMARY   88

STUDY QUESTIONS   89

NOTE   89

5—Selecting Instructional Media   **90**

INTRODUCTION   90

SAMPLE OBJECTIVES   91

GENERAL UTILIZATION FACTORS   91

READING MATERIALS 92
  Textbooks (Traditional) 92 — Textbooks (Programmed) 94

AUDIO AIDS 95
  *Radios, Record Players, and Tape Recorders 95
  Telephones 96*

VISUAL AIDS 97
  *Pictures 97 — Opaque Projectors 97 — Slides and
  Filmstrips 98 — Bulletin Boards 98 — Maps and Globes,
  Charts and Graphs 99 — Chalkboards 100 — Overhead
  Projectors 100 — Realia 102*

AUDIOVISUAL COMBINATIONS 102
  Multimedia Kits 102 — Films and Television 102

COMPUTERS AS TOOLS FOR LEARNING 104
  *Problems in Using Computers in Schools 105
  Advantages of Using Computers in Schools 105
  Developments in CAI 107*

SUMMARY 108

STUDY QUESTIONS 109

NOTES 109

6—Planning Instructional Units 111

INTRODUCTION 111

SAMPLE OBJECTIVES 111

ORGANIZING CONTENT 112
  *Structures of Disciplines 112 — Time-Frames 113
  Concepts 113*

WAIMON KNOWLEDGE STRUCTURES 114

TOPICAL OUTLINES 116

RATIONALES 116

UNIT PLANNING 117
  *What Is a Unit Plan? 118 — The Herbartian Unit 118
  Components of a Unit Plan 119*

ORGANIZING THE PARTS OF A UNIT:
AN ABBREVIATED MODEL 121

DECIDING ON OPTIONAL ACTIVITIES 122

PLANNING FOR EVALUATION AND FUTURE
USE 122

SUMMARY 123

CHAPTER APPENDIX A 125

CHAPTER APPENDIX B 126

STUDY QUESTIONS 127

NOTES 127

7_Planning Daily Lessons 128

INTRODUCTION 128

SAMPLE OBJECTIVES 128

PROS AND CONS OF LESSON PLANNING 129

LESSON PLAN COMPONENTS 130

*Objectives 130 __ Content 132 __ Instructional
Activities 132 __ Materials 133 __ Evaluation 133 __ Time 133
Miscellaneous Components 134*

SAMPLE LESSON PLANS 134

*Concept Lesson, One Period 134 __ Concept Lesson to Be
Carried Over to the Following Day 137 __ Concept Lesson
One (20-Minute Micro-Lesson) 138 __ Concept Lesson
Two (20-Minute Micro-Lesson) 139 __ Analysis Lesson
(20-Minute Micro-Lesson) 141*

SUMMARY 142

STUDY QUESTIONS 142

8_Measurement and Evaluation 144

INTRODUCTION 144

SAMPLE OBJECTIVES 144

BASIC PRINCIPLES AND TERMINOLOGY 145

*Obtain Enough Samples 145 __ Obtain Different Kinds of
Samples 146 __ Check for Validity 146 __ Assess Student
Effort 147 __ Check for Reliability 147 __ Criterion-
Referenced Evaluation 148 __ Norm-Referenced Evaluation 149*

TEACHER-MADE TESTS 149

*Objective Tests 150 __ Multiple-Choice Items 152
Principles for Building Multiple-Choice Items 154 __ True-
False Items 156 __ Matching Items 157 __ Completion
Items 158 __ Preparing the Test and the Students 159
Essay Tests 160 __ Validity and Use of Teacher-Made Tests 164*

STANDARDIZED TESTS 164

General Utilization Factors 167

ALTERNATE EVALUATION PROCEDURES 167

ITEM ANALYSIS 169

CALCULATING GRADES 170

*Grade Contracts 171 __ Preset Levels 171 __ The
"Curve" 171 __ Eyeballing 177 __ Credit–No Credit 179*

GRADING AND SUBJECTIVITY 179

REPORTING GRADES 179

TEACHER EVALUATION 180
  Teacher Performance Tests 181 — Audio and Video Recordings 182 — Interaction Analysis Techniques 182 Student Evaluations 182 — Peer Evaluations 183 Administrative Evaluations 183

SUMMARY 183

STUDY QUESTIONS 185

NOTES 186

9 — Classroom Management 187

INTRODUCTION 187

SAMPLE OBJECTIVES 187

BASIC MANAGEMENT PRINCIPLES 188
  The Goal Is Self-Control 188 — Help Students Be Successful 189

MASLOW'S HIERARCHY OF NEEDS 189
  Physiological Needs 190 — Safety Needs 192 — Love Needs 195 — Esteem Needs 195 — Self-Actualization Needs 197

GUIDELINES FOR PRECLUDING DISCIPLINE PROBLEMS 198

BEHAVIOR MODIFICATION: OPERANT CONDITIONING 201

BEHAVIOR MODIFICATION: REALITY THERAPY 205

THE THIRD PRINCIPLE—HAVE A REASONABLE PLAN FOR DEALING WITH PROBLEMS 207

POTENTIALLY DANGEROUS PROBLEMS 210

HYPERACTIVITY AND CHEMOTHERAPY 210

LEGAL TERMS AND ISSUES 211

SUMMARY 213

STUDY QUESTIONS 215

NOTES 215

10 — Individualizing Instruction 216

INTRODUCTION 216

SAMPLE OBJECTIVES 216

THE SYSTEMS APPROACH TO
INDIVIDUALIZING 216

THE EFFECT OF SELF-INSTRUCTIONAL PACKAGES
ON THE CURRICULUM 219

*The Purpose of Package Programs 219 __ The Teacher as
Advisor 220 __ Packages as Enrichment Activities 220
Remedial Use of Packages 221 __ Extended Absence 221
Partial Package Programs 221 __ Modified Systems
Programs 222 __ Model of a Self-Instructional Package 222*

SUMMARY 231

STUDY QUESTIONS 232

11 _ Managing Co-Curricular Activities 233

INTRODUCTION 233

SAMPLE OBJECTIVES 233

EXTRA PAY 234

TYPES OF SPONSORSHIP 235

*Clubs 235 __ Student Government 237 __ Pep
Groups 237 __ Service Organizations 238
Classroom-Associated Organizations 238 __ Events 238
Trips 238 __ Dances 239*

SALES AND MONEY MANAGEMENT 239

ELECTIONS AND APPOINTMENTS 244

CONTRACTS 245

WORKING WITH OFF-CAMPUS
ORGANIZATIONS 245

ASSEMBLIES 246

DISRUPTION OF CLASSES 247

OBJECTIVES OF EXTRA-CURRICULAR
ACTIVITIES 247

THE SCHOOL CALENDAR 248

SUMMARY 249

STUDY QUESTIONS 249

Appendix 250
Index 267

Preface

This book is based on the idea that students can acquire certain skills and information that will help them become humane and effective teachers. Because this era emphasizes technology and competency-based instruction, we have incorporated into both the content and the structure of the text principles that are central to the uses of technology in education and to the competency-based movement. We have, for example, suggested certain precise instructional objectives at the beginning of each chapter. We have also included a model to help students understand competency-based instruction, examples of a knowledge structure and a self-instructional package, an in-depth look at computer applications in education, and ways of evaluating and maintaining classroom control that are consistent with competency-based approaches.

While we believe there is much of value in the competency-based movement, we do not believe the teaching-learning process is quite as precise or clear-cut as some proponents of the movement imply. Success as a teacher depends as much on the development of personal characteristics conducive to good teaching as on the mastery of specific teaching skills and procedures. A good teacher must, for example, be tolerant of individual differences and opinions, be fair with people, and be receptive to new ideas. These attributes, and others like them, are difficult to specify as precise instructional objectives or to evaluate as specific competencies. Nonetheless, they are as crucial to good teaching as any of the skills and procedures about to be presented.

Many people contributed time, effort, and ideas to this book. We thank Mr. William D. Gattis, Vice-President of the Education Division of Tandy Corporation, who provided information concerning educational technology and much material support; Ms. Barbara Neu, a representative of Educational Activities, Inc., who provided many materials and insights; Dr. Morton

Waimon, Professor of Education at Illinois State University, who developed what we have called the Waimon Knowledge Structure; Mr. Kenneth Lovett, who developed the model knowledge structure and unit plan used in this text; Dr. Edward Streeter, who, in a commencement address at Illinois State University in 1988, clearly enunciated the idea of "educating all the children of all the people"; Dr. Clifford Edwards, Professor of Education at Brigham Young University, and Dr. Larry Kennedy, Professor of Education at Illinois State University, who provided many of the insights that found their way into this text; and the members of the Secondary Education area in the Department of Curriculum and Instruction at Illinois State University who contributed many ideas. In addition, we express our thanks and appreciation to David M. Lorber, who contributed many hours of work and his technical expertise in word processing to preparing the drafts of this text.

Note to Instructors

The sequence of chapters in this text is meant to facilitate your instruction. Chapter 1 is intended to stimulate class discussion concerning some of the basic goals of educators. Chapters 2 and 3 actively involve students in writing instructional objectives for their own subject areas, and Chapters 4 and 5 facilitate whole-class activities, such as demonstrations and discussions of various instructional procedures and instructional media. These five chapters deal with all but one of the areas students need to know about in order to construct instructional units and lesson plans. The area that is omitted is measurement and evaluation.

In previous editions, the topic of measurement and evaluation was dealt with before the planning of instructional units and individual lessons. This sequence makes sense because it is consistent with the instructional models discussed in Chapter 2 and because students need that information to plan complete units and lessons. In this edition the measurement and evaluation chapter follows the planning chapters. The reason for the change is that many instructors include micro- or peer teaching as a part of their course. Such teaching usually emphasizes the use of particular skills and giving students experience in front of a group. Expecting students to prepare and administer tests or quizzes for a micro-lesson distracts them from the main purposes of the experience and reduces their already short instructional time. To minimize this problem, the chapter on measurement and evaluation is presented after the planning chapters. If you do not use microteaching in your course or if you simply prefer the earlier sequence, teach Chapter 8, Measurement and Evaluation, before teaching Chapters 6 and 7. The sequence of the remaining chapters has not been changed.

—1—

The Goals of Education

INTRODUCTION

The goals of education are fairly clear—peace on Earth, good will toward men and women, and perhaps increasing control over our environment. What is less clear is what needs to be done to achieve these goals. As early as about 350 B.C. Aristotle is quoted as saying, "As things are . . . mankind are by no means agreed about the things to be taught. . . . Again about the means there is no agreement."[1] In more recent times (1986), Larry Cuban, in *Teachers and Machines,* pointed out that educators are expected to:

- Socialize all children, yet nourish each child's individual creativity.
- Teach the best that the past has to offer, but insure that each child possesses practical skills marketable in the community.
- Demand obedience to authority, but encourage individual children to think and question.
- Cultivate cooperation, but prepare children to compete.[2]

As a prospective educator, what do you think should be the goals of education? One way to approach the question is to try to explain the qualities you would like to see in your students if you met some of them ten years after you had them in class. As you list certain skills, knowledge, and attitudes, you are actually describing some of your ideas of appropriate goals of education. Other people might well emphasize different points if they were to answer the same question. These differences of opinion account for the never-ending discussion about educational goals.

While there is and always has been some disagreement about educational

1

goals, many of our current goals originated centuries ago, and many have gone from prominence to virtual nonexistence during the course of history. These pendulum-like swings are still with us, and they have a direct impact upon what occurs in the classroom. This chapter explains how some of the most important of these goals developed.

SAMPLE OBJECTIVES

When you complete this chapter, you will be able, in writing, to:

1. Explain the origin of educational goals such as "to educate all the children of all the people" and "to integrate knowledge," and to cite at least two factors that have historically hindered the achievement of each one.
2. Explain at least one major effect that each of the following groups have had on education in the United States: the Committee of Ten on Secondary School Studies (1893), the Committee on the Reorganization of Secondary Education (1918), and the National Commission on Excellence in Education (1983).
3. Develop at least four goals for American schools and, for each goal, provide a rationale based either on historical data or logical argument, explaining why that goal should be included among the most important of educational goals.
4. Give at least two reasons that the very idea of educating makes it difficult to specify specific educational goals and to have students achieve them.

FIVE GENERAL GOALS

There is no shortage of educational goals; people have been formulating them for years. However, certain goals—educating all the children of all the people, providing for individual differences, teaching "the basics," integrating knowledge, and helping students learn to learn—seem particularly basic. Since we have not yet fully achieved these goals, perhaps you will become the educational leader who finds ways to move us forward.

To Educate All the Children of All the People

The idea of educating all children probably has its roots in prehistoric times when, as a matter of survival, parents taught their children how to find food and shelter and how to defend themselves. While prehistoric societies might have tried to teach all the children (universal education), the advent of civilization brought about a shift in goals.

Formal education was made possible when the division of labor allowed some individuals to engage in activities other than those directly related to day-to-day survival. The most important of these activities was mediating with the gods, and the men who did the mediating were the priests. As the need for new priests grew, it is likely that the priests selected as their successors their own sons or the sons of wealthy or powerful families. These few were taught the secrets of the priesthood. Thus, the beginning of formal education contained within it the seeds of educational dualism: the practice of providing one kind of education to a select group (usually the male children of wealthy parents) and providing either a different kind of an education, or none at all, to the children of everyone else. Throughout history, the dualistic approach has been far more common than the universal approach.

The ancient Hebrews (about 800 B.C.) came as close to universal education as mankind was to come until the seventeenth century. The Hebrews required all males to be able to read the Torah (the Five Books of Moses). While the Hebrews excluded females from this requirement, societies for the next 3,000 years were even more dualistic. During most of recorded history, only the sons of the wealthiest families could afford a formal education or were expected to get one.

The universal approach reappeared in colonial America when, in 1642, "the General Court (colonial legislature) of Massachusetts passed a law requiring all parents and masters of children to see that their charges were taught reading, the capital laws, the religious catechism and apprenticeship to a trade."[3] Implementation of the law was slow and erratic, but the pendulum was clearly swinging back to universal education. While the idea that all the children of all the people should be educated is now predominant, dualism is still with us in the context of different kinds of education, such as college-bound versus vocational education or, unfortunately, in isolated cases, racial segregation.

To Provide for Individual Differences

Individual differences have always been apparent, although at times they have been virtually ignored. Plato (427–347 B.C.) was very much aware of the importance of such differences. He explained, in his *Republic,* that social harmony could be achieved only when each person recognized his or her own interests and abilities and then found an appropriate niche in society. Differences in interests and abilities would cause some people to become workers, others soldiers, and still others philosophers. Social harmony would exist because individuals would be doing work appropriate to their talents, and they would therefore be happy (rather than frustrated because the work was too difficult or bored because it was too easy).

It should be noted that during Plato's time education was provided primarily by tutors and almost exclusively to the sons of wealthy citizens. As the tutorial approach gave way to group instruction, it became increasingly difficult to provide for individual differences. Today, as we try to educate all the children of all the people, providing for individual differences is more difficult than ever, but the goal remains.

We should keep in mind that accommodating individual differences rarely means individualizing education. To truly individualize education, we would have to develop instructional objectives that fit the unique interests and abilities of each student. This is not economically feasible in today's schools, nor is it the goal of our education system. Educators frequently group students with similar abilities or interests (reading groups in elementary schools and different programs or tracks in high schools), but usually do little more for students unless they have special needs.

Some schools have experimented with self-pacing: having the same objectives for all students, but allowing students to work toward achievement of those objectives at their own paces. One of the earliest such experiments was conducted in the mid-1920s, in Winnetka, Illinois, and a similar experiment was tried during the mid-1960s at Nova High School in Fort Lauderdale, Florida. The same approach was tried from 1970 to 1980 in the teacher preparation program at Illinois State University. Significantly, while each of these trial programs attracted national attention, all of them have since been replaced by more traditional approaches. Self-pacing poses some very difficult problems with respect to logistics, record-keeping and, most important, student motivation.

Teaching the Basics

The cry of "back to the basics" continues to be heard loudly and clearly. The question is, what are the basics? To the ancient Hebrews, being able to read the Torah was the all-important basic. To the Greeks, the basics included the study of rhetoric (use of the language), dialectics (formal logic), grammar (reading, writing, and literature), mathematics, music, civic responsibilities, and participation in a systematic physical fitness program. The Romans adopted most of the Greek educational program, but they minimized the arts and emphasized rhetoric, particularly public speaking. During the Middle Ages (circa 500–1300) educators reduced the list still more by deleting music and physical education. For them, the basics became the trivium—grammar, dialectics, and rhetoric—and the quadrivium—arithmetic, geometry, music (religious chants), and astronomy. These disciplines, with only a few changes, became the seven liberal arts, and they are still considered the basics of higher education. Clearly, each society decides for itself what the basics are and permits the list to vary as different pressures come to bear.

The Integration of Knowledge

One commonly accepted goal of today's schools is to help students develop into knowledgeable, healthy, and aesthetically aware citizens. This goal was shared by the ancient Greeks, who very strongly believed that most aspects of life are so interrelated as to be inseparable. This view was reflected in the Greek goal of helping individuals develop a sound mind in a sound body, and it was the basis for their two-part curriculum: rhetoric, dialectics, grammar, and music for the mind and systematic physical training for the body.

The interrelatedness of knowledge began to be lost as more knowledge became available and people began to specialize. In 1439, William Byngham founded one of the first schools of education, Godhouse College, in England.[4] Although students in the school were already teachers, Byngham started the idea of student teaching, and it is likely that he advocated that students learn subject-matter as separate disciplines. Later, in 1684, Jean Baptiste de la Salle founded a school of education at Rheims, France. Baptiste de la Salle was among the first to organize subject-matter to facilitate group instruction and to advocate the orderly promotion of students from one unit of subject material to another.[5] These early schools of education became known as normal schools because they set the norm or standard for good teaching practices. The idea of breaking knowledge into disciplines and dealing with each discipline separately became widely accepted, and it continues to dominate education today. Regardless of its advantages, this approach does little to convey to students the interrelatedness of knowledge.

In the first half of the 1900s, some educators in the United States tried to break away from the subject-centered curriculum and return to a more interrelated approach. These educators (known collectively as Progressivists) argued that instruction ought to be interdisciplinary and geared to solving social problems. There was great debate about the wisdom of abandoning the traditional subject-centered curriculum and the methods that had become entrenched over the years, so the Progressive Education Association (of which John Dewey was the major spokesman) planned and conducted what may be the largest-scale longitudinal study ever conducted in education: the Eight-Year Study.

The Eight-Year Study (1933–1941) was conducted to see whether students who participated in "progressive" high-school programs would perform as well in college as students who participated in traditional programs. In the first phase of the study, more than 300 colleges and universities were persuaded to waive the usual subject-area and Carnegie unit entrance requirements for students who participated in the study. (A Carnegie unit reflects the completion of at least 120 clock hours in a subject within a school year.) Then, 30 high schools, public and private, large and small, were selected, the only requirement for selection being that the schools had to agree to experiment with a progressive curriculum.

The second phase of the study involved matching each graduate of the 30 schools with another student in the same college who had graduated from a school not in the study and who had, therefore, met the usual entrance requirements. A total of 1,475 matched pairs were studied, and by 1941 the results were in. "Graduates of the thirty schools had higher grade point averages, received more academic honors, and were found to be more precise, systematic, and objective thinkers than their matchees."[6] Finally, empirical data supported the contention that alternative approaches could succeed in preparing students for college.

With such results, the reader may wonder why educators went back to the subject-centered approach with its emphasis on the separateness of knowledge. Part of the answer lies in the reluctance to depart from tradition; teaching separate subjects has been the rule for hundreds of years. Another part of the answer lies in the convenience of dividing knowledge into separate subjects. It is easier to concentrate on one thing at a time, and therefore it is easier to teach and to learn one thing at a time. Still another part of the answer lies in the difficulty of determining the specifics of the various "progressive" experiments that were implemented in the 30 schools.

Unfortunately, none of these reasons changes the fact that we are still far from our goal of enabling students to interrelate all that they learn.

Learning How to Learn

Another commonly accepted goal is to teach students to learn how to learn so that they can continue to acquire new skills, knowledge, and insights throughout their lives. Ironically, education has historically engaged more in indoctrination than in education. Throughout the Middle Ages and into the 1800s, teachers presented students with information or sets of beliefs or laws (often the Bible) and expected them to memorize all or part of the material and to believe it without question. Intellectual curiosity and creativity have been consistently opposed by most educational systems.

The Greeks lit the light of learning with their spirit of inquiry. Philosophers such as Socrates, Plato, and Aristotle believed that people could learn about themselves and the world around them by applying logic, by hypothesizing, and by observing. Socrates gave us the dialectical method (the use of questions and answers but with terms rigidly defined and topics narrowly limited), and Aristotle gave us syllogistic reasoning, wherein major and minor premises lead to conclusions. These learning tools virtually disappeared during the Middle Ages, but they re-emerged during the Age of Enlightenment (1550–1760) with the work of such scholars as Galileo and Sir Francis Bacon. They believed that knowledge could be acquired by the "scientific method," which consists of five steps: (1) identifying the problem, (2) forming a hypothesis or probable solution, (3) gathering data by observing and/or experimenting, (4) interpreting the data, and (5) drawing conclusions.

Even after the Age of Enlightenment, few educators taught their students to use logic or the scientific method to verify what they were taught. It was easier to indoctrinate than to educate. Ultimately, the Progressivists, led by John Dewey, did advocate this approach. Dewey wanted students to engage in reflective or critical thinking, which was essentially the use of the scientific method. The Progressive approach continues to be in conflict with a "basics" approach (Essentialism), and at any given time one or the other is dominant. Currently, the Essentialist approach is dominant.

FORMAL STATEMENTS OF EDUCATIONAL GOALS

The five educational goals just discussed are among the most important that we are working toward, but we rarely see them in writing. If fact, since formal education was, for thousands of years, only for the very few, there was little need to formally state any educational goals. It is likely that when the Roman emperor Antoninus (86–161 A.D.) first decreed that all towns should provide for the salaries of teachers through municipal taxes,[7] that he had certain educational goals in mind and certain expectations of the teachers. If so, your authors have yet to find a record of them.

In the United States there have been numerous goal statements, beginning with the legislation passed in Massachusetts in 1642 requiring "all parents and masters of children to see that their charges were taught reading, the capital laws, the religious catechism and apprenticeship to a trade."[8] Since 1642, a few legislative acts and committees have had a great impact on education and on educational goals in the United States, and some of them are described below. In reading through them, try to determine whether they moved us nearer to, or further from, any of the five goals just discussed, or whether they defined new goals.

The Morrill Act (1862)

By the mid-1700s the Industrial Revolution had begun, and there was a growing need for people who were able to read simple instructions and who could operate the machinery that was increasingly being used. The secondary schools of the day were still patterned after the "Latin grammar schools" established in Massachusetts in 1647, which in turn were patterned after the Latin grammar schools of medieval Europe. These schools were attended by students who had completed a dame school (the equivalent of an elementary school) and who were going on to higher education. By the mid-1800s, the needs of the country had broadened. Unfortunately, the dualism of the past was alive—formal education for the elite and something different or nothing at all for everyone else. The need for workers grew so great that Congress stepped in, even though the Constitution makes no provision for federal involvement in education. In 1862, Congress passed and President Lincoln signed into law the first Morrill Act.

The Morrill Act (sometimes known as the Land-Grant Act) helped establish agriculture and other practical arts as legitimate educational goals. It did this by granting 30,000 acres of federal lands to each state per congressional representative. States were to sell all or part of the land, invest the capital forever, and use the interest to finance instructional costs (building and maintenance costs were excluded) for colleges to provide classes and train teachers in vocational technology courses. In 1890, a second Morrill Act was passed. It specified that federal support for land-grant institutions was to continue and that racial exclusion was not to be practiced (we were, and still are, working on educating all the children of all the people).

The Committee of Ten (1893)

In 1893, the National Education Association tried to formalize the purpose of American high schools. At the time, the population in the United States was almost 76,000,000, and there were approximately 52,000 high school students. (As of 1987, the population was estimated to be 242.2 million, with about 30 million in high school.)[9] The number in 1893 was small, but it was growing quickly as states passed compulsory education laws. The committee was to recommend goals for high schools and help decide whether they should continue to focus on college preparation or become more comprehensive. Among the committee's more important recommendations were these:

1. all pupils should pursue a given subject in the same way and to the same extent as long as they study it at all;
2. every subject should cultivate the pupil's powers of observation, memory, expression, and reasoning;
3. the function of the high schools should be to prepare pupils for the duties of life as well as to prepare them for college; and
4. colleges and scientific schools should accept any one of the courses of study as preparation for admission.[10]

In addition to presenting its recommendations, the committee also presented models of four high-school programs designed to prepare students for college. The effect of the committee's recommendations and models was to keep the primary focus of high schools on college preparation (where it is today) and to emphasize the importance of mastering separate subjects (which we still do today). Obviously, the recommendations of the Committee of Ten have had a lasting impact.

The Committee on College Entrance Requirements (1899)

In 1899 the Committee on College Entrance Requirements of the National Education Association reiterated a triple function of the secondary school:

1. Preparation for life.
2. Preparation of teachers for the common schools.
3. Preparation for college.[11]

That they additionally attempted to paint a more congenial educational picture by stating that programs should be flexible, have a variety of electives, and take into account the students' abilities, points up the NEA's growing concern for and influence over the conditions of learning.

The Commission on the Reorganization of Secondary Education (1913)

By 1913 the Commission on the Reorganization of Secondary Education, appointed by the NEA, recommended what was to become probably the most famous statement of the purposes of the high school. Labeled the "Seven Cardinal Principles of Secondary Education," these aims were memorized by countless numbers of prospective teachers as part of their pre-service training. In an informal study conducted and replicated eight times, with separate groups of twenty to forty prospective teachers and teachers in the field who attempted to construct their own set of aims for the high school, at least six of the original seven principles were *still* on those groups' final lists of worthwhile aims for today's youngsters.[12] A summarized version of the seven cardinal principles follows:

1. *Health.* Good health habits need to be taught and encouraged by the school. The community and school should cooperate in fulfilling the health needs of all youngsters and adults.
2. *Command of fundamental processes.* The secondary school should accept a responsibility for continuing to teach and polish the basic tools of learning, such as arithmetical computation, reading, and writing, that were begun in the elementary school.
3. *Worthy home membership.* Schools should give students an understanding of the interrelationships of the family in order for the give and take to be a healthy, happy affair. Proper adjustment as a family member will lead to proper acceptance of responsibility as a family leader in later life.
4. *Vocation.* The secondary school should teach students to appreciate all vocations. The basic skills of a variety of vocations should be made available to students who have the need or desire for them.
5. *Citizenship.* The students' basic commitment to proper citizenship must be fostered and strengthened during the adolescent years. The secondary school needs to assume this responsibility not only in the social sciences but in all subjects.
6. *Proper use of leisure time.* The students should be provided opportunities while in secondary school to expand the available possibilities for leisure time. (The commission felt that leisure time properly used would enrich the total personality.)
7. *Ethical character.* The secondary school should organize its activities and personal relationships to reflect good ethical character, both to serve as an exemplar and to involve the student in a series of activities that will provide opportunities to make ethically correct decisions.[13]

The seven cardinal principles were an attempt by a group of educators to use the needs of society and the individual as a basis for describing what secondary schools should accomplish. Other attempts were subsequently made to identify the central goals of schooling, and a few of the most noteworthy are described in the paragraphs that follow. Depending upon the prevailing issues of the particular time and place, the statements made by these groups show slight changes in emphasis and style. They are therefore best looked at in terms of the social situation in which they were articulated.

The American Youth Commission (1937)

By 1937 the country was deep in the Depression, and educators were looking at education in terms of how it could help students get and keep jobs. The principle of vocational preparation became predominant: "American youth need opportunity for economic independence. They need information on how to prepare for, find, and hold a satisfying job."[14]

The Educational Policies Commission (1938)

In 1938 the Educational Policies Commission set forth a series of goals arranged in four major divisions with subsections concerning "the educated man." The four main divisions included (1) self-realization, (2) human relationships, (3) economic efficiency, and (4) civic responsibility. A typical goal format under the civil responsibility subsection was: "The educated person respects the law."[15]

The National Association of Secondary School Principals (1947)

After World War II, a shift in priorities increased the emphasis on science. John S. Brubacher credits Herbert Spencer with a large part of the responsibility for this shift because Spencer's essay, "What Knowledge Is of Most Worth," drew wide attention. Spencer's opinion was that, in spite of the commonly held position that the liberal arts are the most worth studying, the priority should actually be on the practical, and he felt the knowledge of most practical worth was science.[16] Certainly the wartime development of radar, sonar, rockets, and atomic bombs did nothing to undermine this popular opinion.

In 1947 the National Association of Secondary School Principals delineated the "Imperative Needs of Youth." These goals repeated, in essence, the seven cardinal principles and added statements on appreciating aesthetics, becoming an intelligent consumer, and understanding the methods and influence of science. The thrust of the list of goals had changed from the general goals we examined at the beginning of this chapter to command of fundamental processes and a re-emphasis on rationality, clear expression of thoughts, and reading and listening with understanding.[17]

The National Defense Education Act (1958)

The first half of the 1950s saw few calls to refocus educational goals, but that calm was shattered on October 4, 1957, when the Soviet Union launched Sputnik, the first manmade earth satellite. Americans were shocked. How could the Russians beat us into space? Why were our schools not preparing better scientists? Strident calls for a more rigorous curriculum and for a greater emphasis on science and mathematics were heard across the land. In 1958 Congress once again involved itself with educational goals by passing the National Defense Education Act (NDEA).

The NDEA made hundreds of thousands of dollars available to schools that were willing to develop and expand science and mathematics programs and, later, foreign language programs. With the support of federal dollars and the public's perception of need, many new programs and materials were developed for teaching students and training teachers in these areas. Achievement in math and science became an important educational goal. The idea of integrating knowledge was virtually ignored, as were individual differences. Students interested in the social sciences or in the arts, for example, received little benefit from the new thrust.

The Elementary and Secondary Education Act (1965)

By 1965 attention had shifted from winning the space race to reforming our own society. President Lyndon Johnson called for the building of a "Great Society," which included, among other things, helping children of low-income families catch up academically to children of middle-income families. Passage of the Elementary and Secondary Education Act in 1965 provided money for programs such as Project Head Start (emphasis on preschool and primary education for children of low-income families) and Upward Bound (emphasis on middle and secondary education for low achievers). Such programs provided more intensive help to disadvantaged students than had been provided earlier; they typically focused on the basics of reading, writing, and arithmetic, but the long-term results of these programs and the programs started under the NDEA have been disappointing.

From 1972 to 1986, the National Assessment of Educational Programs of Princeton, New Jersey, conducted a study of 150,000 students. Results of the study were tabulated and released in June 1988. The results showed that:

1. More than one-fourth of 13-year-old middle schoolers cannot handle elementary school arithmetic.
2. Nearly one-third of eleventh graders say they generally do not understand what the math teacher is talking about.
3. Only 6 percent of 17-year-olds can handle algebra or multistep math problems.
4. Scores for blacks and Hispanics, despite modest gains, lag 7 to 11 percent below those for whites.[18]

During the mid-1980s, disappointment over low scores on standardized achievement tests (the latest yardstick of educational excellence) prompted calls for a revision of educational goals. More important, the new voices represented large segments of the population, and the changes called for are clear and specific.

The National Commission on Excellence in Education (1981)

Questions concerning the ability of the United States to compete with the rising economic powers in Asia and Europe, as well as concern over low test scores, prompted yet another national commission to study education. In 1981, T. H. Bell, the U.S. Secretary of Education, appointed the National Commission on Excellence in Education. It studied the effectiveness of education in the United States and made its report in 1983. The title of the report, "A Nation at Risk: The Imperative for

Educational Reform," foretold its contents. The report concluded that our education system left much to be desired. Some of the facts cited are the following:

1. International comparisons of student achievement, completed a decade ago, reveal that on 19 academic tests, American students were never first or second and, in comparison with other industrialized nations, were last seven times.

2. Some 23 million American adults are functionally illiterate by the simplest tests of everyday reading, writing, and comprehension.

3. About 13 percent of all 17-year-olds in the United States can be considered functionally illiterate. Functional illiteracy among minority youth may run as high as 40 percent.

4. Average achievement of high school students on most standardized tests is now lower than 26 years ago when Sputnik was launched.

5. The College Board's Scholastic Aptitude Tests (SAT) demonstrate a virtually unbroken decline from 1963 to 1980. Average verbal scores fell over 50 points and average mathematics scores dropped nearly 40 points.[19]

6. In many other industrialized nations, courses in mathematics (other than arithmetic or general mathematics), biology, chemistry, physics, and geography start in grade 6 and are required of *all* students. The time spent on these subjects, based on class hours, is about three times that spent by even the most science-oriented U.S. students, i.e., those who select 4 years of science and mathematics in secondary school.

7. "Minimum competency" examinations (now required in 37 states) fall short of what is needed, as the "minimum" tends to become the "maximum," thus lowering educational standards for all.[20]

The commission also felt that while "*the average citizen* today is better educated and more knowledgeable than the average citizen of a generation ago,"[21] the average graduate of our schools and colleges today is not as well-educated as *the average graduate* of 25 or 35 years ago, when a much smaller proportion of our population completed high school and college."[22] In essence, the report said that education standards in our country were too low, that mediocrity was becoming the rule rather than the exception, and that things must change quickly if we are to continue to be a world power. Here are some of the recommendations that the commission made to improve educational standards:

1. "That state and local high school graduation requirements be strengthened and that, as a minimum, all students seeking a diploma be required to lay the foundations in the Five New Basics by taking the following curriculum during their 4 years of high school: (a) 4 years of English; (b) 3 years of mathematics; (c) 3 years of science; (d) 3 years of social studies; and (e) one-half year of computer science. For the college-bound, 2 years of foreign language in high school are strongly recommended in addition to those taken earlier."[23]

2. "That schools, colleges, and universities adopt more rigorous and measurable standards, and higher expectations, for academic performance and student conduct and that 4-year colleges and universities raise their requirements for admission."[24]

3. "That significantly more time be devoted to learning the New Basics. This will

require more effective use of the existing school day, a longer school day, or a lengthened school year."[25]

Note that the recommendations made in the "Nation at Risk" report are different than the recommendations and goal statements made by previous commissions and groups. The recommendations are for specific and observable changes—a delineation of Five New Basics (math, English, science, social science, and computer science), a specific number of years of study for each of these subjects, and more instructional time for everything.

THE EFFECT OF BROAD GOALS

Legislative acts and commission reports such as those listed cause many people to wonder about the value of these broad aims. After all, educational goals have been formulated for thousands of years, and we still have not reached consensus. What is the point of continuing to state such goals? Why is achieving these goals so difficult? Are these the goals that dictate curriculum decisions in individual school districts?

The answer to the first question is easy. We began this chapter by asking you to try to list qualities you would like to see in your students if you met them in the future. You probably had some difficulty specifying those qualities. Societies experience the same difficulty magnified by the number of people involved. Nevertheless, general directions do emerge, and educators try to focus on what our society deems important at the time. Meanwhile, some of the goals have remained alive for centuries and should provide a foundation for your work as an educator.

The answer to the second question is more difficult. One problem is that some people believe that if we teach all students the same things, they will all come out of the schools very much alike in their abilities and beliefs. This idea might be diagrammed as in Figure 1.

A shining example of the impact of this goal is the study of American history, which is mandated by all states in the Union. This particular course has traditionally been a curricular inclusion because many Americans have felt that youngsters should have a knowledge and appreciation of their country's past. If all students learned similar things, they might all end up with similar attitudes.

FIGURE 1

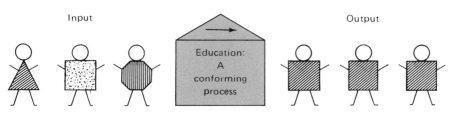

FIGURE 2

The problem with this view of the education process is that, as each succeeding generation learns about its past, it tends to reject much of what its predecessors held near and dear. Looking again at the requirement that all students study American history, it can be seen that, although the original goal was to make Americans of different generations more alike in their knowledge and appreciation of their past, things are not working out quite as expected. Today students learn that, while Washington championed freedom, he also kept slaves; that only some of the colonists supported the Revolution, while others were outright Tories and still others were neutral; that many Americans treated the Indians and the Mexicans badly; and that industrialists were less than fair to their workers during the late 1800s and early 1900s. Each generation of graduating students is quite different as a result of formal education. Schools do change people, for better or for worse. A more accurate diagram of formal education might well look like that outlined in Figure 2.

Obviously, the two effects of education are quite different. Changes could be made in our education system that would increase the uniformity in thinking among graduates. For example, we could admit to the schools only particular students (such as the sons of the very wealthy). This would increase uniformity of the "product" because, since the students were more alike before schooling, they would tend to be more alike after schooling. We would, of course, have to give up the goal of educating all the children of all the people, and we would have to forget about teaching students to learn to learn. Creative thought and uniform thought are at opposite ends of the continuum.

We could also choose to indoctrinate rather than to educate. If we wanted students to simply believe what we told them, rather than to question and to critically examine ideas and beliefs, we could, again, guarantee greater uniformity. Our Pilgrim ancestors might approve. Would you?

The fact is that some of our most treasured goals focus on individual freedoms. Those goals sometimes conflict with our equally treasured goals of giving students the skills, knowledge, and attitudes that we believe they will need to live happy and successful lives. We are continually trying to reconcile these basic conflicts.

Finally, there is the question of whether the broad goals dictate the curriculum decisions made in individual schools. The answer is, no, not much. The reasons are fairly clear. One reason is that teachers tend to teach not only the *way* they themselves were taught, but *what* they themselves were taught. The rewording of a broad goal by a commission in Washington, D.C., does not necessarily bring about a change in a tenth-grade English class in Normal, Illinois.

Another reason is that local school decisions are very much influenced by people who have local power or who are very vocal. For example:

1. The president of a PTA thinks sex education is needed and influences a community action group to push for it. Pressure is exerted through appropriate channels until a sex-education course is adopted by the board.
2. Women in an affluent suburb of a large city picket and petition until courses in women's studies are offered.
3. A parents' organization decides that the schools should have more microcomputers so they hold fund-raisers, purchase the computers, and give them to the schools, expecting that computer-related courses will be offered.

Whatever the general goals are, one thing is certain. We are living in an age of accountability, and teachers must translate broad goals into specific statements. Teachers must be able to explain to students, parents, and administrators what specific goals Johnny and Mary and Sue are working toward. Goals such as integrating knowledge and learning to learn are admirable, but they are long-range goals. Teachers have to state their specific course goals: to explain what students will be able to do after successfully completing the course that they were unable to do before.

The business of specifying instructional goals is so important that the following two chapters are devoted to it. Stating precise instructional objectives in various domains and at various levels puts a working edge on broad educational goals.

SUMMARY

Of the many broad goals that provide the foundation for education in the United States, five of the most basic are: (1) educating all the children of all the people, (2) providing for individual differences, (3) teaching "the basics," (4) integrating knowledge, and (5) helping students learn to learn. Achievement of these goals is hindered by the fact that, while attempting to provide an education to all students, we find it economically and logistically impossible to fully achieve all of the other goals.

In attempting to provide direction to education in the United States, the federal government (which has no constitutional mandate to deal with education) has passed legislation, such as the Morrill Act and the National Defense Education Act, that provided the financial resources for educators to meet needs felt nationwide. Federally appointed commissions and national organizations have issued reports, such as The Nation at Risk, which have prompted other changes in the ways schools operate. These forces have brought consensus, at least concerning some issues, among most educators. For example, most high school curriculums are similar and the content of many courses is also similar. While part of this consensus is due to the ever-present pressure of college entrance requirements, part of it is also due to greater consensus among the American people concerning what the next generation needs to know.

Educational reform measures from coast to coast are reflecting demands for greater rigor and greater uniformity in the schools. While few advocate indoctrinating students instead of educating them, teachers still are under increasing pressure to demonstrate that their students are able to do specific things after instruction that they were unable to do before. Precise instructional objectives are becoming increasingly important.

STUDY QUESTIONS

1. What basic conflicts come into play when educators work toward achieving each of the five goals of education?
2. Why did the ancient Greeks include physical education and music in their educational program?
3. Name and explain the effects of at least two pieces of federal legislation that have fostered changes in the goals or methods of education.
4. Name and explain the effects of at least two national committee or commission reports that have fostered changes in the goals of education.
5. Taking each of the seven cardinal principles individually, explain why it is or is not relevant today.
6. Why was the Eight-Year Study conducted, how was it conducted, and what were its findings?

NOTES

1. Benjamin Jowett, trans., *The Works of Aristotle, Politics,* Book VIII, Ch. 2, Vol. X (Oxford: Clarendon, 1921), p. 1338.
2. Larry Cuban, *Teachers and Machines* (New York: Teachers College Press, 1986), p. 2.
3. *Encyclopaedia Britannica,* 12th ed. s. v. "history of education—United States."
4. J. A. Johnson, H. W. Collins, V. L. Dupuis, and J. N. Johansen, *Introduction to the Foundations of American Education* (Boston: Allyn and Bacon, 1979).
5. J. Mulhern, *A History of Education,* 2nd ed. (New York: Ronald Press, 1959), p. 407.
6. Daniel Tanner and Laurel Tanner, *Curriculum Development,* 2nd ed. (New York: Macmillan, 1980), p. 367.
7. Wayne Dumas and Weldon Beckner, *Introduction to Secondary Education* (Scranton, Pa.: International Textbook, 1968), p. 14.
8. *Encyclopaedia Britannica,* s. v. "history of education—United States."
9. Mark S. Hoffman, ed., *The World Almanac* (New York: Pharos Books, 1988), p. 227.
10. *Report of the United States Commissioner of Education,* vol. 2, parts III and IV, 1892–1893, pp. 1474–75.
11. *National Education Association Proceedings* (Washington, D.C.: National Education Association, 1899), pp. 635–636.

12. Walter D. Pierce, unpublished informal survey of broad goal setting by college students, Illinois State University, 1988.

13. U.S. Bureau of Education, *Cardinal Principles of Education,* Bulletin No. 35 (1918), pp. 5–10.

14. H. R. Douglass, *Secondary Education for Youth in Modern America* (Washington, D.C.: American Council on Education, 1937), p. 137.

15. Educational Policies Commission, *The Purpose of Education in American Democracy* (Washington, D.C.: National Educational Association, 1938), pp. 50, 72, 90, and 108.

16. John S. Brubacher, *A History of the Problems of Education* (New York: McGraw-Hill, 1947), p. 16.

17. National Association of Secondary School Principals, *The Imperative Needs of Youth of Secondary School Age,* Bulletin No. 31 (March 1947).

18. "Education," *Time* 131, No. 25 (June 20, 1988): 79.

19. David P. Gardner, ed., *A Nation at Risk: The Imperative for Educational Reform,* A Report to T. H. Bell, Secretary of Education (Washington, D.C.: U.S. Department of Education, 1983), pp. 8–9.

20. Ibid., p. 20.

21. Ibid., p. 11.

22. Ibid.

23. Ibid., p. 34.

24. Ibid., p. 27.

25. Ibid., p. 29.

2

Writing Precise
Instructional Objectives

INTRODUCTION

In 1921, Boyd H. Bode spoke of the need for educators to give "consideration to what constitutes a good life in the social order."[1] He was concerned that rather than having broad educational goals that would result in good people living good lives in a good society, educators might focus on simplistic, perhaps even superfluous goals, because dealing with such goals is less difficult.[2] He had good reason for concern, and prospective teachers should have the same concern.

Broad goals must be narrowed before they can be achieved. To travel is a broad goal; in order to achieve it, the traveller must narrow it, that is, decide to travel to London or to Paris. The same is true of broad educational goals. Before they are usable in the classroom, they must be narrowed into instructional objectives. Bode was concerned that we might narrow the goals so much that we would lose sight of the original intent. That we might, for example, concern ourselves so much with teaching students to describe "democracy," that we would forget about the larger goal of teaching them how to act as citizens in a democracy.

This chapter will examine: (1) two approaches to instruction, the "field" theorists (Gestalt, Perceptual, and Cognitive) and Behaviorism, and their effect on moving from broad goals to instructional goals, (2) a way to conceptualize the instructional process so that parts of it can be analyzed and improved, and (3) what is meant by the term "precise instructional objective."

SAMPLE OBJECTIVES

When you complete this chapter, you will be able, in writing, to:

1. Explain at least one major difference between the approaches to education advocated by the field theorists and the Behaviorists.
2. Diagram a four-stage model of instruction, label each stage, and explain the purpose of each stage.
3. Explain and exemplify each of the three parts of a precise instructional objective.
4. When given a series of instructional objectives, correctly label at least 80 percent as: (a) lacking an observable terminal behavior, (b) lacking a minimum acceptable standard, (c) lacking both an observable behavior and a minimum acceptable standard, (d) asking for different behaviors, or (e) acceptable as written.
5. Given a specific topic, write three objectives, each of which contains an observable terminal behavior, conditions (when necessary), and a minimum acceptable standard of performance.

FIELD LEARNING THEORY VERSUS BEHAVIORISM LEARNING THEORY

Some educators maintain that education differs from instruction because education is open-ended and continuous, whereas instruction is closed-ended and finite. A few educators (such as Ivan Illich in *Deschooling Society*) have even argued that schools as we know them are not needed.[3] However, we do have schools, and the significant point of debate has always focused on what should be going on in them. Should we follow an approach that tries to keep the broad goals intact as much as possible, or should we specify narrower, more easily achieved goals? At the risk of oversimplification, the first approach is that of the field psychologists and the second that of the Behaviorists. What follows is a brief look at both views.

Gestalt, Cognitive-Field, and Perceptual-Field Psychology

"Gestalt" is a German word that means a whole that has properties that exceed the sum of its parts. When applied to education, the basic idea is that the goal of education is to do more than simply teach specific facts and skills. No one doubts that having facts and skills is important, but the extent to which a person acquires them only partly accounts for the things that person does or does not do throughout life. Other factors—attitudes, health, and even appearance—also influence what a person does or does not do.

Field psychologists, such as Max Wertheimer, Kurt Koffka, Wolfgang Kohler, and Arthur Combs, argue that each person's goals and previous experiences (their perceptual field) have a great effect on what that person actually learns, regardless of what is covered in class. On this basis, Gestaltists believe that instructors should make concerted efforts to connect ideas and pieces of information so that students are more likely to perceive wholes. By analogy, rather than just laying bricks, teachers should help students see the overall design of the house. Further, teachers should take into account the previous experiences and goals of students in planning and providing instruction. Gestaltists want to teach the "whole person," and their ideas have been endorsed by such educators as Jean Piaget and John Dewey.[4]

The Gestaltist approach is more easily used at the primary levels (K–3) than in the upper grades. One reason for this is that, as students' knowledge-bases expand, they can go into greater depth in specific areas. This leads to the departmentalization and separate course offerings that characterize instruction at the higher grade levels.

Another factor complicating use of the field approach is the fact that, for better or for worse, people assess the quality of education on the basis of test scores and, particularly, scores on standardized achievement tests. In order to improve test scores, specific skills and knowledge must be taught and students' mastery of them assessed. This is done more easily with narrow instructional goals than with broad ones, so schools are increasingly behavioristic.

Behaviorism

Behaviorism grew out of the classical conditioning experiments conducted by Ivan Pavlov in the 1890s. Pavlov's success in getting a dog to salivate at the sound of a bell fascinated psychologists. The idea was pursued to see whether humans could also be made to react to specific stimuli. The work of Pavlov and other psychologists, particularly the guru of Behaviorism, B(urrhus) F(rederick) Skinner, was parallelled by the success of American industry during the early 1900s.

Behaviorism with its stimulus-response approach, requires that learning tasks be broken down into small steps taken sequentially. The Industrial Revolution brought with it the same step-by-step approach. For example, to build a car, each part is built and then the parts are assembled sequentially. Since each step in the process is discrete, it is possible to analyze each step in order to make it more efficient. This systems analysis approach is at the heart of Behaviorism. The idea of using the successful industrial model in the schools, parallelled by work of the behavioral psychologists, gave rise to the development of teaching machines and programmed learning and, at the same time, to the idea of stating instructional goals precisely.

Points to Consider

As indicated, some educators have reservations about the behavioristic approach. They fear that so much attention will be focused on the small steps that the larger goals will be forgotten—that we will lose sight of the forest for the trees. Other educators have reservations about the behavioristic approach because they believe that it results in the manipulation of students, as teachers manipulate stimuli in order to get the students to respond as desired. They believe that while it is interesting that

Pavlov could get dogs to salivate, an education should do something other than turn students into automatons who respond without thinking.

While these reservations are legitimate, the fact is that we are living in an age of accountability. Parents, administrators, taxpayers in general, and teachers themselves want to be sure that time and effort on everyone's part are not being wasted in school. They want to know what it is that Johnny and Mary will be able to do when they complete a particular course that they were unable to do before taking the course. In response to calls for more accountability, educators (even in the lower grades) are being called upon to specify instructional objectives that can be achieved within a semester or a year and then to demonstrate that the objectives have been achieved.

It is virtually a certainty that new teachers will find it both necessary and useful to specify relatively narrow instructional goals. Doing so does not mean that they must ignore broad goals or that they intend to turn their students into stimulus-response subjects. It simply means that by using a generally behavioristic approach, they will be better able to specify particular instructional goals and to help their students achieve them. They are likely to find, as have many educators, that they can blend some of the ideas of the field theorists and the Behaviorists. Ironically, one tool that will help them analyze the instructional process and see where such blends might make sense is an instructional model—a tool that epitomizes the behavioristic approach.

FOUR-STAGE MODELS OF INSTRUCTION

Conceptual models, such as four-stage models of instruction, help educators visualize a whole by delineating each of the parts and showing the relationship of the parts to the whole. This visualization then helps in analyzing the strengths and weaknesses of the instruction process. The parts that make up typical four-stage models of instruction are: (1) specification of instructional objectives, (2) preassessment of students to determine their beginning abilities relative to the objectives, (3) instructional activities intended to help students achieve the objectives, and (4) evaluation to determine whether students have achieved the objectives.

These steps are not very different from the steps taken to achieve any goal. For example, when you get up in the morning you have to decide what to wear so you consciously or unconsciously specify an objective—typically, to dress appropriately for some activity. Next, you consciously or unconsciously assess your current dress and determine that your pajamas or nightgown are not likely to be appropriate. Then, you do something to achieve the objective—you select and put on the clothes that you think will be appropriate. Finally, you engage in the planned activity and, if you were dressed appropriately for it, you achieved your objective.

Since the steps are so basic to achieving any goal, it is somewhat surprising that it was not until 1970 that they were formally depicted as parts of an instructional model. It was then that Popham and Baker, in *Systematic Instruction,*[5] and Kibler,

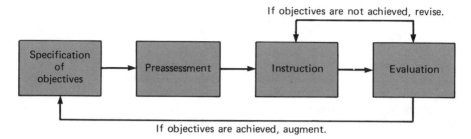

FIGURE 3   A Goal-Referenced Instructional Model with Courses of Action Dictated by Evaluation of Results

Barker, and Miles, in *Behavioral Objectives and Instruction,*[6] depicted these four stages in schematic diagrams. Popham and Baker used the diagram in Figure 3 to show the model and its self-correcting features.

The diagram by Kibler, Barker, and Miles is very similar. Using the title "General Model of Instruction" and somewhat different labels, they included a *feedback loop* to examine the first three stages when such an examination was indicated by the results of the evaluation. The General Model of Instruction is illustrated in Figure 4.

There is little substantive difference between the two models, and either can be used effectively. The major thrust of both is the division of instructional planning into four parts. The rest of this chapter concerns the factors that should be considered as teachers formulate instructional objectives, and how objectives can be written so that they clearly communicate instructional intent.

PRECISE INSTRUCTIONAL OBJECTIVES

Ralph Tyler (research director for the Eight-Year Study) is credited with coining the term "precise instructional objective." Since Tyler, other educators (including Robert Mager, James Popham, Eva Baker, and Paul Plowman) have written extensively advocating the use of such objectives.[7] Since the purpose of precise instructional

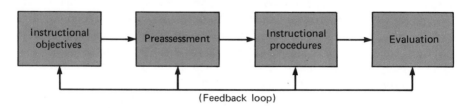

FIGURE 4   A General Model of Instruction

objectives is to clearly communicate instructional intent, we will begin our discussion by looking at sources of instructional intent.

Sources of Instructional Intent

Ralph Tyler, the "father" of precise instructional objectives, suggested that educators should consider three major sources of input for objectives: societal needs, subject-matter needs, and student needs.[8] Those three sources are still appropriate.

We have already seen how some of our current broad educational goals have roots that go back to the dawn of civilization and how our society as a whole has identified educational goals (by providing dollars for specific kinds of programs and by publicizing the results of national commissions). Teachers need to keep these broad goals in mind, but to write the kind of objectives Tyler advocated, they need to also turn to sources closer to home, such as their own school districts and individual schools.

In the process of developing instructional objectives, most school districts ask teachers to get together on the basis of common grade levels or common subject-area interests. Typically, district administrators also provide teachers with objectives that have already been formulated either locally or by educators elsewhere. Sometimes it is appropriate to adopt some of those objectives as they are, but often they can be adopted after some modification. Sometimes, of course, teachers must do the whole job themselves.

To consider societal needs with respect to instructional objectives, teachers should first ask themselves whether the objectives being considered are compatible with community goals. Some communities are composed primarily of factory workers, others of farmers, still others of white-collar workers. Regardless of type, every community wants a good education for its children, but different communities prefer to emphasize different skills and areas of knowledge. To find out if they are focusing on the educational objectives of their community, teachers should share their ideas with parents and other community members. In addition to whatever response they get, they are doing a great deal to forge good school-community relations. They are demonstrating their recognition of the fact that parents and other concerned citizens have parts to play in educating students and should have a voice in planning the educational program.

One word of caution. Teachers may find out some things that they do not like. For example, they may find that the community depends largely on one industry and, in order to keep that industry, water or air pollution problems are minimized or overlooked. The school board may not want environmental concerns discussed in the schools. Similarly, teachers might find that the community is fundamentalist with respect to religion and wants teachers to give as much emphasis to creationism as to evolution.

Teachers who find serious conflicts with what they believe students should be taught have a number of choices, but two are dominant: (1) adjust the objectives and teaching to the standards of the community, or (2) seek employment in a district with objectives closer to their own. When teachers sign a contract, they accept the obligation to follow lawful administrative mandates. Teachers are free to work within the system to change those mandates, but if they ignore them, they can be fired for insubordination regardless of their justification.

Another question teachers might ask is how relevant their proposed objectives are to the realities of college entrance requirements, employment requirements, and such social needs as tolerance and the ability to communicate, and the ability to think logically as in the application of cause-effect reasoning and syllogistic reasoning. Students, parents, and fellow educators can help determine relevance.

A second source of objectives is the subject-matter itself. Although the integration of knowledge is one of the most fundamental of all educational goals, teachers are employed to teach courses within one or two academic disciplines such as mathematics, English, or the physical sciences. In the early 1960s, some educators (such as Jerome Bruner) advanced the idea that each discipline had its own structure—its own unique set of organizing principles.[9] Most educators have failed to see any such unique set of organizing principles in the disciplines, but there are some patterns that might help structure objectives.

For example, U.S. history is typically taught chronologically, with a focus on dates and major wars. How many of those dates do you remember now? What were the causes of the War of 1812? If you learned about the colonial period triangular trade route, can you relate it to today's international business community? History can be taught in ways that might help students acquire more useful knowledge. For example, a teacher could follow a topical approach and show students how some aspect of human endeavor (such as communications, the arts, transportation, or education) changed over time. This approach might help students to better integrate knowledge because it draws upon information from various disciplines. Teachers must help students convert information into useful knowledge. They can begin to do so by examining the content of what they teach and asking which elements will be important to students ten years after those students leave the classroom. In fact, that might be the most crucial question a teacher can ask.

The student population is the third source of objectives. We are not talking here about the specific students in a specific class. The objectives for those students, as well as most of the instructional materials, will be in place before the teacher meets the students. We are talking about the needs of students typical of those in a specific class.

To determine the extent to which proposed objectives will meet student needs, the teacher must ask what those needs are. For example, students will typically have very little need to name the first ten presidents of the United States (unless they are on a quiz show). However, being able to describe the division of powers in the federal government might help a student to better understand the conflicts that often exist between the legislative and executive branches; being able to balance a checkbook or a diet might make daily life easier.

Another aspect of student needs concerns their academic level. The objectives for college-bound students differ from the objectives for students not bound for college. This truth raises the age-old question of dualism, but it would be foolish to pretend that everyone has the same academic abilities or aspirations. Once we move beyond minimal competencies ("the basics"), it makes sense to adjust objectives to the abilities of students. Considering the needs and abilities of students can and should make a real difference in the educational objectives.

After writing down their ideas, teachers should seek further input by scanning current texts in their subject-area and checking curriculum guides and resources units. Having compiled what will probably be a lengthy list of ideas, the teacher is ready to begin converting the list into a set of precise instructional objectives.

THE BASIC PARTS OF PRECISE INSTRUCTIONAL OBJECTIVES

Observable Terminal Behavior

The first step in transforming the raw material into precise instructional objectives is to specify an *observable terminal behavior* for each objective. An observable terminal behavior describes, in terms of activities that a person can actually see and measure, exactly *what a student will be expected to do at the end of instruction*. Experience has shown that terms such as "define in writing," "underline," and "diagram" are more effective in describing expected behaviors than are terms such as "know," "learn," and "understand." The terms in the second group are not directly observable and can be interpreted in a number of ways. Consider the following examples:

1. You will know the difference between prose and poetry.
2. You will define, in writing, the terms *prose* and *poetry* and illustrate each definition with the name of an example.

Since the word "know" in the first objective represents a behavior that is not directly observable, the student cannot determine how the teacher expects the knowledge to be demonstrated, and neither the teacher nor the student can ascertain when or if the objective is finally achieved. If no observable behavior is stated, the objective is useless in terms of telling students exactly what is expected of them: it does not convey instructional intent.

The second objective contains an observable behavior: "define in writing." Since both teacher and students can now describe how achievement of the objective is to be demonstrated, it becomes easier to plan instruction that will help students acquire the necessary skills, easier for students to focus their efforts on achieving the specified skills, and easier for the teacher and the students to determine when, in fact, the objective *is* achieved.

It should be noted that words such as "know," "learn," "understand," "grasp," and "discern" do not necessarily have to be avoided when writing precise instructional objectives. If such words are necessary to convey instructional intent, the teacher may use them but should be sure to include an explanation of how the implied behavior is to be demonstrated. Consider, for example, the following objective.

> You will demonstrate an understanding of prose and poetry by writing the definitions of these terms and illustrating each definition with the title of an appropriate example.

The objective contains an observable terminal behavior, but it is unnecessarily wordy. In many instances words such as "learn" and "understand" are superfluous: they do not assist in clarifying the instructional intent. The fewer words used to clearly convey the instructional intent, the less chance there is for misinterpretation.

Some terms, such as "identify," "differentiate," and "solve," are less ambiguous than are such terms as "know" and "learn," yet they describe purely mental activities—activities that go on in the student's head—and are therefore not directly observable. To make these terms less ambiguous, the teacher must again be sure to specify a means by which the activities can be observed: "identify in writing," "differentiate by recording on a checklist," or "record on paper the step-by-step procedure." Indicating to students what specific activity will be required to demonstrate the competence overtly not only sharpens the mental picture students have of what is expected of them, but also tends to reduce anxiety. The expected behavior is now clear.

Sometimes it makes sense to have students demonstrate a competence orally. While this kind of competence demonstration has its place, its disadvantages must be kept in mind. If an objective requires a student to "state orally" certain specifics, the reliability of the competence demonstration is compromised if other students hear the recitation. It would be illogical, for example, to write an objective that stated, "The student will state orally three measures of central tendency," unless provisions were made for each student to demonstrate the competence privately. If the competence were demonstrated in a classroom setting, the teacher would be unable to differentiate between those students who actually understood the material and those who were merely parroting what they heard others say.

Since it is likely that a large number of the objectives will be demonstrated in writing, it may be advantageous to state at the beginning of the list of objectives that all objectives will be demonstrated in writing unless specified otherwise. This procedure eliminates the need to include the words "in writing" in virtually every objective.

Conditions

Once the observable terminal behavior is decided upon, the teacher is in a position to add any special limitations or freedoms that will exist when the behavior is demonstrated. Conditions frequently refer to time limits or to the use of aids or special equipment, but they can refer to whatever factors are considered important to the demonstration of the terminal behavior. A physical education teacher, for example, might consider it important to specify "using a regulation baseball" in an objective concerning the hitting of line drives to avoid any question as to whether a baseball or a softball is to be used. Again, the function of conditions is to clarify further the student's mental picture of the constraints or other conditions that will affect the demonstration of the specified competence. Consider the following objectives.

You will be able to:

1. Describe, in writing, at least two possible advantages associated with the use of precise instructional objectives.
2. Using only notes, describe, in a paper of no more than two pages, at least two possible advantages and two possible disadvantages associated with the use of precise instructional objectives.

The first objective contains an observable terminal behavior ("describe, in writing"), but students do not know if they will be expected to memorize the required information or if they can simply open a text and copy what they need. In the second objective doubts are removed. The condition that notes may be used is stated clearly, and there is little room for misunderstanding. Likewise, the specification of length ("in a paper of no more than two pages") gives students an even more complete description of the constraints.

While statements of conditions are usually quite helpful and are sometimes absolutely necessary to avoid misunderstandings, some care must be taken in their use. Preconditions such as "after a lecture" or "after reading Chapter Ten" usually weaken an objective because they limit the sources from which a student may draw information in formulating responses. Certainly it would not be the teacher's intention to penalize a student for having acquired information or skills outside the class, and yet conditions such as those just mentioned imply such a penalty. If, on the other hand, the limitation is crucial to the objective for some specific reason, such preconditions must be included.

There are few instances in which the prerequisites for an objective need to be included in the objective itself. Generally, a precise instructional objective should not concern itself with how a student acquires the knowledge or skill to demonstrate a particular competence. The manner in which a student prepares for eventual demonstration of a competence falls within the realm of instructional activities. At this point in formulating objectives, the teacher's main concern is specifying the competence itself as clearly and concisely as possible.

Another point to remember is that it makes little sense to attempt to state all conditions for all objectives. For example, the condition "with no aids" will probably be common to many objectives. To include the words "with no aids" in each and every objective, however, would be both repetitive and distracting. A more logical solution would be to state the conditions common to most objectives at the beginning of the list of objectives and to discuss the general nature of these conditions with students prior to instruction.

As a general rule, the teacher should state conditions whenever there is a possibility that doubts or misunderstandings may arise. If there are any doubts whether conditions are needed in a particular objective, they should be included. If no conditions are specified in the objective, adding constraints at the time the competence is to be demonstrated may result in strong student resentment.

Minimum Acceptable Standard

The last element included in a complete precise instructional objective is a minimum acceptable standard of performance. The teacher must decide how well each of the observable behaviors must be demonstrated for it to be deemed acceptable.

Given the kind of behavior called for in the objective, the minimum acceptable standard can be stated in quantitative terms, qualitative terms, or both. As the name suggests, quantitative terms specify amounts or numbers and qualitative terms specify particular points or aspects that are sought. The following are examples of objectives using quantitative and/or qualitative minimum acceptable standards.

You will be able to:

1. Given four sets of symptoms, diagnose, in writing, the correct disease in *at least three* of the cases.
2. Write *at least ten* precise instructional objectives, each of which contains *an observable terminal behavior, conditions,* and *a minimum acceptable standard.*
3. Explain, in writing, the proper use of the wood lathe including (a) *the procedure for mounting material,* (b) *the proximity of the rest block to the material,* (c) *the speed of the chuck,* (d) *the proper use of the tool bit,* and (e) *safety precautions.*

The first objective utilizes only a quantitative standard (at least three). The second example combines a quantitative standard (at least ten) with a qualitative standard (contains an observable terminal behavior, conditions, and a minimum acceptable standard). The third contains a qualitative standard that describes the minimum elements necessary in a student explanation (points a through e).

A common misconception concerning minimum acceptable standards is that the specification of allowable time or lengths of answers is, by itself, sufficient to clarify what is expected as a minimally acceptable performance. Generally this is not so. Consider the following objectives.

You will be able to:

1. Describe, in a paper of no more than two pages, the results of World War II.
2. Type at least two letters in one class period.

In the first objective students could argue that they should receive credit for achieving the objective for writing simply, "The Allies won." This answer would meet the condition "in a paper of not more than two pages," but it confuses conditions with minimum standards because the teacher failed to include a minimum standard. According to the second objective, the student could turn in two messy, error-filled pages at the end of the period and be upset if they were not accepted. In neither objective did the quantitative limitations convey the true minimum standards. The teacher did not state the complete instructional intention.

If, however, time or length is a consideration for achievement, then it can be a minimum standard. For instance, in the objective "You will be able to run the 100-yard dash in 13 seconds," thirteen seconds is certainly the minimum acceptable standard. Similarly, a teacher who is teaching how to summarize can include "in less than one page" as part of a minimum standard.

Qualitative standards present a more involved problem for those writing objectives, for they often imply subjective judgments, and it becomes difficult to describe the particular attributes or characteristics that must be included in the terminal behavior demonstration if that demonstration is to be declared acceptable. For example, the objectives stated in the instances given are improved as additional qualitative standards are added.

You will be able to:

1. Describe, in a paper of no more than two pages, the results of World War II in terms of at least two economic developments in France and Germany.
2. Within one class period, type a one-page personal letter and a one-page business letter, using the block style, with no typographical errors.

As rewritten, the objectives begin to communicate instructional intent more clearly and minimize the chances for misunderstandings. As more standards are added, the picture of the desired end product will become more and more clear in the mind of the student. Trying to include every possible point, however, would make the objective so cumbersome that it would be virtually useless.

For instance, in attempting to establish qualitative standards for either of the two objectives given, the teacher will undoubtedly consider many factors such as logical organization, completeness, relevancy, neatness, spelling and punctuation errors, and other considerations that are either too common or too vague to specify. Common standards as well as common terminal behaviors and common conditions can be stated at the beginning of a list of objectives, thus eliminating the obligation of stating them for each objective.

Of course, the task of specifying standards for logical organization, completeness, relevancy, or other similarly nebulous factors is admittedly difficult; in fact, in some instances it may even be impossible. While it is desirable to communicate clearly to the student exactly what will be sought in the response or skill demonstration, at the same time it is necessary to keep the objective to a reasonable length.

Sometimes the length of an objective becomes a problem. Sentences, including objectives, get longer as an idea is embellished with descriptions, examples, and sometimes other ideas. These embellishments are intended to clarify the main idea, but, if they give the reader too many things to keep in mind, they have the opposite effect. Generally, sentences or objectives longer than about 25 words tend to be difficult to comprehend. Therefore, whenever possible, objectives should be written as single sentences no longer than 25 words. In the objective concerning the results of World War II, for example, the parameter "in terms of at least two economic developments in France and Germany" gives students a clearer picture of how they are to orient the answer. Adding the words, "See the handout for further minimum standards," would allow the teacher to describe further minimum standards without loading down the objective with material that might detract from readability and interest.

The fact that all possible qualitative standards are not included in each objective should not be taken as an abdication of the teacher's right or professional obligation to make judgments concerning overall quality, and this point should be made clear to students. The teacher should simply acknowledge the fact that many instructional objectives deal with complex concepts or human behaviors and that the objectives are therefore attempts to convey, as far as possible, the true instructional intent by specifying as many pertinent parameters as makes good sense. If students are expected to refer to particular ideas, points, or aspects when demonstrating a competence, those points should be identified in the objective, but terms such as "main ideas," "most important points," and "major aspects" should be used with the understanding that the teacher is willing to accept the student's opinion regarding these matters. A teacher who is not precise in describing terminal behaviors or minimal acceptable standards should not hold the students accountable for the consequences of misinterpretation.

PRACTICE IN WORKING WITH OBJECTIVES

PRACTICE EXERCISE 1: CHARACTERISTICS OF OBJECTIVES

Many of the following objectives are stated in unacceptable form. Use the following rating scale to pinpoint the weakness(es) in each objective, rewrite the objective in acceptable form, and check your responses with those furnished. An objective may be rated using more than one response. (Note: It can be argued logically that, if an objective contains no observable behavior, then there is no way for it to contain a minimum standard. This is because, if it is impossible to observe *what* the student is going to be able to do, then it is impossible to determine *how well* he or she has to do it.)

Rating Scale

1. Lacks an observable behavior
2. Lacks a minimum acceptable standard
3. Lacks conditions
4. Contains all three necessary elements

You will be able to:

1. Know the democratic principles upon which our country is founded.
2. Know the names of both U.S. senators from your home state.
3. Be an alert and an aware citizen.
4. Given a microcomputer and a diskette, correctly run a specified program.
5. Prescribe appropriate medication for a surgery patient.

6. Take an active role in society.
7. Demonstrate typing skill by retyping two letters in class, using block style, without errors.
8. Write a proper personal letter.
9. Understand the plight of the poor people in our country.
10. List orally the three branches of our federal government in class.
11. List orally the strengths and weaknesses of the United Nations.
12. Understand two steps in the committee process.
13. Appreciate the benefits of competency-based instruction.
14. Sincerely believe in just one reason to participate on a committee.
15. Demonstrate a comprehension of behavioral objectives by achieving a score of at least 80 percent on a forced choice test dealing with behavioral objectives.

Rating Scale Answers

1. 1, 2, 3
2. 1, 3 ("both" is a quantitative minimum standard)
3. 1, 2, 3
4. 4
5. 3
6. 1, 2, 3
7. 4
8. 2, 3 ("proper" does not prescribe a precise minimum standard)
9. 1, 2
10. 4
11. 2, 3 (how many strengths and weaknesses?)
12. 1, 3
13. 1, 2, 3
14. 1, 3
15. 4 (technically correct but somewhat ambiguous)

The following objectives are examples of rewrites based on the original and contain an observable behavior, minimum standard, and conditions. It is expected, of course, that rewrites may vary considerably from these models.
You will be able to:

1. Write, in class, all requirements for election and lengths of term for U.S. congressmen.
2. Write the names of both U.S. senators from your home state.
3. Select a current legislative issue, write a one-page letter to your U.S. senators expressing your views on that issue, and give at least two reasons for those views in the letter.

4. (No changes needed.)
5. Given a hypothetical description of a surgery situation, prescribe the medication necessary.
6. After reading the details in the local paper, write a letter to its editor that expresses your views on a current local problem and contains at least two rationales for those views.
7. (No changes needed.)
8. Write a one-page personal letter containing at least a heading, salutation, body, and closing, without grammatical error.
9. State orally at least three factors inhibiting the elimination of poverty within our country.
10. (No changes needed.)
11. List, in writing, with no aids and within thirty minutes, at least two strengths and two weaknesses of the United Nations.
12. Describe, in writing, at least two steps in the committee process.
13. Describe, in writing, at least three benefits of competency-based instruction to students.
14. Describe orally to the class at least one reason to participate on a committee.
15. Recall and/or apply information concerning the structure of precise instructional objectives well enough to answer correctly at least 80 percent of a series of multiple-choice questions concerning such objectives.

SELF-TEST: REWRITING POORLY STATED OBJECTIVES

Rewrite each of the following objectives so that they contain an observable behavior, minimum standard, and conditions.

1. You will develop good instructional objectives.
2. You will know why behavioral objectives are important.

Checking the Rewritten Objectives

1. Look at the rewritten objective. Ask the question, "Does this objective tell me what the student is going to be able to do after the lesson that I can observe?" If it does, then the objective includes an *observable behavior.*
   In objective 1, the word "develop" is imprecise. A person could develop objectives in his or her head but that would be unobservable. It would be better to say "develop and write," "state orally," or just "write."
   In objective 2, the word "know" is not observable. Observable behavior could be "stated orally," "explain," "describe in writing," or "demonstrate understanding by taking a test."
2. Second, ask if the rewritten objectives answer the question, "How well does the student have to demonstrate the observable behavior?" If the

objective answers this question, then the objective has a *minimum standard.* In objective 1, "good" does not give us a minimum standard.

3. Third, ask if the rewritten objective answers the question, "Under what circumstances will the student demonstrate the observable behavior?" If the objective answers this question, then it has the necessary condition or conditions.

Possible Rewrites

You will be able to:

1. Write, without aids and within ten minutes, two behavioral objectives, each of which contains an observable terminal behavior, any necessary conditions, and a minimum acceptable standard.
2. State orally in class at least two reasons for the wide acceptance of behavioral objectives by educators.

SELF-TEST: CHARACTERISTICS OF OBJECTIVES

Use the following rating scale to pinpoint the weakness(es), if any, in each of the following objectives:

Rating Scale

1. Lacks an observable behavior
2. Lacks a minimum acceptable standard
3. Lacks conditions
4. The objective is acceptable

You will be able to:

1. Write a critical reaction to *Moby Dick.*
2. When asked by the teacher, state orally the names of two wartime presidents.
3. Recite the Pledge of Allegiance with no errors.
4. Demonstrate a knowledge of proper tool use by selecting a saw with which to cut plywood.
5. Understand quadratic equations well enough to solve, on paper, any three that are given, without the use of aids and within thirty minutes.
6. Demonstrate easy mathematical skills with at least 80 percent accuracy.
7. Understand fully the terms *volt, ohm,* and *alternating current.*
8. Demonstrate good physical condition, in part, by running the mile in less than six minutes.
9. Translate written French into written English.
10. Be proud to be an American 85 percent of the time.

**Answers to Self-Test on Characteristics
of Objectives**

1. 2, 3
2. 4
3. 3
4. 2, 3
5. 4
6. 1, 3
7. 1, 2, 3
8. 3
9. 2, 3
10. 1, 3

SUMMARY

In order to work toward the achievement of broad goals, the teacher must formulate objectives that are relatively narrow and short-term. The field theorists have reservations about narrow goals because they believe, as did the ancient Greeks, that a person's life experiences are so interrelated as to be inseparable. The field theorists would like to teach the whole child; during the 1920s and 1930s, the Progressivists worked toward this end. Yet the continuing expansion of knowledge has made specialization a necessity, and this specialization fits well with the idea of narrower goals.

During the first half of the 1900s, the success of American industry and the work of behavioral psychologists (such as Pavlov and Skinner) attracted the interest of educators. The systems analysis approach seemed to be a way to improve education; soon many educators were working diligently to try to define precise instructional objectives that focused on important abilities rather than on superfluous information. Ralph Tyler suggested that educators turn to society, to the subject matter, and to students as sources of curriculum input. That suggestion is still a good one, but perhaps the single most important question that can be asked about an objective is how useful will its achievement be to the student ten years later.

The key elements of a precise instructional objective are an observable terminal behavior, a minimum standard of performance and, if needed, conditions. These components should constitute a single sentence, preferably of no more than 25 words. The observable terminal behavior must be some behavior that will be demonstrated at the end of the instructional unit and that is overt and public (such as writing or orally stating). The minimum acceptable standard may be either quantitative (two out of three or 80 percent) or qualitative (in which certain key aspects are identified). Typically, the quantitative standards are used with the lower-level objectives and the quantitative standards with the higher-level objectives.

Once objectives are written, they should be checked for clarity by asking a typical student what he or she would need to do in order to achieve the objective. If the student is not sure, the objective needs polishing. Before use, the objectives should be approved by the appropriate administrator. Each teacher's objectives must fit into the curriculum for the entire school.

STUDY QUESTIONS

1. In the minds of many educators, there is a difference between education and instruction. What is that difference, and how would it be likely to affect day-to-day teaching?

2. What differences would be likely in the instructional plans and activities written by field theorists versus those of Behaviorists?

3. What are the origins and purposes of typical four-stage models of instruction?

4. Ralph Tyler suggested that educators turn to three sources for ideas for educational objectives. Explain what those three sources are and why they are or are not sufficient.

5. Explain at least three arguments for and at least three arguments against stating instructional objectives precisely. Then defend your own position.

6. Explain the differences between quantitative and qualitative standards, and cite two examples of each.

NOTES

1. Daniel Tanner and Laurel Tanner, *Curriculum Development,* 2nd ed. (New York: Macmillan, 1980), p. 101.
2. Ibid.
3. Ivan Illich, *Deschooling Society* (New York: Harper & Row, 1971).
4. Wayne Dumas and Weldon Beckner, *Introduction to Secondary Education* (Scranton, Pa.: International Textbook, 1968), pp. 130–134.
5. James Popham and Eva Baker, *Systematic Instruction* (Englewood Cliffs, N.J.: Prentice-Hall, 1970), pp. 13, 18.
6. Robert J. Kibler, Larry L. Barker, and David T. Miles, *Behavioral Objectives and Instruction* (Boston: Allyn and Bacon, 1970), p. 13.
7. See Robert Mager, *Preparing Instructional Objectives* (Palo Alto, Calif.: Fearon, 1962); James Popham and Eva Baker, *Establishing Instructional Goals* (Englewood Cliffs, N.J.: Prentice-Hall, 1970); and Paul D. Plowman, *Behavioral Objectives* (Chicago: Science Research Associates, 1971).
8. Tanner and Tanner, *Curriculum Development,* p. 86.
9. Jerome Bruner, *The Process of Education* (Cambridge, Mass.: Harvard University Press, 1959).

Classifying and Using Precise Instructional Objectives

INTRODUCTION

As the needs of society, students, and the subject-matter itself are considered, the list of possible instructional objectives may seem endless. Most teachers come to the conclusion that they will not have enough time to help students achieve all of the objectives that could be listed, and they are right. There is always more that could be done than there is time in which to do it. This fact simply emphasizes the need to be selective in the objectives that are put on the final list.

The purpose of precisely stating instructional objectives is to clarify instructional intent so that teachers and students work toward the same clear goals. A key question then focuses on the instructional intent. Given the current propensity to judge educational excellence on the basis of test scores, teachers might consider it reasonable for their main instructional intent to be to help students learn a great deal of factual information and enable them to apply that information, particularly on pencil-and-paper tests. Is this the main goal we should work toward?

No one will deny that students must be able to recall and apply information, but there is a difference between "necessary" and "sufficient." A teacher's task is to help prepare students for life, and life consists of more than recalling information and applying basic skills on pencil-and-paper tests. The facts and skills that students learn are analogous to individual bricks. By themselves they have limited utility, but if they are joined together properly, they can become parts of a beautiful cathedral. A teacher's job is not simply to lay on brick after brick. It is to help build cathedrals—to help students integrate knowledge, learn to learn, and become human beings who will make the world a better place.

In order for a society to flourish, it must have citizens with a variety of abilities. Although some, and perhaps most, of a teacher's work will be directed at helping students acquire skills and knowledge, teachers can help students develop various abilities. For example, they can help students learn to make intelligent decisions and distinguish between fact and opinion. Teachers can also help students become more tolerant and understanding. These things can be done if teachers analyze their instructional objectives and make sure that those objectives require more than the simple recollection of information. This chapter will help teachers classify instructional objectives on the basis of the kinds of thinking they require of students.

One of the best known classification schemes was developed in 1956 and described in a book edited by Benjamin Bloom entitled *Taxonomy of Educational Objectives, Handbook I: Cognitive Domain.*[1] "Bloom's taxonomy" (as it is popularly known) is divided into three domains, and each domain is divided into levels. The cognitive domain, delineated in *Handbook I,* concerns the acquisition and manipulation of factual information. The affective domain, delineated in *Handbook II,*[2] concerns commitment toward values and attitudes. The psychomotor domain, delineated in a book entitled *A Taxonomy of the Psychomotor Domain,*[3] concerns the development of physical skills.

SAMPLE OBJECTIVES

When you complete this chapter, you will be able to:

1. List, in writing, each major level of the cognitive, affective, and psychomotor domains (knowledge).
2. Describe, in writing, the distinguishing characteristics of each level of the cognitive domain (comprehension).
3. Given an instructional topic, write one precise instructional objective at each level of each appropriate domain (synthesis).

THE TAXONOMY AND ITS USE

The taxonomy of educational objectives was developed to help educators classify objectives according to the skills and abilities they elicit from students. When working with any of the taxonomic domains or levels, teachers must keep in mind that they are working with a theoretical division of skills and abilities. It is extremely difficult to analyze the working of the human mind, and there are likely to be some objectives that do not seem to fit neatly into any specific level or even any specific domain. The possibility of haziness in classification does not seriously lessen the usefulness of the taxonomy because most objectives *will* fit into one or another domain and level. Further, classifying objectives according to the taxonomic divisions enables teachers to see whether they have included a reasonable range of skills and abilities, even if a few objectives are misclassified.

THE COGNITIVE DOMAIN

The cognitive domain is divided into six major levels, each of which is divided into sublevels. The following discussion is intended to give the teacher enough skill to make initial classifications of objectives for the purposes mentioned. Studying the material that follows and completing the exercises will enable the teacher to examine and defend the variety of thinking skills included in objectives.

Knowledge

The first and most fundamental level of the cognitive domain is knowledge. At this level students are expected simply to recall information to which they have been exposed or to recognize information presented. The main skill emphasized by objectives written at this level is simple recollection. Listed below are some examples of objectives written at the knowledge level.

You will be able, in writing and under test conditions, to describe:

1. At least five parts and three formats characteristic of business letters.
2. The unit of metric measure corresponding to (not equivalent to) pounds, ounces, quarts, gallons, inches, yards, and miles (e.g., miles/kilometers).
3. The steps that a bill goes through to become a U.S. law.

Comprehension

The second level of the cognitive domain is comprehension. It is the view of many educators that this level is the one most emphasized in today's schools. If this view is correct, our level of emphasis is disappointing because the comprehension level is low in the hierarchy of intellectual skills. This level indicates that the student can not only recall information, but that the information has meaning to the student.

Bloom includes three kinds of intellectual skills in the comprehension level. The first of these is *translation*, the ability to make a one-for-one conversion from one symbol form or language to another. The second skill is *interpretation*, the ability to generalize or paraphrase information. The third skill is *extrapolation*, the ability to make predictions based on the information presented. Examples of observable behaviors reflecting each of these skills are as follows.

You will be able, in writing and under test conditions, to:

1. Translate the formula for converting degrees Fahrenheit to degrees Celsius from sentence form to mathematical statement form.
2. Describe what is meant by the tone of a letter and cite examples of two tones.

3. Given the long-term effects of the National Defense Education Act (1958), explain two likely long-term effects of the current reform movement in education.

Application

The third level of the cognitive domain is application. Application is essentially the act of using rules, principles, or generalizations in a rather mechanical way to complete a task. It is useful to think of the student understanding a principle or rule at the comprehension level and then using the principle or rule in a practical situation at the application level. Examples of objectives written at the application level follow.

You will be able, under test conditions, to:

1. Given unorganized components of a business letter and a specific business letter format, organize the components according to the specified format and type the letter without error.
2. Given a series of temperatures in degrees Fahrenheit, convert, in writing, at least 80 percent of them to correct degrees Celsius.
3. Given a hydroponic growing area no larger than one square foot, within a two-week period, grow a plant at least two inches tall either from seed or from a seedling no taller than one-quarter-inch tall.

Analysis

The fourth level of the cognitive domain is analysis. Many educators consider analysis to be the first of the higher cognitive levels. Bloom includes three kinds of skills in the analysis level. The first of these is the analysis of *elements*. This skill is demonstrated by breaking down a whole (the problem, material, or sample) into its constituent parts or elements. The second skill is the analysis of *relationships*. This skill is demonstrated by describing relationships between or among elements. The third skill is the analysis of *organizational principles*. This skill is demonstrated by describing the organization or structure of a whole.

Sometimes the line between application-level and analysis-level tasks is not clear. One of the key points of difference lies in the complexity of the task. At the application level, the task is so clearcut that there is little question as to which rules, principles, and procedures need to be used. The focus is upon using them correctly. At the analysis level, the task is more ambiguous. The elements, relationships, and organization principles sought are not so obvious and may not call clearly for the use of this or that rule or procedure.

The line between analysis- and evaluation-level tasks is also sometimes unclear. The key difference here is objectivity. The assessments made during an analysis are wholly objective. One test of the objectivity of the analysis is to ask whether three equally qualified experts would probably come to the same conclusion. If the task is truly one of analysis, experts would tend to arrive at the same conclusion. At the evaluation level, the conclusion reached might be wholly subjective. Examples of objectives written at the analysis level follow.

You will be able, in writing and under test conditions, to:

1. Given a magazine article, identify which passages of the article are based on assumptions and which are factual.
2. Read short essays written by two political leaders and explain at least two differences in their political points of view, citing supporting passages from the given essays.
3. When given an advertisement, explain what the most likely target population is and why, and what technique is being employed.

Synthesis

The fifth level of the cognitive domain is synthesis. Synthesis, in this context, means the creation of something new from previously existing elements or principles. Bloom mentions three kinds of synthesis products. The first is *unique communications*. These would consist of oral or written efforts in which the student effectively conveys ideas, feelings, or experiences to others. The second kind of product would be *a plan or a proposed set of operations*. Such plans or sets of operations would be assessed by whether they met specified requirements. Those requirements could be given to the student or developed by the student along with the plan or set of operations. The last kind of product is the *derivation of a set of abstract relations*. A typical example would be the derivation of a hypothesis.

Although students will be using knowledge and skills already mastered as the basis of their synthesis activities, the teacher must not confuse the simple accumulation of related parts for synthesis. For example, the task of creating a nutritious menu might be accomplished simply by selecting X foods from Y food groups. Such an activity might be appropriate at the application level. If, on the other hand, the task was to create a dish that would appeal to and meet the nutritional needs of a particular kind of person (a nine-year-old boy, or a high school girl), the complexity of the task increases significantly. Guard against confusing application-level objectives with the more complex synthesis-level objectives. The former focus on the use of rules and principles in a mechanical way; the latter focus on creativity and higher-level thinking. Some objectives written at the synthesis level follow.

You will be able, under test conditions, to:

1. Compose, for your local newspaper, an original editorial of no more than one page, in which you describe a series of changes in the local governing structure that would make it more democratic.
2. Write a unique short story (no more than three pages) that can be properly classified as a comedy, is set in the 1950s, has at least two major characters, and has a happy ending.
3. Given a topic and a time frame, write a plan for a concept lesson that includes at least one precise instructional objective and with content and instructional activities likely to help students achieve the objective.

All of these objectives demonstrate how activities at the synthesis level can be used to help students integrate knowledge. For example, in order to write an acceptable lesson plan, the student needs to know about the topic assigned and how to organize and write a lesson plan. Teachers should be sure that their course objectives include synthesis-level objectives. The task is more than just laying brick upon brick. The bricks have to be joined together. Synthesis-level objectives help accomplish that task.

Evaluation

The last and highest level of the cognitive domain is evaluation. It forms a bridge to the affective domain. Evaluation in the cognitive domain is defined as the formation of a value judgment (*evalu*ation), but the most important part of the activity is not the judgment itself; it is the justification of that judgment. Students will be making judgments throughout their lives. The purpose of evaluation-level objectives is to help students learn to justify their judgments. The justification can consist of logical reasoning (cause-effect or syllogistic), references to specific facts or examples, or the use of specific criteria, but it should not reflect a lack of thought (e.g., "My father believes this so I believe it too"). Guard against confusing analysis-level and evaluation-level objectives. In the former case, three equally qualified experts would be likely to arrive at the same conclusion. In the latter case, all three might have different opinions and equally strong, but different, rationales. Examples of objectives written at the evaluation level follow.

You will be able, in writing and under test conditions, to:

1. Given two business letters, explain in less than two pages which one you believe is more effective and support your decision by citing at least three specific facts or examples.
2. State your position with respect to whether students in the U.S. should learn the metric system and defend your position by citing at least three factual or cause-effect arguments.
3. Explain which economic system you believe has the greatest longterm growth potential and support your belief by citing at least three factual or logical arguments that are consistent with accepted knowledge.

THE AFFECTIVE DOMAIN

When *Taxonomy of Educational Objectives, Handbook I* was published in 1956, most educators readily accepted the concept of three domains of endeavor and just as readily accepted the levels within the cognitive domain. Most educators agreed then, and still agree, that one of their primary responsibilities is to help students acquire and manipulate factual information. However, when David Krathwohl edited *Handbook II* in 1964, many educators were confronted with a question.

Most educators agree that affects such as emotions, attitudes, and values exist and profoundly affect human endeavors. Most educators also agree that a typical classroom, with its many human interactions, is one of the places where attitudes and values can be shaped. The question was how much, if any, instructional time and effort should a teacher focus on building or changing feelings, attitudes, and values.

Consider the following points. First, teachers have a great deal to do with the feelings, attitudes, and values that are developed in their classrooms regardless of whether they do or do not state affective objectives. Factors as varied as the way they dress and act, the way they expect students to dress and act, and the way they interact with students all work to shape students' feelings, attitudes, and values. For example, teachers who act dictatorial or use the language carelessly convey a different message to students than those who treat students as responsible people or take care to use the language properly. The instructional objectives also help shape attitudes, feelings, and values. If the objectives focus primarily on low-level skills or seem irrelevant to students, attitudes in the class will be different than if the focus of the objectives is on the attainment of high-level abilities that are clearly relevant and important to the students. Separate objectives that focus purely on attitudes, feelings, and values may not be needed.

Second, many people believe that it is the prerogative of parents or churches to develop attitudes, feelings, and values and that schools should focus on cognitive development. Though teachers are permitted to encourage mainstream values—for example, honesty and reverence for life—they may inadvertently cause a holy war by espousing a more complex or specific moral stance. Given the absolute separation of church and state and the great diversity of moral thought in the United States, it is presumptuous to stand up and shine the light of Truth on everyone else.

Third, the only way to assess the attitudes or values people have is by observing what they do or say. Teachers who decide to write objectives in the affective domain must select observable behaviors that they believe will reflect particular attitudes or values. If they happen to select inappropriate behavioral indicators, their assessment of the affect will be distorted.

Fourth, what should teachers do with information about the achievement or lack of achievement of affective objectives, if such information can be acquired? For example, it would be difficult to defend the raising or lowering of a test score because the student did or did not demonstrate a particular attitude, and the same would be true of a final grade. In this age of accountability, teachers must be able to demonstrate that their grades were reported objectively and that they were not biased by questionable determinations of whether the student had or had not acquired certain attitudes, feelings, or values.

Finally, there is a conflict between the purpose of precise instructional objectives and the nature of objectives in the affective domain. The general purpose of precise instructional objectives is to clarify instructional intent so that teachers and students can work toward the same clear goals. Inherent in this idea is the fact that the students must know what the objectives are before instruction begins. Knowing the affective objectives, students could demonstrate the specified behaviors only to please the teacher and stop demonstrating them as soon as the course ends. The same thing may happen with objectives in the cognitive domain, but there at least teachers are more certain of the validity of the behaviors being observed.

Given the problems described, many teachers choose not to write objectives in the affective domain. Regardless of whether they write such objectives, teachers should understand the affective domain because it describes the progression of commitment that we all go through as our attitudes, feelings, and values develop. Therefore, we will look briefly at each of the five levels of the affective domain and see what a typical objective might look like at each level.

Receiving

The lowest level of the affective domain is receiving. At this level the student is aware of the existence of a condition or problem and is willing at least to listen attentively to what others have to say about it. The element of commitment is not present, and the behavior is somewhat analogous to "sitting on the fence." Though aware of an issue, the student has not yet made a decision about it. An objective at this level might be for the student to demonstrate a willingness to learn about drug abuse by contributing to an introductory discussion on the subject.

Responding

The second level is responding. At this level the student is willing to go along with an idea or a value (such as being willing to follow school rules), actively volunteers to respond, and takes satisfaction in the response. The level of commitment is minimal, and the behavior is analogous to jumping off the fence but holding on to it and being ready to jump back at any moment. An objective at this level might be for the student to display an interest in solving drug-related social problems by taking a stand in classroom discussions against drug abuse.

Valuing

The third level is valuing. Here the student demonstrates that the attitude has been accepted and is consistently preferred over competing attitudes or values. The commitment is clear: the student has walked away from the fence and is willing to be identified as holding the attitude or value. An objective at this level might be for the student to indicate a commitment to social reform by becoming an active member of a community service organization such as Students Against Drunk Driving.

Organization

The fourth level is organization. As students become more aware of values, they eventually recognize that conflicts between values do arise and must be resolved by setting priorities on values. To do so, students should use higher-level cognitive thinking, which will enable them to resolve value conflicts in a logical and defensible manner. They will then have greater confidence in their decisions. This level is a direct link between the cognitive and the affective domains. An objective at the organization level might be for the student, when confronted with a conflict between staying active in a music group and leaving the group because of its tolerance of drug use, to weigh the likely outcomes of each course of action and decide which will be in his or her best long-term interest.

Characterization

The highest level of the affective domain is characterization. At this level a person's value system has been internalized so that behavior clearly reflects the values held. When we think of a miser or a spendthrift, we are thinking of someone who has reached the characterization level. Each has embraced a particular value so completely that every thought and action exemplifies the value. Since students are in the process of developing their value structures, few will reach the characterization level while still in high school. An objective at this level might be for the student to demonstrate a continuing commitment to the idea of social reform by studying to be a physician who specializes in drug abuse.

THE PSYCHOMOTOR DOMAIN

The psychomotor domain is concerned with the development of motor skills and neuromuscular control. Objectives in the psychomotor domain often contain elements of the cognitive or affective domain (and vice versa), but the dominant characteristic and intent of the student's response is a physical movement. The curricular areas in which psychomotor skills receive major emphasis include typing, shorthand, home economics, industrial education, art, music, and, of course, physical education. It is important to keep in mind, however, that virtually all other curricular areas depend, to one degree or another, on psychomotor skills because speaking, gesturing, writing, and eye-hand coordination are all examples of psychomotor domain skills.

This psychomotor domain taxonomy, developed by Anita J. Harrow in 1972,[4] represents a model of viewing, explaining, and classifying the neuromuscular development stages through which students pass. As with the cognitive and affective domain taxonomies, this psychomotor domain taxonomy depicts a continuum of simple to complex achievements, and its use can greatly facilitate the conceptualization and sequencing of appropriate objectives and experiences. The levels of the psychomotor domain taxonomy are as follows.

Reflex Movements

Reflex movements are involuntary actions that are elicited ordinarily as a response to some stimulus. Ordinarily educators are not concerned with this level of responding unless a particular student has some impairment that limits proper execution of the movements. These movements are part of the repertoire of all normal children and are developed to a sufficient degree so that more complex psychomotor skills can be developed from them with little difficulty.

Basic-Fundamental Movements

Basic-fundamental movement patterns are developed in the first year of life. These movements build on the reflex movements and consist of such behaviors as grasping, reaching, manipulating objects, crawling, creeping, and walking. Ordinarily, basic-fundamental movement patterns are learned naturally, without training. Again the educator need have little concern regarding the formulation of objectives for this level unless a particular student is observed having problems in this area. Special education teachers may be required to provide appropriate activities for their students with regard to basic-fundamental movements, especially where muscular or visual impairment exists.

Perceptual Abilities

In reality, perceptual ability refers essentially to cognitive functioning. Its inclusion in the psychomotor taxonomy is based on the fact that perceptual and motor functions are inseparable. Without proper perceptual skills, students are unable to make adequate motor responses. The taxonomy is divided into the following categories of perception that lead directly to motor behaviors.

Kinesthetic discrimination consists of one's perceptual judgments regarding one's body in relation to surrounding objects in space. It involves the ability to recognize and control the body and its parts in movement while maintaining balance.

Visual discrimination involves a number of components that are necessary for proper psychomotor execution. The first of these is visual acuity. This involves the ability to distinguish form and fine details and to differentiate between various observed objects. Second is visual tracking, which is the ability to follow objects with coordinated eye movements. Following the movement of a ball is an example of this. Third is visual memory. This is the skill to recall from memory past visual experiences or previously observed movement patterns such as dance routines or swinging a baseball bat. Figure-background differentiation is the fourth category of visual discrimination. Here, the learner is able to select the dominant figure from the surrounding background. Evidence that the individual can differentiate figure and background occurs when he or she is able to identify the dominant object and respond to it. Ball catching and hitting thrown balls can be accepted as evidence that the individual can differentiate figure and background. Consistency is the last category of visual discrimination. This is the ability to recognize shapes and forms consistently even though they may have been modified in some way.

Auditory discrimination involves the ability of the learner to receive and differentiate among various sounds and their pitch and intensity, distinguish the direction of sound and follow its movement, and recognize and reproduce postauditory experience such as the notes that can be used to play a song on the piano.

Tactile discrimination is the learner's ability to differentiate between different textures simply by touching. Being able to determine the slickness or smoothness of an object or surface may be essential to properly executing psychomotor movements where the body must come in contact with surfaces in the process.

Coordinated abilities incorporate behaviors that involve two or more of the perceptual abilities and movement patterns. At this level the student is able, for example, to differentiate between the figure and the ground and to coordinate the visually perceived object with a manipulative movement such as in the act of kicking a moving soccer ball. Remember that the actual kicking of the ball is the psychomotor evidence that there is a coordinated discrimination ability.

It should be obvious that perceptual abilities are not actually observable phenomena. Evidence that these abilities exist depends on various movements and cognitive tasks. The following are examples of objectives written at the various levels in the perceptual abilities category:

You will be able to:

1. Without any outside assistance, walk the full distance across a balance beam and back without falling, on each of five tries (kinesthetic discrimination).
2. From an audio recording of a symphony orchestra, list the names of 80 percent of the instruments playing in any 30-second segment of the recording (auditory acuity).
3. Catch 95 percent of the baseballs batted from a distance of approximately fifty yards (coordinated activities).

Physical Abilities

The physical abilities of the learner are essential to efficient execution of psychomotor movements. Physical abilities constitute the foundation for the development of skilled movements because of the demands placed on the various systems of the body during the execution of these psychomotor skills. Underdeveloped physical abilities can be serious limiting factors in developing highly skilled movement. The physical abilities include endurance, strength, flexibility, and agility.

Endurance is the ability of the body to supply and utilize oxygen and to dispose of increased concentrations of lactic acid in the muscles. The lack of endurance reduces the learner's ability to perform movements efficiently over long periods of time. Development of endurance requires strenuous activity on a sustained basis.

Strength is the relative ability to exert tension against resistance. The development of strength is accomplished ordinarily through gradually increasing the extent of the resistance through the use of weights and springs. The student's own body can also be used as resistance in exercises such as pull-ups and push-ups. Maintenance of strength requires the learner to utilize the muscles continually. Obviously the strength required to perform various psychomotor movements depends upon the nature of these movements as well as on the ability of the learner. For example, a greater amount of strength is required for wrestling than for fencing. In wrestling, strength is developed relative to size. In addition to wrestling, sports that require a good deal of strength include football and gymnastics.

Flexibility refers to the ability of the learner to engage in wide range of motion in his or her joints. Flexibility depends greatly upon the extent to which muscles can be stretched during movement and not result in injury. Hurdlers, gymnasts, and dancers are among those who are most concerned about flexibility.

Agility is the learner's ability to move with dexterity and quickness. Agility is involved with deftness of manipulation, rapid changes of direction, and starting and stopping activities. Typing, playing the piano or other musical instruments, and playing basketball are activities that require a good deal of agility. The following are examples of objectives written at the different levels of the physical abilities category:

You will be able to:

1. Following the Harvard-Step Test, have your recovery period pulse count decrease to a point at or above the next highest classification level when compared with the norms (endurance).
2, Execute correctly fifty push-ups and fifteen pull-ups with no more than five minutes' rest between the push-ups and pull-ups (strength).
3. While sitting on the ground in the hurdler's position, touch your extended foot with your fingers and hold this position for ten seconds (flexibility).
4. Complete the run-and-dodge course in less than twenty seconds (agility).

Skilled Movements

A skill is essentially a degree of efficiency in performing a specific but reasonably complex psychomotor behavior. Ordinarily, learning is associated with skill development. The classification of skilled movements consists of two separate continuums, one vertical and one horizontal. The vertical continuum involves the degree of difficulty of the particular movement and is referred to as the levels of skill mastery for each of the levels of complexity. The levels of complexity include simple adaptive, compound adaptive, and complex adaptive. Each of these levels of complexity has the following mastery levels: beginner, intermediate, advanced, and highly skilled.

Activities included in the skilled movement category are those that involve an adaptation of the inherent movement patterns listed in the basic-fundamental movements level. The difference between the two levels is that, with skilled movements, the concern is with evaluating the learner's performance in terms of the degree of proficiency, whereas the basic-fundamental movements level is concerned with whether the learner can simply perform the movement.

Remember, in differentiating among the three categories of skilled movements, that the first involves a limited amount of sensory information and only a portion of the performer's body or body parts. The second involves the extension of the body parts through the use of an implement or tool. The third incorporates total body movement, in many instances without a base of support, and necessitates the making of postural adjustments due to the unexpected cues.

With regard to mastery levels in executing skilled movements, there is a horizontal continuum from beginner through intermediate and advanced skill levels to the highly skilled. At the beginner skill level, the learner is able to perform the skill with some degree of confidence and similarity to the movement expected. This stage is somewhat beyond the trial-and-error learning of initial attempts at the learning task. When the learner can minimize the amount of extraneous motion and execute the skill with some proficiency, he or she is categorized as being at the intermediate skill level. Once the individual can perform the skilled movement efficiently and with confidence and achieve almost the same response each time, his or her skill level is judged to be advanced. At this level, the student's performance is usually superior in quality when compared with similar performances of his or her peers. Highly skilled performances are usually limited to those individuals who use their skills professionally. In this case the individual is totally involved in the use of his or her skill. At the highly skilled level, factors such as body structure, body function, and acuity of sensory modalities and perceptual abilities become critical. Proper execution of the skills depends heavily upon each of these components.

The following are examples of behavioral objectives written at the different levels of the skilled movements category.

You will be able to:

1. In a five-minute timed test, type at a rate of 40 words per minute and make no more than five errors (simple adaptive skill).
2. From a distance of 20 feet, putt a golf ball into the cup 25 percent of the time (compound adaptive skill).
3. Execute properly the following dives with a point rating of at least 4.5: forward one and one-half, one-half gainer, and one-and-one-half forward twist (complex adaptive skill).

Nondiscursive Communication

This category of behaviors consists of nonverbal communications used to convey a message to an observer. These movements involve such nonverbal expressions as facial expressions, postures, and complex dance choreographies. Two subcategories are included: expressive movement and interpretive movement.

Expressive movement is composed of many of the movements that are used in everyday life. The basic types of expressive movement include posture and carriage, gestures, and facial expressions. These means of expression are used to indicate the individual's internal emotional state. Expressive movements as such are not usually incorporated into the formal curriculum. However, they are used in modified form by learners in the area of fine arts and are included in the taxonomy for this reason. The teacher will not ordinarily write behavioral objectives for the purpose of accomplishing expressive movements.

Interpretive movements are art forms. They can either be aesthetic, where the movements are performed for the purpose of creating for the viewer an image of effortless, beautiful motion, or they can be creative movements that are designed to communicate some message to the viewer. In both cases, the performer must have a highly developed level of skill in movement with a knowledge of body mechanics and have well-developed physical and perceptual abilities. The following is an objective at the interpretive movements level. You will be able to:

> Create your own movement sequence to a piece of music of your own selection, which contains recognizable rhythmic patterns, keeps time with the music, and communicates a message to the viewer on a contemporary social theme (interpretive movement).

It should be noted that for many movements there are several components. In such cases the learner may be instructed and evaluated on either one or all of the components that make up a skill. Dividing the movements into component parts allows for more accurate evaluation and also provides the learner with more specific details that can be used to make movement corrections. Analysis of subcomponent skills is particularly useful for the highly skilled performer. However, for the beginning learner, a good deal of confusion may result from too much detailed analysis of inefficient movements. The more advanced learners become, the more they are likely to benefit from detailed analysis.

TESTING OBJECTIVES FOR CLARITY

Once the teacher has ascertained that the objectives are technically correct and provide for student development at a variety of cognitive levels, he or she should test to see if they communicate the instructional intent clearly. On occasion the teacher may become so involved in the instructional process that the *means* to the ends are communicated to students as objectives rather than the ends themselves. Phrases such as "will read" and "will attend" are almost sure giveaways that the objective is more a learning activity than an objective. Objectives do not specify how information or skills will be acquired, only the ultimate behavior sought.

Mager[5] suggests that one way to test the clarity of a precise instructional objective is for the writer to consider whether another competent person could, on the basis of the written objective(s), differentiate among students who can and those who cannot demonstrate the competence described with the same degree of precision as could the writer of the objective(s).

Another way to test objectives for clarity is to ask other people (co-workers, friends, or students) to read each objective and discern what they think they would have to do to demonstrate the competence. If their interpretation differs, or if the teacher has to explain, "What I really meant was...," the misleading objective(s) should be rewritten. This second method is particularly useful if students are used as readers, since they will be more representative of the potential "consumers" than anyone else. It may be, for example, that the level of reading difficulty of the objectives is inappropriate for the potential users. If a fellow teacher reads the objectives, this factor may pass unnoticed; if students read the objectives, they will be quick to point out that they cannot understand what was written and intended.

For the purpose of clarity, when presenting objectives to students for large units of instruction, it is best to reveal those objectives that describe the ultimate instructional intent rather than the enabling objectives. Consider the following.

You will be able to:

1. Write the definitions of the terms *fact* and *opinion*.
2. When given a series of statements, label, in writing, those that are facts and those that are opinions.
3. When given a newspaper editorial, underline all statements of opinion and explain, in writing, why those statements are opinion.

Of these three objectives, the last best describes the terminal objective. The first two may serve as objectives for individual lesson plans, but the last more accurately reflects the ultimate instructional intent of the teacher. The teacher may well choose to include only the last objective on a list of course objectives given to students. The connection between the first two and the final objective could, and should, be pointed out to students at the time those objectives are used in particular lessons, but the crucial terminal behavior is expressed in the last objective.

USING PRECISE INSTRUCTIONAL OBJECTIVES

Once teachers have (1) gleaned ideas for instructional objectives by considering the needs of society, students, and the subject-matter, (2) converted those ideas into precise instructional objectives, and (3) classified the objectives into domains and levels to ensure that students will develop a range of skills and abilities, the next step is to get administrative approval to use them. Administrators in a school are charged with, among other things, seeing to it that an approved curriculum is implemented. For this to happen, the objectives of various courses must complement one another; administrators can help see that they do, but only to the extent that they are aware of the objectives of each teacher. It is, therefore, prudent for each teacher to get administrative approval for course objectives and to thereby minimize the chance of jeopardizing the success of that part of the curriculum.

After getting administrative approval for the objectives, the next step is to communicate those objectives to students. One way to do this is to include the objectives, a tentative content outline, and a calendar in a course syllabus for the semester.

Such a handout might consist of a brief overview of the course; the half dozen or so most important objectives, including those at the higher cognitive levels; policies that will be followed concerning such things as written assignments, homework, and making up tests; grading procedures; and a tentative, week-by-week schedule of planned activities (material to be covered in class, out-of-class assignments, and important dates such as test dates and due dates). During the first or second class meeting, time would be well spent discussing the entire syllabus with students. Such a discussion will convey to students the facts that the teacher has a definite sense of purpose, is thoroughly prepared, and intends to follow a businesslike approach.

During such a discussion, the focus should be on the course objectives. The teacher should show that the objectives are relevant to the students' needs and demonstrate how each of the activities will help the students achieve the objectives. As the tentative schedule is discussed, the teacher should point out that the planned activities will be associated with specific instructional units and that they will be discussed in greater detail as each unit is begun.

The advantage of this approach is that it provides students with "the big picture." It tells them some of the most important things they will be able to do when they successfully complete the course. Since a teacher's success depends on the success of the students, it is a good idea to give them reasons to be successful; the teacher can do so by demonstrating to students how achievement of the objectives will be beneficial to them (even if they do not go on to college). A teacher who doubts the relevance of the objectives will find it difficult to persuade students to cooperate in the instructional activities. Think carefully about the objectives and focus on those that are clearly relevant. The objectives should induce students to cooperate.

Finally, teachers should try to develop clear and independent thinkers. Students must be given opportunities to voice their ideas, and teachers must be prepared to act on those ideas. With respect to discussing a course syllabus, it means that teachers should encourage students to react to the course objectives. Students should be told of the rationale behind the plan and should be asked for their ideas about changing, adding, or deleting objectives to make them more relevant and about changing other parts of the syllabus. The fact that significant thought and effort went into selecting the objectives and organizing the course will not be lost on the students; it will communicate a seriousness of purpose on the teacher's part. The fact that student input is solicited will also make an impression; it will tell students that they are considered adult enough to think seriously about the work ahead. Asking for input does not obligate a teacher to make changes, but if students' input *can* be incorporated, they will have a degree of ownership in the course, and that will be an inducement to them to see the plan succeed.

AN OVERVIEW OF COGNITIVE LEVELS

I. COGNITIVE DOMAIN—BENJAMIN S. BLOOM (1956)

1.00	Knowledge	Simple recall. No understanding necessary.
2.00	Comprehension	Limited understanding. Demonstrated by translation, interpretation, and extrapolation.

3.00	Application	Utilization of rules, principles, and procedures to accomplish a task.
4.00	Analysis	Identification of components within a whole, recognition of relationships among those components, and recognition of the organization of the whole.
5.00	Synthesis	Combination of parts into a new and unique whole.
6.00	Evaluation	Making, defending, and supporting value judgments.

II. AFFECTIVE DOMAIN—DAVID R. KRATHWOHL (1964)

1.0	Receiving	Sensitization to the existence of certain phenomena and the willingness to direct attention to them.
2.0	Responding	Stage at which students will become sufficiently involved in a subject or activity that they will seek it out and gain satisfaction from working with it or engaging in it.
3.0	Valuing	Stage at which behavior is motivated not by the desire to comply or obey but by the individual's realization that some attitude or value has become important to him or her.
4.0	Organization	The resolution of value conflicts and the beginning of the organization of a value system hierarchy.
5.0	Characterization	Stage at which the commitment to a value hierarchy has become internalized and thus controls the individual's behavior. The values constitute part of the individual's life-style.

III. PSYCHOMOTOR DOMAIN—ANITA J. HARROW (1972)

1.00	Reflex movements	Movements or actions elicited in response to some stimulus, but without conscious volition on the part of the learner.
2.00	Basic-fundamental movements	Actions such as reaching, crawling, and walking that are inherent motor patterns are based upon the reflex movements of the learner and that emerge without training.
3.00	Perceptual abilities	Recognition of and discrimination among various perceptual modalities such as kinesthetic, visual, auditory, and tactile modes and coordinated abilities such as eye-hand coordination.

4.00	Physical abilities	Functional characteristics of organic vigor (endurance, strength, flexibility, and agility) that when developed provide the learner with a sound, efficiently functioning instrument (his or her body) to be used when making skilled movements.
5.00	Skilled movements	Development of increasing degrees of skill or mastery of movement patterns learned at earlier stages of development.
6.00	Nondiscursive communication	Use of movement to communicate. Includes such movements as facial expressions, postures, gestures, and modern dance choreographies.

PRACTICE IN CLASSIFYING OBJECTIVES

PRACTICE EXERCISE 1: THE DOMAINS

Classify each objective as belonging to the cognitive (c), affective (a), or psychomotor (p) domain.

You will be able to:

___ 1. Explain, in writing, which of two possible solutions to the problem of social unrest is most likely to eliminate the problem.

___ 2. Recite the Emancipation Proclamation from memory with no more than two errors.

___ 3. Thread a movie projector so that, when the projector is turned on, the film will not flicker.

___ 4. Show increased interest in band music by attending eight out of the ten concerts offered during the year.

___ 5. Given thirty quadratic equations, solve correctly, on paper, at least 80 percent of them.

___ 6. Demonstrate concern for the democratic principles of free enterprise by orally stating these concerns.

___ 7. Show a growing interest in art by participating extensively in discussions about art forms.

___ 8. Transfer bacteria from a culture to a petri dish in a manner that produces properly spread colonies and no contamination.

___ 9. Write an original short story that has appropriate sentence structure and organization and that meets the requirements of heightened action.

___ 10. Given a series of paintings, explain, in writing, which one is best and why.

Answers to Practice Exercise 1

1. C	5. C	8. P
2. C	6. A	9. C
3. P	7. A	10. C
4. A		

PRACTICE EXERCISE 2: COGNITIVE LEVELS

Classify each objective into its level within the cognitive domain. Check your responses against the answers provided. Resolve any discrepancies by further study, analysis, or consultation with your instructor or peers. Always classify the objectives at the highest level implied.

Levels of the Cognitive Domain

1. Knowledge
2. Comprehension
3. Application

4. Analysis
5. Synthesis
6. Evaluation

You will be able to:

_____ 1. Given three garments of varying prices, choose the garment you consider to be the best buy and give three written reasons for the decision based on the construction of the garment.

_____ 2. List, in writing, at least five factors that led up to the Spanish-American War.

_____ 3. Given a new list of possible reasons for World War I and World War II, classify them, in writing, under World War I or World War II with no errors.

_____ 4. State, in writing, four common ingredients in pastry.

_____ 5. Given the necessary material, compare, in writing, the state welfare program in Illinois to that in California on at least five points.

_____ 6. Explain, in writing, using at least five examples, why many Blacks moved to the North at the end of the Civil War.

_____ 7. Given comprehensive material on the waste of natural resources, write an original legislative bill calling for conservation of natural resources.

_____ 8. Given necessary materials, develop a unique, written ten-year plan for the economic development of a hypothetical country.

_____ 9. On a ten-minute written quiz on ceramics, explain three ways of hand-building a pot.

_____ 10. Given sculptures done by peers, choose one that you judge to be best and defend that choice by citing, in writing, at least three points of superiority in the selected piece.

___ 11. Given the names of two Cubist painters, contrast and compare the styles of each painter in a one-page paper citing at least four similarities and three differences.

___ 12. Solve 90 percent of the two-digit multiplication problems on a written math test.

___ 13. Calculate and write down how much 1 gram of N HCl will have to be diluted to prepare 500 ml of 0.5N solution.

___ 14. Given a list of tasks that must be done during an eight-hour period, create a written work plan that organizes the tasks so that the time will be used efficiently to complete them.

___ 15. Use Robert's *Rules of Order* to conduct a class election without any violations of procedure.

Answers to Practice Exercise 2

1. 6	6. 2	11. 4
2. 1	7. 5	12. 3
3. 4	8. 5	13. 3
4. 1	9. 2	14. 5
5. 4	10. 6	15. 3

PRACTICE EXERCISE 3:
PSYCHOMOTOR LEVELS

Classify each objective into its level within the psychomotor domain. Check your responses against the answers provided. Resolve any discrepancies by further study, analysis, or consultation with your instructor or peers.

Levels of the Psychomotor Domain

1. Reflex movements
2. Basic fundamental movements
3. Perceptual abilities
4. Physical abilities
5. Skilled movements
6. Nondiscursive communication

You will be able to:

___ 1. Given bacteria cultures, petri plates, wireloop, and Bunsen burner, transfer bacteria from the culture tubes to the petri dishes using proper streaking techniques and preventing contamination.

___ 2. Type 40 words per minute in a three-minute timed test with no errors.

___ 3. Drive an automobile in heavy traffic properly executing a right turn, a left turn, a lane change, a stop, and a parallel park.

___ 4. Draw at least 25 Old English letters demonstrating correct proportion and style.

___ 5. Dance the waltz in proper time.

—— 6. Given a series of ten pictures, point to the dominant figure (as opposed to background figures) in at least eight instances.

—— 7. Without any outside assistance, demonstrate a unique dance routine that is coordinated with at least four minutes of music and that communicates the theme of "war."

—— 8. Show an increase in grip strength of five pounds after two weeks of training.

—— 9. Swim 1,000 yards in less than 19 minutes and have a heart rate of no more than 120 beats per minute after one minute of rest.

—— 10. While battling against a complete defensive team, hit a pitched baseball safely three out of ten times.

Answers to Practice Exercise 3

1. 5	6. 3
2. 5	7. 6
3. 5	8. 4
4. 5	9. 4
5. 5	10. 5

SUMMARY

The publication of *Taxonomy of Educational Objectives, Handbook I: Cognitive Domain* in 1956 and the publication of *Handbook II: Affective Domain* in 1964 increased the ability of educators to examine objectives in order to ensure that they focused upon the achievement of skills and abilities at varying levels of complexity. Although the lines between the domains and between the levels within them are sometimes unclear, the notion of separate domains and levels is, itself, useful.

The cognitive domain deals with the acquisition and manipulation of factual information and it is divided into six levels: knowledge, comprehension, application, analysis, synthesis, and evaluation, with all the levels being cumulative. The focus of the lowest level is on simple recall. At the comprehension level, the focus is on understanding as evidenced by the ability to translate, interpret, or extrapolate, and at the application level the focus is on the rather mechanical use of rules, principles, and procedures. The knowledge, comprehension, and application levels make up the lower-level cognitive skills.

At the analysis level, the focus is upon identifying elements, relationships, or patterns of organization within a whole that are not clear or obvious. Identifying the clear or obvious requires only lower-level skills. While analysis level tasks require students to read between the lines and to determine which rules, principles, and procedures to use and how to use them, the tasks are objective enough that if given to independent experts, the experts would be likely to reach the same conclusions.

The synthesis level focuses upon the creation of a unique communication, plan, or idea. Though the emphasis here is upon creativity, the teacher must provide clear minimum acceptable standards by which the student's effort can be objectively assessed.

The evaluation level focuses upon making and then justifying a value judgment. The point is to enable students to logically defend their choices. At this level, experts might disagree but each would have a logical reasons for his or her choice.

The affective domain concerns the development of attitudes, feelings, and values. Educators disagree about the need to write objectives in the affective domain, but not about the fact that everyday teacher actions and interactions help to shape students' attitudes, feelings, and values.

The levels within the affective domain extend from simple awareness (receiving), to minimal commitment (responding), open commitment (valuing), the prioritizing of values (organization), and making one's life congruent with one's beliefs (characterization). Achievement at each of these levels depends on the selection of some observable behavior that the teacher assumes reflects the attitude, feeling, or value in question.

A structure of the psychomotor domain was written by Anita Harrow and published in 1972. The levels within it extend from reflex movements through skills such as walking and running (basic-fundamental movements); skills such as auditory and tactile discrimination (perceptual abilities); characteristics such as strength, endurance, flexibility, and agility (physical abilities); skills such as typing and playing tennis (skilled movements); and the use of bodily movements alone to express ideas, emotions, and situations (nondiscursive communication).

After precise instructional objectives are written, they should be classified and, if necessary, adjusted to ensure that a range of skills and abilities are developed. Ideally, the objectives should move students from teacher-directed, lower-level skills to student-directed, higher-level skills. Finally, the objectives should be approved by the administration to ensure that they fit into the overall curriculum.

The following checklist might be useful as a way of verifying the adequacy of the objectives:

1. Is the objective a single sentence, preferably of twenty five words or less?
2. What is the single observable behavior? Underline it.
3. Is the behavior to be demonstrated under controlled conditions so there will be no question about who did the work? (No group work or homework assignments.)
4. What is the minimum acceptable behavior? Circle it.
5. Is the standard reasonable in light of the ability level of the students?
6. Could a parent or someone else who is not a specialist in the subject evaluate achievement of the objective as well as the teacher could?
7. If there is a series of objectives, are they labeled as to level and arranged from the lowest level to the highest level?
8. Describe at least two ways in which achievement of the objective will help the student better understand the world outside of school.
9. How does the objective help the student integrate knowledge or learn to learn?

STUDY QUESTIONS

1. What major purpose is served by classifying instructional objectives?
2. What characteristics differentiate tasks at the analysis and evaluation levels from tasks at the application and synthesis levels?
3. Name and explain two of the major points of contention concerning the stating of objectives in the affective domain.
4. What characteristic of nondiscursive communication differentiates it from other levels of the psychomotor domain?
5. What are three ways by which educators can test their objectives for clarity?
6. Why is it wise for a teacher who is developing his or her own instructional objectives to have those objectives approved by the appropriate administrator?

NOTES

1. Benjamin S. Bloom, ed., *Taxonomy of Educational Objectives, Handbook I: Cognitive Domain* (New York: David McKay, 1956).
2. David R. Krathwohl, ed., *Taxonomy of Educational Objectives, Handbook II: Affective Domain* (New York: David McKay, 1964).
3. Anita J. Harrow, *A Taxonomy of the Psychomotor Domain* (New York: David McKay, 1972).
4. Ibid.
5. Robert F. Mager, *Preparing Instructional Objectives* (Palo Alto, Calif.: Fearon, 1962), p. 52.

__4__

Selecting Instructional Procedures

INTRODUCTION

If broad educational goals (such as learning to learn and integrating knowledge) are kept in mind, it follows that students need to acquire and be given opportunities to apply skills and knowledge. The kinds of opportunities provided depend, in part, upon the abilities of the students, so assessing those abilities is important. Once this is done, appropriate instructional activities can be planned.

Instructional procedures can be placed into two broad and sometimes overlapping categories: those that are teacher-directed (such as lectures or demonstrations) and those that are (or can be) student-directed (such as discussions or projects). Typically, teacher-directed procedures are used to provide information quickly, and student-directed procedures are used to give students opportunities to use that information.

This chapter begins with an examination of preassessment purposes and techniques. Then, procedures that apply to most instructional situations are examined. Finally, a variety of teacher-directed and student-directed procedures are discussed. Please note that, as was the case with the domains and levels of Bloom's taxonomy, the divisions of teacher-directed and student-directed instructional procedures are not always distinct.

SAMPLE OBJECTIVES

When you complete this chapter, you will be able, in writing, to:

1. Describe at least two student skills or abilities that should be preassessed to help ensure students' success in class, and two or more ways to assess such skills or abilities.

2. Explain the purpose of set induction and cite at least two ways that effective sets can be induced.
3. Explain what is meant by stimulus variation and cite at least two ways by which stimuli can be varied.
4. Describe at least three features that will enhance the effectiveness of a lecture or a demonstration and explain how those features contribute to effectiveness.
5. Describe at least three different classes of questions and explain when the use of each would be most appropriate.

PREASSESSING ACADEMIC STATUS

When teachers develop instructional objectives, they make some assumptions about the abilities of the students they expect in their classes. For example, while some variation in the academic abilities of the students is expected, the teachers and the administrators who assigned the students to the classes assume that the students will generally be functioning at a particular level. What would happen if the assumption was wrong? Suppose, for example, that a teacher walked into a junior-level class and found that many of the students were reading far below grade level and could make little sense of the text, or that the students did not have the math abilities that were expected? Conversely, and less likely, suppose that the students were reading far above grade level or had already mastered the skills that the teacher planned to teach? What would happen in either of these cases would depend upon what changes, if any, were made in the objectives and procedures, but the point is that no changes would be made if the teacher did not take the time to preassess the students' achievement level.

If students do not possess the background prerequisite to the new knowledge and skills they will be learning, it will be difficult, perhaps impossible, for them to learn the new material. One way to determine the extent to which students have mastered the prerequisite knowledge and skills is to administer evaluation instruments that sample their knowledge and skills. Questions for such tests can be developed by examining the texts that students used in preceding course work, by talking with the teachers of those courses, and by analyzing examinations that students have taken. This information, plus the teacher's own expectations of prerequisite skills, should provide the basis for a short but effective preassessment test. It is often helpful to include at least one short-answer question to assess students' writing abilities.

A preassessment test should yield important information. The teacher hopes the results will prove that most students have the necessary prerequisites and that activities can proceed as planned. If the results indicate that many students do not have the necessary prerequisites, there is a problem; depending on its severity, administrative help may be needed to solve it.

If the students lack the skills needed, the teacher must decide on a course of action. One choice is to modify the course objectives by adding remedial objectives that would cover the prerequisites. Taking the time to help students achieve these remedial objectives would leave less, and perhaps too little, time for students to achieve all of the original objectives. A second choice is to go ahead with the planned objectives, even though many of the students will have great difficulty.

Strong arguments can be made for taking the time to work on prerequisites, and equally strong arguments can be made for going ahead, but before a teacher makes either decision the administration should be consulted. Administrators' responsibilities include the approving of course objectives and the evaluation of teachers' performance. Once course objectives have been approved and become part of the curriculum, any major change in those objectives may affect other parts of the curriculum. An administrator may have a good reason for wanting to leave objectives unchanged or for welcoming changes, and a teacher could upset carefully made plans by making unilateral changes.

Further, administrators assess the performance of teachers. It reflects a high degree of professionalism to take the time to preassess students and to suggest courses of action based upon the preassessment results. Moreover, if it is necessary to go back and cover prerequisites (to take the students from where they are), and administrative approval to do so has been obtained, a teacher can undertake the remediation without fear of being accused of failure to have students achieve all of the course objectives by the end of the semester or year. The reason that all course objectives might not have been achieved is that some of the available time was spent covering the prerequisite skills and knowledge. If it is decided to move ahead without remediation, and students perform poorly, at least the teacher has pointed out to the administration that the students were unprepared for the work. A teacher can control either time or achievement, but not both. If given sufficient time, a reasonably competent teacher can help virtually all students achieve the course objectives. If the teacher must work within a limited time-frame, then fewer students can be helped.

It is possible that a teacher will decide, on the basis of preassessment, that students could and should work on objectives more sophisticated than those originally planned. Again, before making any major changes in course objectives, it would be wise to consult with the appropriate administrator.

Regardless of whether the preassessment results cause a teacher to back up, proceed as planned, or jump ahead, the writing sample acquired via the short answer question will be useful. If students cannot use the language properly, then it might be necessary to add work on this area to the other objectives. All teachers have a responsibility to help students improve their use of the language. If students lag in such development, that deficiency may very well have a detrimental effect on their overall performance; they may have the right information but be unable to express it. Identifying this as a problem area early gives a teacher the opportunity to help students overcome the problem.

ADDITIONAL SOURCES OF INFORMATION

Virtually every school keeps a cumulative record of each student. That record usually includes standardized achievement test scores, attendance records, past grades and, sometimes, anecdotal records. Anecdotal records are descriptions of specific events or comments about the students. Some teachers feel it is useful to look through the folders of their students to find out about particular strengths and weaknesses. Other teachers feel that they want to assess students on the basis of their current performance and that information in the cumulative folders might bias that assessment. In any case, many teachers now avoid adding anecdotal records to students' files for fear that those records may one day be used in a court of law. Defending a value judgment can be difficult.

PREASSESSING MAINSTREAMED STUDENTS

"Mainstreaming" refers to placing students with special needs into regular classrooms. In 1975, Congress passed the Education for All Handicapped Children Act (Public Law 94-142). This law not only provided for the education of all handicapped students, it also provided: (1) that those students should be educated in the least restrictive environment (a regular classroom rather than a special education classroom to the extent possible), (2) that individualized educational plans should be devised for such students, and (3) that all evaluation procedures for screening students for special services must be nondiscriminatory. In order to comply with Public Law 94-142, teachers should not only examine the cumulative folders of such students, but also talk with the appropriate guidance counselors and special education teachers.

While the adjustment of terminal behaviors might be time consuming, the possible adjustment of minimum acceptable standards poses the real problem. Some of the mainstreamed students may have learning disabilities that make it difficult for them to meet the standards set for others in the class. If a teacher has such students in class, he or she should first check with school administrators to find out if a policy has been established regarding the adjustment of standards for mainstreamed students. If no policy has been established, the teacher should work with special education teachers or guidance counselors to develop a set of objectives that are reasonable for the student and for the subject and grade level in which the student has been placed. It is *not* suggested that the teacher should abandon grade standards to accommodate the mainstreamed student(s). If mainstreamed students simply cannot meet reasonable standards for a particular subject at a particular grade level, consideration should be given to placing them in another class (perhaps a special education class) to give them a fair chance at success.

The more teachers know about the beginning abilities of their students, the more they will be able to select appropriate learning activities and help students succeed. Preassessment can provide the information. Now we will look at learning activities.

THE STANFORD SKILLS

Good teaching results from a combination of skills, knowledge, and attitudes that cannot be precisely described; it is an excellent example of the whole being greater than the sum of the parts. Nevertheless, teacher education is based upon the fundamental principle that, to the extent that teaching is a science, it can be systematically analyzed and improved. The four-step instructional models discussed previously can aid in isolating specific parts of the instructional process for examination. The rest of this chapter will focus on the third step: instruction.

Over the years there have been numerous attempts to identify the best teaching procedures, and there will undoubtedly be many more. This is not an attempt to advocate any one of them. No instructional procedure works best for all people, at all times, and under all conditions, but some procedures are better suited for some things than for others.

In the mid-1960s a group of educators, including Dwight Allen, James Cooper, and others at Stanford University, developed the idea of microteaching, that is, teaching mini-lessons to peers in order to develop specific instructional skills. Those skills became known as the "Stanford skills," and a few of them are described below because they can be used in a wide variety of instructional situations.

Set Induction

All lessons have beginnings, but some beginnings are more effective than others. For example, think about a math lesson that starts: "Open your books to page 109." The effect on students is likely to be deadening. It prompts thoughts such as "more of the same," or "only 204 pages left to go." In contrast, think about a math lesson that begins: "If you had the choice of getting a penny a day with the total doubled each day for a month, or a million dollars, which would you choose?" The second beginning is more likely than the first to stimulate students' interest.

An effective beginning of a lesson stimulates student interest, focuses that interest on the topic at hand, and actively involves the students. Asking a good question is one way to do this. To effectively induce a favorable mind-set the question must be complex enough to require thought, but not so complex for students to answer before learning the information to be taught. Rhetorical questions generally do not facilitate good set inductions. A rhetorical question is one to which no answer is expected or to which there is only one reasonable answer. An example is, "How many of you think that helping people is generally good?" Since the answer is obvious, few students will bother to think about it, so its value in inducing a favorable set is minimal.

There are other ways to induce a favorable set. A teacher could, for example, briefly review the main points covered the previous day, or relate a brief story or anecdote that relates directly to the upcoming lesson. The point, in any case, is to stimulate interest, focus the interest on the topic at hand, and to involve the students. Usually a minute or two is all that is necessary to do the job. It is also appropriate to use these same techniques during a lesson as shifts are made from topic to topic.

Communicating the Objective

Though it is true that most lessons build upon one another and that there may be some carry over from day to day, the teacher's planning and the students' learning will be easier if the instructional objective for each lesson is made clear. A good way to do this is for the teacher to communicate the lesson's objective to them. This can be done by writing the objective on the board or by orally explaining it, but in any case, a moment or two should be taken to ask a student to paraphrase the objective. This will help to ensure that students do, in fact, understand what they are supposed to be learning during the lesson.

Stimulus Variation

Most people are able to learn about the world around them via their five senses: sight, sound, taste, touch, and smell. Unfortunately, educators sometimes forget to use as many of the five senses as possible. For example, students can learn about Hawaiian luaus by reading about them, by seeing pictures of them, by hearing about them, or by participating in one. Which way would be most effective? Why?

Not all subjects lend themselves to learning via taste, touch, or smell, but even the use of gestures, voice inflections, and visual aids can help. As it happens, there is room for variety in the provision of instruction in all subjects. If instructional objectives include the range of cognitive abilities that they should, achievement of those objectives will *require* the use of a variety of instructional procedures and materials.

Further, regardless of how successful any given single instructional procedure may be originally, its effectiveness will eventually pale with continued use. Variety is the spice of life. Lessons should be spiced up with a variety of activities, but the activities should be carefully planned. The teacher should know how the activities will directly contribute to the achievement of specific instructional goals.

Closure

Just as every lesson has a beginning, every lesson has an end. There is a big difference, however, between a planned ending and having the bell ring while the teacher is in mid-sentence. There are two major purposes of closure. The first is to give students a sense of accomplishment—a feeling that they took a step in the right direction—that they accomplished something more than just attending another class. The second purpose is to relate the information just learned to information learned previously, to previous experiences, or to information yet to be learned and to events likely to happen. This bridge-building helps students put those bricks together. It helps to create a whole out of the parts.

There are other skills that Allen and the Stanford team identified, but those will be encountered as various procedures are discussed. Further, other educators have modified and reordered some of these basic skills. For example, Madelin Hunter has formulated a mastery learning program that begins with review of the previous day's work. It then moves to anticipatory set to focus attention and stimulate student participation, to the input and modeling of new information and skills, a check for understanding, and then guided and independent practice. There are still other config-urations of the basic skills, but they all fall into one of two broad categories—teacher-directed or student-directed. The following instructional procedures are primarily teacher-directed.

TEACHER-DIRECTED INSTRUCTIONAL PROCEDURES

Teacher-directed instructional procedures are used to provide instruction with little active student participation. During the early 1970s, some educators felt that indirect instruction was more valuable than direct instruction, since students were more involved and were "thinking" more. While this view is still held by some educators, at least as many believe in the virtues of direct instruction. Undoubtedly, a blend of the two, depending upon the instructional objective, is most useful.

Teacher-directed instructional procedures are most often used to help students achieve low-level objectives. These objectives usually call for students to acquire information, and it is appropriate for teachers to provide that information via lectures, demonstrations, and other teacher-directed activities. Lessons of this kind are also used to help students develop concepts. Sometimes "telling" lessons are referred to as concept lessons.

To keep the terminology clear, in this book a concept is defined as any group of things, concrete or abstract, that have enough characteristics in common to make up a unique set. For example, the word "tree" is a concrete concept. The word may bring to mind pine trees, maples, or oaks, but it does not call to mind dandelions or roses. All trees (with only a few exceptions) have enough characteristics in common to differentiate them from other plants, so they make up a unique set. An example of an abstract concept would be democracy. That term may bring to mind governments such as our own or those of France and Great Britain, but it does not bring to mind the government of Fascist Germany or Communist China (except as negative examples). Teacher-directed activities are useful in helping students understand concepts and in helping them link those concepts together into broader generalizations.

Formal and Informal Lectures

Lectures at the secondary level have fallen into some disrepute, simply because too many lectures were poorly done by too many teachers. A good lecture—one that is well planned and delivered smoothly and with conviction—can be an exciting learning experience and will be perceived as such by students. The line between such a lecture and an artistic performance is very fine indeed, and the extensive use of lectures must be reserved for the teacher with the personality and ability to do such work. It is possible for almost any teacher to plan and orchestrate a lecture that is cohesive and polished and that will capture the interest of all but the most reluctant student. The time spent in planning such a lecture, however, precludes all but an occasional use of this method by most teachers.

Rather than striving for the perfect "formal" lecture, that is, a lecture in which students do little except listen to a virtuoso performance, most teachers do better to concentrate on identifying those points, skills, and procedures that will enable them to deliver an "informal" lecture, that is, one that provides for student participation rather than passive student reception. This approach has the advantages of being well within the capabilities of most teachers, ensuring student interest, and thus being more useful. From this point on, the term *lecture* refers to the informal lecture unless stipulated otherwise.

Uses of Lectures. Lectures are used appropriately to (1) quickly and concisely present a great deal of new and integrated information, (2) clarify relationships among general points or between specific causes and effects, (3) explain procedures, and (4) point out inferences, inductions, deductions, and assumptions. It is reasonable to ask why the teacher should not simply use handouts to convey this information, since most students can read and comprehend at a rate of about 250 words per minute, whereas most can listen and comprehend at a rate of only 150 per minute. In many situations in which lectures are used, a handout would be as appropriate or even more appropriate; however, in other situations, particularly those in which the teacher may wish to add emphasis by voice inflection, or to make instant modifications on the basis of student reactions, lectures are clearly an appropriate instructional experience. Additionally, the informal lecture allows for spontaneous student responses and questions, and thus points can be clarified as they are raised by the students.

Planning Lectures. There are a number of appropriate lecture-planning procedures. Perhaps the most common is to construct a word or phrase outline. As the first step in this process, the teacher describes the specific instructional objective students will be able to achieve after listening to and participating in the lecture.

The kinds of objectives for which lectures are most appropriate are generally those at the low cognitive levels. For example, you will be able to:

1. Explain in writing six causes of World War I.
2. Write, in your own words, the definition of ethnocentrism and illustrate it with at least two examples.

The objectives are appropriate to lectures because their terminal behaviors are not time consuming (and thus do not infringe on the time available for the lecture) and do not require much, if any, student practice. With such objectives, students can be expected to demonstrate successfully the desired behavior simply by virtue of having been exposed to the information.

The objective will serve as the standard against which all prospective constituent elements of the lecture will be compared. Those elements that contribute clearly to student achievement of the objective will find their way into the word or phrase outline, whereas those that contribute little or nothing will be discarded. This procedure assures cohesiveness in the lecture and facilitates evaluation of the lecture's effectiveness. The outline may consist of short sentences, phrases, or even single words. Many teachers have found that they can lecture most effectively if they reduce their notes to a minimum. Voluminous notes, either in the form of lengthy outlines on sheets of paper or many brief items on index cards, tend to inhibit rather than to help the lecturer. Faced with detailed notes, many beginning teachers tend to refer to the notes more often than necessary, simply because they are there. In some cases the referrals become so frequent that the lecturer is, in effect, reading the notes. Additionally, voluminous notes tend to tie the lecturer to the podium, increase the probability of losing one's place, and decrease the opportunities the lecturer has to look at the audience while speaking. Extensive notes, in most cases, simply do not add to the smoothness and polish of a final delivery.

The lecture outline should serve to spark memory, not as a source of new information. The outline contains the key phrases, facts, figures, names, dates, and so on that are at the heart of the material; it should organize the material into logical blocks and to subdivide these blocks into manageable sizes to facilitate student learning. When giving an initial lecture, it may be helpful to make notes concerning the approximate length of time each part of the lecture should take.

Another part of planning concerns checking the content for its suitability for the student's level. It is easy to make notes without realizing that the students may not be familiar with certain terms, especially those that are technical or complex. If such terms are used in the outline, they should be starred or otherwise noted to remind the teacher to define and explain them.

During the planning of lectures, consider the use of appropriate instructional aids. Almost any lecture will hold student attention longer when the lecturer includes pictures, maps, graphs, cartoons, or similar support materials. The time to consider the use of such aids is when the lecture is being planned, and appropriate steps in ordering should be taken early.

There are two parties in an informal lecture: the students and the lecturer. Teachers who use this learning mode can often increase their effectiveness by working with students to ensure that common-sense notetaking procedures are used. For example, the teacher can hand out a list of instructions, such as the one here.

1. Each set of lecture notes should start on a separate page and carry the date and title of the lecture (as well as the lecturer's name if a guest is presenting the lecture).
2. A consistent outline format should be used, such as the following:

   I. Major topic (the purpose of outlining)
       A. Subheading (logical organization of content)
           1. Explanations (sequential steps: causes and effects, etc.)
               a. Further explanations

3. Notes tend to be more useful if the students attempt to write down only major areas and points rather than to copy the lecture word for word.
4. They should look for techniques such as restating, rephrasing, and listing of points on the board or overhead projector as clues that these are major points.
5. Contextual clues such as "There are *three* main facts here..." are often used at the beginning of a series of points and can facilitate the outlining of the information.
6. The development of a personal shorthand system for abbreviating frequently used words and phrases can save considerable time.
7. There are advantages to writing neatly enough that recopying the notes is not

necessary. Students can read and study neatly written notes in less time than it takes to recopy them. Some students, however, find that the act of recopying or rephrasing notes assists in learning.

8. Space may be allowed, as the notes are being taken, to add personal thoughts, comments, questions, and reactions.

9. Some students, particularly visually handicapped students, may benefit from taping the lectures.

Delivering the Lecture. After considerable effort has been made to prepare material for a lecture, the teacher may find that the students will deem the mode ineffective because of delivery or style. Lectures, as with any other instructional procedure, are enhanced by the stimulation of student interest *at the very beginning.* This initial interest arousal is enhanced by involving students as directly as possible and should "tune them in" to what the lecture is about. There is some evidence that teachers who can initiate lessons well can elicit more learning than teachers who do not concentrate on the initial stages of a presentation.[1]

Language usage can also contribute to or detract from the effectiveness of a lecture. Using language of appropriate complexity and formality is an art worth practicing. If new words are to be introduced, clear definitions should be made so that students will understand their meanings in the context in which they are used. Using complex language early in the lecture will cause students to "tune out" because they feel the lecture is going to be "over their heads," making it difficult to recapture their interest.

Good lecturers will often explain to students how the lecture is organized (cause-effect relationships, chronological order, easy-to-difficult, concrete-to-abstract, rule-example-rule). This helps students orient their thinking and organize their notes.

The effectiveness of lecturers is increased by visual reinforcement of verbal information. If students *see* important facts, figures, names, and dates as well as *hear* them, the probability of their being remembered increases. Furthermore, varying the stimulus can, in itself, be a device helpful in refocusing the attention of students whose interest may be wavering. Among the most common kinds of visual aids are prepared posters, chalkboards, overhead projectors, and opaque projectors. These devices are easy to use and provide sufficient latitude for creative utilization.

The ways in which the voice is used also influence effectiveness. Voice inflections, for example, can place emphasis on particular points and can dramatize quotations and asides. By varying the pitch and volume of the voice, lecturers add the variety necessary to capture the interest of the students. Rate, too, is important. Although most people can listen and comprehend from about 125 to 150 words per minute, a lecture is intended to instruct, and to do so properly, the rate at which the lecture is delivered should be slower, from 110 to 130 words per minute. The rate of delivery depends on the purpose and complexity of the material. In the case of most lectures, the teacher should allow time for students to listen to what is being said, comprehend what they hear, and relate new information to what is already known.

This last step cannot be done when the material is complex or if it is delivered at too fast a rate.

All teachers *can* improve their lecture delivery techniques. By taping segments of a speech and dividing the number of words spoken by the number of minutes elapsed, the words per minute can be calculated. It will also become apparent if there is a tendency to vary delivery rate. If there is a tendency to mispronounce particular words, to use personal pronouns, or insert words such as "you know" or "uh," listening to recorded lectures will make it immediately apparent. Teachers simply do not realize their own idiosyncracies until they listen to themselves and analyze what they hear.

Just as the use of formal visual aids adds to the interest of a lecture, so do physical movements. Appropriate hand and arm movements can help punctuate sentences and emphasize important points. Moving from behind the desk or podium and walking about can provide visual stimulation, but all these movements must stop short of being distracting. The use of a videotape recorder to detect and correct inappropriate physical movements can be revealing and beneficial.

The use of numerous and relevant examples has been shown to facilitate student understanding of content. Generous use of examples, nonexamples, analogies, and illustrations will help to keep student interest high and produce more learning.

When students are actively involved, their interest is higher, and the teacher can assess responses for students' understanding. Student participation is best encouraged by careful planning. Procedures found helpful to many teachers include preparing sets of key questions to be asked at appropriate places in the lecture. The experienced teacher is constantly aware of nonverbal clues and student behaviors that indicate confusion. Having students reiterate points by answering questions will often clarify important points for students who are still struggling with a new idea.

A good lecture concludes with a summary and review of the main points. While this activity can be done orally, it may be helpful to students if the teachers makes use of visual aids. Visual reinforcement helps to emphasize important points, and it gives students a chance to double-check notes, fill in points they may have missed, and correct errors.

In summary, the lecture is one of the most often used instructional procedures. Lectures have the advantage of enabling a teacher to present to students a large body of information in a relatively short period of time, and they are relatively easy to direct and control.

Possible disadvantages are that lectures can encourage passive, rather than active, student participation; that they may not provide much of the student-teacher interaction needed for proper evaluation of the instructional process; that they can foster unquestioning acceptance of presented material; that they may not capitalize on student curiosity or creativity; and that they tend to center more on the content than on what the student is to do with the content.

Questioning

The judicious use of questions can be the basis for valuable instructional experiences. Questions can be used to find out how well students understand a particular block of information, to shift student attention from one point to another, to increase retention of important points by isolating and emphasizing them, and to point students in the right direction before starting assignments. Perhaps their most valuable use, however, is to elicit high-order thinking on the part of students as questions are asked that call for analysis, synthesis, and evaluation skills and to provide practice for students in formulating and orally communicating specific answers to specific questions.

Using the following steps of the "overhead" questioning technique may prove helpful in increasing the effectiveness of questions:

1. *State the question clearly and precisely.* A question such as, "What about microcomputers?", for example, gives the student little direction for an answer. It is necessary to ask a follow-up question to clarify the first question. It would be better to ask, "How does a microcomputer differ from a large computer?" or "How could a microcomputer be used in this class?"

2. *Pause after asking the question and allow it to "hang overhead."* When the teacher asks questions in a classroom, it is beneficial for all students to think about the answer. To encourage this kind of attention, the teacher should ask the question clearly and then pause before calling on someone. The pause gives students a chance to think about the question and encourages all students to do so since they do not yet know who is to answer.

3. *Call on students at random.* Since it is desirable for all students to think about the questions, the teacher should not follow any pattern when calling on students. Any pattern, be it a seating arrangement, an alphabetical arrangement, or any other kind of sequence, has the effect of reducing attention on the part of those students who feel they will not be called upon.

4. *Provide immediate feedback to students.* The teacher should indicate the appropriateness of student answers. If an answer is not wholly correct, try to use the part that is correct or state the question to which the given answer would have been appropriate. If students are assured that their responses have value, active participation will continue.

Categorization of Questions. The nature of questions may be varied to ensure differing types of responses from students. One convenient way of categorizing questions to see the frequency of a particular type is to compare them with the divisions of the cognitive domain. The following examples may be helpful in placing questions into appropriate categories and are also indicative of the types of objectives for which this procedure is appropriate:

1. *Knowledge (or simple recall).* "What are the three basic parts of a precise instructional objective?"
2. *Comprehension (or understanding).* "What is meant by the term *in loco parentis?*"
3. *Application (for using information).* "Traveling at 55 miles per hour, how long would it take to get from New York to Los Angeles?"
4. *Analysis (or pulling an idea apart).* "What words or phrases does the author of this article use that cause the article to be biased?"
5. *Synthesis (putting together something new).* "How would you have improved upon Germany's strategy during the Battle of Britain?"
6. *Evaluation (or making and defending a judgment).* "Who do you think our best president was, and why?"

Another way to categorize questions is according to their essential function.

1. *First-order questions.* A first-order question may be defined as any question that has served its purpose as soon as an acceptable answer is given. Any of the six categories of questions described earlier can be considered first-order questions if their answers are clear-cut and if no further elaboration is elicited or desired.

2. *Probing questions.* A probing question is asked to encourage students to go beyond their initial responses to explain themselves further. An example of the use of a probing style might be, "Good, you're right so far, now can you give us an illustration?" By asking students to provide examples, illustrations, rationales, and so on, teachers can frequently determine the depth of students' understanding of material more accurately than by using first-order questions alone. A follow-up probing question often begins with "why."

3. *Open-ended questions.* An open-ended question has no definite right or wrong answer. A question such as "What do you think about the probability of extraterrestrial life forms?" is asked to encourage students to go beyond the recollection or explanation of previously acquired information and to hypothesize, project, and infer. Such questions are particularly well suited to the initiation of discussions.

4. *Convergent questions.* Convergent questions are arranged in a series and are designed to "converge" on a particular point or idea. For example, questions such as "Are there fewer or more farmers now than twenty years ago?" and "How do farm subsidies affect consumer prices?" could be used to help students focus attention on the issue of government farm subsidies. Convergent questions may be used to induce a principle or deduce an answer.

5. *Divergent questions.* Divergent questions, as the name implies, are asked to draw a student's attention away from one point and allow it creative freedom to settle on a different but related point. Divergent questions are particularly useful in inspiring student discovery of analogous situations. "What present-day parallels do we have, if any, to the Athenian agora?" is an example of an analysis-level question being used to stimulate divergent thinking.

Encouraging students to ask questions is a skill that can be manifested in numerous ways. The teacher can assist students in phrasing questions and make it clear that questions indicate a willingness to learn, not ignorance, on the part of students. The teacher can respond to students' questions thoroughly, courteously, and in a friendly manner and indicate the importance of students' questions by comments such as "That was a good question because...." Finally, the teacher must *never* humiliate a student who gives a wrong answer.

Demonstrations

Demonstrations have the unique advantage of enabling students to observe the demonstrator engage in a learning task rather than simply talking about it. A correctly conducted demonstration, whether of some laboratory procedure, physical skill, or other action, is often a stimulating instructional experience because it demonstrates a living model. A typical objective calling for a demonstration might be, "You will apply an arm splint that meets Red Cross requirements to a 'subject' within three minutes."

To make demonstrations effective, the teacher must often break down entire processes into component parts and decide what aspect of the skill, process, or procedure will be demonstrated in the time available. This is necessary because most demonstrations are a part of a larger task that cannot be demonstrated in its entirety during usual school time allotments. For instance, one demonstration in home economics may include the selection of a dessert, say, a cake, and include the exact choice of type of cake, possible substitutions of ingredients, proper blending procedures, and possible pitfalls. Including baking time and frosting may not be possible in the usual time allotment.

Having decided what can adequately be demonstrated within the time allowed, the teacher should then proceed to plan the component parts of the demonstration. Depending upon the nature of the demonstration, initial steps may include an overview description of the skill, process, or procedure. If machinery or equipment of any kind is to be used, the safety aspects are stressed. An outline of main points is often written on the chalkboard for quick reference, or students may be given handouts containing this information. Very detailed descriptions are often not necessary because students are able to understand terms, labels, and relationships easily as they view the demonstration.

During planning for the actual demonstration, the teacher will need to test all the equipment to be used to be sure it functions properly. Before the demonstration is conducted, the environment is arranged so that all students can see what is happening. If small instruments or fine manipulations are called for, schools so equipped often use a closed-circuit TV camera or videotape equipment. Many classrooms in which large numbers of demonstrations take place are equipped with overhead mirrors above demonstration tables. Effective demonstrations blend verbal skills with accompanying psychomotor skills. Gifted demonstrators are able to use the full range of questioning skills, drawing students' attention to crucial steps and to the way in which various steps are carried out. Exaggerated movements are to be avoided; they might confuse or mislead students as they attempt to practice the movements later.

Demonstrations that can be followed by immediate student practice appear to have maximum effectiveness. If it is not possible to provide for immediate practice, a review is necessary before delayed practice is begun. If no student practice is available, perhaps an alternative experience would be as effective as a fully prepared demonstration. If the length or complexity of the demonstration prohibits immediate practice, the teacher could divide the demonstration into two parts. The biggest asset of a demonstration is its ability to guide and precede students' actual involvement in a similar experience.

When the demonstration involves valuable or potentially dangerous material or equipment, the teacher must carefully weigh the dangers and benefits involved. If material or equipment is too dangerous or too valuable, it may be wise to choose a different procedure. Students are in school to learn, but not in an environment where they take unnecessary risks.

As students practice the skill or procedure, the teacher should provide individual corrective feedback and encourage students to assess their own performances. This is particularly important when dealing with mainstreamed students. Good teaching demands, of course, that allowances be made for individual differences that may affect the way in which instructions are carried out. For example, if the instructions begin, "Using your right hand," left-handed students may find such a movement awkward. In addition, allowance must be made for deviation among students' approaches. Not all students exhibit the same techniques in practice, and for some students certain procedures may come easily. If a particular student's idiosyncrasy is deemed detrimental to later performance, however, it warrants early correction.

One effective way to conclude a demonstration is to conduct a short questioning session covering specific procedures, terms, labels, and cause-effect relationships. If the practice of the demonstrated skill or procedure is to result in some product (as opposed to resulting in the improvement of some process), examples of satisfactory and unsatisfactory products should be made available so students can compare and contrast their own products with the models. Opportunities for creative responses in the product's development should be encouraged as long as established standards are maintained.

Guest Speakers

The chief purposes of inviting guest speakers into the classroom are to expose students to experts in particular fields, especially individuals who may have views different from those already explored in class, and to help motivate students. Making use of such people in the classroom—a controlled situation—establishes a direct contact between the classroom and the real world.

To maximize the usefulness of guest speakers as an instructional experience, the teacher should involve students in the process of choosing the guest speaker. When the class identifies a need in a particular area in which a speaker can provide a unique contribution, a list of potential speakers is compiled. The names of the prospective speakers are then cleared through the principal or other appropriate administrator, and permission is obtained to invite them to speak to the class. On the list should be persons who can fit such a visit into their schedule. Administrators may be able to suggest individuals who are willing to speak to classes and who have been well received in the past.

It is a good learning experience for students when they can get in touch with the prospective speaker. Among the things the prospective speaker may wish to know will be the age and grade level of the students, the topic being studied, how much the students already know about the topic, what type of unique contribution he or she might make, and the specific time, date, and topic.

It requires effort to prepare students for a guest speaker. If the speaker is to discuss a relatively new topic, it is usually possible to have students read available relevant information or discuss the topic. This gives students a matrix in which to work, thereby increasing their interest and enabling them to ask more intelligent questions. Some speakers prefer to respond to questions written by students before the talk. The quality of such questions depends upon the students' having experience in the content area prior to the speaker's visit.

On the appointed day the speaker will appreciate a student escort, who will meet the speaker at the entrance to the school and guide him or her to the classroom. In the few moments before introducing the speaker, the teacher can determine the approach the speaker will take. It is proper to suggest that time be left for a question-and-answer period after the presentation. If the teacher wishes to make a tape recording of the presentation, the permission of the speaker must be obtained.

After the presentation is complete, the teacher should tie the loose strands together and bring about closure. Points may have been made that will require further study, and aspects of the content presented may need to be related to previously learned material and to the instructional objective underlying the presentation. If students do not suggest writing a thank-you note, the teacher will want to remind them and discuss a procedure for writing it.

The division between teacher-directed and student-directed procedures is not always clear. The teacher-directed procedures described are useful for quickly conveying information. The facts, figures, names, dates, sequences, relationships, and examples constitute the concepts students are trying to learn.

The next section describes student-directed activities. These procedures can help students achieve higher-level objectives by giving them the opportunity to apply skills and knowledge. The more practice students are given in using skills and knowledge and in expressing and defending ideas, the better they will be able to function as informed and thinking citizens.

STUDENT-DIRECTED ACTIVITIES

One of the main concerns of the Progressivists and the field theorists has been that students are not given enough opportunity to integrate and use knowledge. The most commonly used instructional procedures continue to be telling and testing; those procedures emphasize low-level intellectual skills, such as the recollection of specific information and the most basic application of skills and knowledge. The field theorists believe that regardless of how effective telling and testing might be, students need more opportunities to develop higher-level skills.

Ultimately, it is the development of such higher-level skills as analysis, synthesis, and evaluation that most benefits students and society. Those skills cannot be developed without specific facts, figures, names, dates, sequences, and the other components of a well-developed database, but such a database does not automatically lead to the development of higher-level skills. Students need to be shown how to combine pieces of information into meaningful wholes, how to voice and defend positions, and how to critically analyze what they hear and see. Once these skills have been introduced, they must be developed by the students themselves. For this development and practice, student-directed instructional procedures are the most useful.

One reason why student-directed instructional activities are not used more often is that, in terms of the amount of information covered, they are more time-consuming than teacher-directed procedures. If students are asking questions and exploring ideas, less information will be covered than if they are listening to lectures. On the other hand, if student-directed techniques are used, students will be better able to use and remember the information learned.

Discussions

Discussions differ from usual conversation in that their intent and content are more carefully delineated and structured. Conversations that occur spontaneously are usually not intended to achieve specific objectives and are therefore essentially random. Instructional discussions have a specific purpose and direction. Their function is to help students achieve specific objectives. Typical of objectives calling for one or another kind of discussion are the ones that follow:

You will be able to:

1. Describe, in writing, the contents of a survival kit to be taken into the mountains by hikers planning a two-week camping trip.
2. Describe orally either a strength or a weakness in a given political system and explain why it is a strength or a weakness.

The skills and information necessary to achieve these two objectives can be acquired by students in a number of ways, one of which is the discussion. For example, using a discussion to give students practice in analyzing the components of survival kits in general will directly contribute to their ability to compile such components into a kit for any given situation later. The second objective can be achieved directly in a discussion since each student can be given the opportunity to participate and hence demonstrate the required behavior.

General Discussions.   The least specific of the discussion types is the general discussion. As in the other kinds of discussions, the purpose of general discussion is to give students practice in on-the-spot thinking, clear oral expression, and asking and responding to questions. Such discussions are also useful for assessing the diversification of views and exploring ideas.

The teacher's initial step is to gather together and make available to students appropriate background information, materials, and sources. The success of a discussion as an instructional experience depends upon the degree to which students are informed and prepared. Without background in the topic, students will be unlikely to make good contributions to a discussion. Proper procedure often leads to the recording of key questions for use in stimulating or changing the direction of the discussion. By using key questions, the teacher can guide discussions along those lines most likely to contribute to student achievement of the instructional objectives.

Since one of the aims in discussions is to encourage student-to-student communication, it can be helpful to arrange desks or chairs in such a way that students can comfortably see each other. Circular, semicircular, or horseshoe arrangements are useful.

The teacher should explain certain discussion ground rules. Some of these ground rules may be that contributions will be impersonal; that ideas, not the people who suggest them, will be the focus of the discussion; and that common social courtesies will be observed. If there are consistent violations of the rules, students may wish to establish a process for helping their peers who are lax in proper participation procedures.

It is common for teachers unconsciously to allow one or two students to monopolize the discussions. This problem can be avoided by asking for the comments and opinions of those students who do not volunteer to participate, but care should be taken not to force such participation. If students feel threatened, their participation will decrease rather than increase. Asking for opinions rather than for specific facts is a good way to encourage participation without posing a threat.

The problem of digression often emerges in general discussions. Some digressions that lead away from the objective may deal with information that has meaning and relevance for the students. The teacher must decide whether the digression is important enough in its own right to allow it to continue.

Guided or Directed Discussions.   A directed discussion is appropriate if students are to be guided through a series of questions to the discovery of some principle, formula, relationship, or other specific preselected result. In guided discussions students are given practice in inductive or deductive, step-by-step thinking, and since the thinking is convergent, the net result is to lead the students toward a common revelation of a major principle or conclusion.

There is some danger in using directed discussions because the teacher has already determined what the students are to discover. If students become too frustrated in the chain of logic leading to the discovery, they may react with the attitude, "Why didn't you just say so in the first place?" and the value of the experience will be lost. Many teachers who use this technique feel that using it for only ten- or fifteen-minute blocks of time works best. Once the conclusion is reached or the principle is discovered, a shift to another instructional experience to make use of that conclusion or principle logically follows. It has also been found helpful to begin guided discussions with a statement such as, "There is an underlying point here..." or "Let's see if we can reach a conclusion concerning...." Statements such as these help set the stage for the guided discussion and minimize the possibility of students' seeing the experience as guesswork.

An analogy might be made between a guided discussion and a computer-assisted instruction program. In each case the most likely student responses to questions must be anticipated and appropriate questions (or instruction) planned. Both are designed to provide reinforcement to the student for correct answers and are built around a series of sequential steps. The important difference is that in a guided discussion the teacher very closely monitors the interaction and can modify the remaining questions to capitalize on some unexpected student response.

If used cogently, guided discussions can provide an additional rich instructional experience. Students enjoy discovering and solving, and once they have "discovered" a principle, they remember it longer than if it is simply explained to them.

Reflective Discussions. Reflective discussions are used to assist students in developing analytical skills, arriving at alternative explanations, finding solutions to selected problems, and classifying ideas into major categories. These skills relate directly to objectives at the higher cognitive levels (i.e., analysis, synthesis, and evaluation). A typical objective for a reflective discussion might be, "You will explain orally how some aspect of daily life would differ if we lived under a socialistic government."

When using reflective discussions the teacher should define a particular problem relative to the instructional objective, then devise a series of open-ended questions to encourage a variety of possible responses. Additional specific questions will be generated and asked spontaneously during the discussion.

To help maximize the benefit from reflective discussions, one student can be delegated to list the identified main points of each response on the chalkboard. To supplement this listing, the teacher can elicit from the class appropriate headings for clusters of responses that have points in common. In this way, as students are given practice in classifying ideas and in analysis skills, a basis is provided for predicting and hypothesizing solutions to the original problem.

Unlike guided discussions, which can often be conducted at a rapid rate since the teacher has prior knowledge of the result, reflective discussions should be conducted at a relatively slow pace and include periods of silence. Time must be allowed for students to consider alternate possibilities and to think about the ramifications of those possibilities. Many teachers complain that the slowness of reflective discussions is a serious drawback and that the discussions take time that can be used in more valuable ways. Other teachers feel the "thinking" time required is one of the strongest attributes of reflective discussions and use the discussions frequently. In deciding how often to use them, the teacher must weigh these factors and balance time used against the opportunities for divergent responses, large-scale student participation, practice in classification, and reflection.

Inquiry Discussions and the Scientific Method. Inquiry discussions are used to provide students with opportunities to use an analytical approach for reasoning and acquire new information with a minimum of help from the teacher. In inquiry discussions students practice critical thinking, gathering and analyzing data, and drawing conclusions on the basis of evidence rather than intuition.

It is vital that students have access to appropriate resources (e.g., books, maps, instruments, graphs) if inquiry discussions are to be worthwhile. Such materials are used most effectively if they are available in the classroom, but if this is not practical, they could be placed on reserve in the school library or in other central locations.

Inquiry discussion is often used in conjunction with what is called the *scientific method*. The steps of the scientific method are usually stated in a form such as the following:

1. Identify the problem.
2. Formulate a hypothesis (a probable solution or explanation).
3. Gather, evaluate, and categorize available data.
4. Reach some conclusion (either reject or support the hypothesis) on the basis of the evidence acquired.
5. Take some action appropriate to the results (write a letter to an appropriate party concerning the implications of the conclusions or let other interested parties know of the results) so that students will be reinforced for their efforts.

When used as part of the scientific method, most inquiry discussions will be just one part of an overall scheme including several types of instructional experiences. An inquiry discussion will prove valuable at each of the five phases of the scientific method, but using the method itself could occupy a widely varying amount of class time. To facilitate use of this method, the teacher can establish a timetable with the class, ensuring that the investigation will move along smoothly and will conclude by a certain date. Time is allowed for consolidation sessions during which progress to date can be evaluated and future plans refined.

When used as a single-period experience, an inquiry discussion follows the same scientific method in longer-term investigations, but the data-gathering process is abbreviated, with all information coming directly from the students (usually based on their experience and their assigned reading). To keep this process from deteriorating, the teacher must be alert for incorrect, incomplete, or misleading student input. When misinformation is detected, the teacher may be able to use the instance to generate students' interest in finding out more from sources at hand or from sources available for an out-of-class venture. For purposes of inquiry discussions, it is usually inappropriate for the teacher to act as a major source of information. A better role is that of resource person—one who helps point students to the sources of information—rather than as a supplier of data. This is in contrast to guided discussions, in which teachers not only provide information but also direct students to predetermined outcomes.

For example, assume that a teacher adopted the objective, "Each student will describe, in writing, at least five sources of information needed by a modern world leader to function effectively." This objective might be achieved partially by providing students practice in determining what kinds of information the president of the United States needs and how that information is, or might be, acquired. This session lends itself to an inquiry discussion. Consider the following steps.

1. *Identify the problem.* As a beginning point the teacher could ask students how they think the president gets information relevant to decisions he or she makes. This line of questioning usually results in a number of ideas, but the need to pinpoint more specifically the kind of information being discussed will almost certainly emerge. The type of information available from newspapers, for example, is different from that available from top-secret dispatches. Once the problem is restated precisely, the second step can be taken.

2. *Formulate a hypothesis.* Through the use of questions some probable hypothesis can be structured. The teacher should not leave the impression that all possibilities are equally valid, thus precluding the need for further analysis. All ideas concerning a hypothesis may be accepted, but the class should decide on a limited number for further investigation.

3. *Gather, evaluate, and categorize available data.* It is at this point that inquiry discussions may prove difficult to complete within a single class period. Ideally, students should search out all types of data and subject them to a detailed analysis. If only a single class period is to be used, the teacher must make extensive use of questions and clues and must encourage students to analyze their own answers. By questioning, sufficient data can often be acquired and analyzed. If sufficient data are not acquired after questioning, data-gathering teams may be necessary and analysis postponed to a subsequent time.

4. *Reach some conclusion.* Once the data are gathered and analyzed, the class is ready to reach a conclusion. The acquired facts are related to the original hypothesis. Properly handled, the facts should support or reject the hypothesis. In the process, students will have acquired practice in the skill of applying the scientific method to a problem, and they will have engaged in analytical thought.

5. *Take some action.* A logical application of the practice just engaged in would be to have students demonstrate the lesson's objective by casting it in a hypothetical situation. (For example, "You are now the president of the United States. How will you organize your information-gathering machine and of what will it consist?")

If, when an inquiry discussion is initiated, students realize they do not have sufficient information to reach intelligent conclusions, intervening plans for obtaining additional data emerge. Once the data have been acquired, the class reviews the initial steps and proceeds through the remaining steps. For teachers who utilize the scientific method inquiry approach, acquisition of the data is as important as producing the result.

Exploratory Discussions. Exploratory discussions have almost as unstructured a framework as general discussions, but there are some important differences. Exploratory discussions are intended to enable students to discuss controversial issues (such as premarital sex, use of illegal drugs, and abortion) without fear of censure. Such discussions help make students aware of the other students' views and can thus help them become more tolerant of differing notions.

When exploratory discussions are conducted, the teacher must define the topic clearly with the understanding that there will be no negative criticism of other students' views during the discussion. That does not preclude disagreement and alternative views, but if a tone of ridicule emerges, students will become reluctant to voice further opinions, thus defeating the purpose of the discussion. While the later scrutinizing of a general class feeling is not threatening to individuals and can cause little harm, the scrutinizing of a particular student's opinion or comment may cause negative attention to be focused on him or her and may thus cause an unintended and undesirable reaction.

One of the problems of exploratory discussions is that they are often explorations into the affective domain, and a precise definition of what was gained by students is difficult. Students may feel that little was accomplished. To minimize these difficulties, the teacher can synthesize the various contributions and use them as a basis for further instructional experiences that are more precisely defined. There may be few concrete accomplishments directly attributable to an exploratory discussion, but there may be many students who are enlightened by the variety of opinions held by their peers and who are thus given new insights.

Exploratory discussions may also be used in conjunction with a resource person knowledgeable in the area to be studied. The function of such a person would be to present new ideas and opinions to which students could respond.

Evaluation of Discussions. Discussions are time-consuming instructional procedures in relation to content gained by students, especially in comparison with experiences such as reading assignments or lectures. The advantage most forms of discussion have over information-gathering procedures, however, is that they capitalize upon student curiosity and creativity, encourage participation, and allow for development of higher-level thought processes.

Discussions, like all instructional procedures, must be evaluated to determine effectiveness. The best way to judge a discussion is to determine if students can achieve the instructional objective for which the discussion was chosen as the learning activity.

Practicing teachers find it useful to note which students do or do not contribute to discussions and what types of contributions are made by individuals, for comparison with evaluation results. It is sometimes found, for instance, that, even though students did not participate vocally in a discussion they were involved mentally and developed analytical skills. Nonparticipation may indicate that the student needs special, individualized help, but it may also mean that these students are simply thinking about what is being said. By comparing evaluation results with patterns of participation, it may be possible to determine which students need the maximum amount of encouragement to participate, since participation, in their case, aids learning.

The quality of students' responses is a valid indicator of the effectiveness of discussions. When students make comments indicative of muddled thinking or misconceptions the teacher should be alert to a need to clear up the confusing points or misconceptions. On occasion, however, students make such comments purely for effect—to impress their peers or to elicit special attention from the teacher. If it becomes clear that a student is engaging in "artificial" participation, attempting to take care of the problem during the ongoing discussion is likely to produce denials or challenges by the concerned student and should be avoided. A private conference is usually more fruitful.

Effective evaluation of discussions takes thought, but the potential for improvement makes the effort worthwhile. The more discussions are used and evaluated, the more polished the teacher will become in their use. By providing for student demonstrations of instructional objectives and by keeping track of participation, the teacher can polish their ability in this instructional procedure.

Brainstorming

Brainstorming is an instructional procedure similar in many ways to an exploratory discussion. Brainstorming is used to generate a wide variety of creative ideas concerning a problem in a short period of time.

To conduct a brainstorming session, the teacher must act as a facilitator. The facilitator's primary responsibility is to see that proper procedures are followed. Brainstorming uses relatively few, but crucial, rules. After the problem is identified, the facilitator explains that the point of the brainstorming session is to acquire as many creative ideas as possible. Everyone is encouraged to contribute any idea regardless of how strange it may seem. The facilitator makes it clear that no idea or contribution is to be discussed, evaluated, or criticized during the brainstorming session and that each idea suggested will be added to a written list of ideas.

The effectiveness of brainstorming sessions depends on rapid pace, short duration, and close adherence to the rule that no idea or contribution during the brainstorming is to be discussed. At the end of the session the class will have a number of suggestions written down relating to the central topic. The facilitator then helps the class divide the ideas into general categories and move into an exploratory discussion in which the various ideas are discussed. If such discussion is allowed to interrupt the brainstorming session itself, the necessary freewheeling atmosphere is inhibited.

One common use for brainstorming sessions is to acquire seed material for more complex tasks, such as synthesizing. Thus, the teacher might use a brainstorming session to help students generate ideas with which to build a rationale for or against suggested governmental legislation.

Panel Discussions

An instructional procedure in which the teacher plays a reduced role is the panel discussion. Panel discussions permit a small group of students to delve deeply into an area of interest and then to act as a source of information for the rest of the class.

To arrange a panel discussion, a small group of students (six or fewer) is identified as participants on the panel, and one student acts as chairperson. If needed, assistance is provided in dividing up research responsibilities and setting up a time schedule. Responsibilities on the panel are assigned commensurate with the abilities of the students. For some students, providing specific references and sources may be necessary.

When the panel is ready to act as an authority, the chairperson or other moderator may follow several courses of action. One common approach is for the moderator or chairperson to explain briefly what the panel is prepared to discuss with the class, to introduce each of the panel members and identify his or her special areas of interest, and begin accepting questions from the class.

An alternative approach uses the moderator or chairperson to introduce briefly the topic to be discussed and then to introduce each of the panel members, allowing each about five minutes to discuss or explain his or her particular area of interest. The moderator or chairperson then summarizes the findings and opens the panel to questions and comments from the class. This procedure has the benefit of providing the rest of the students with information upon which to base questions.

In both approaches the moderator or chairperson ensures that all panel members participate on an equal basis and that sufficient time is left for a final summation. Time is also allowed for the teacher to bring the panel discussion to a close near the end of the class period and establish the relationship of the discussion to the instructional objective.

Sociodramas

Sociodramas are useful for dramatizing particular social problems and for increasing student empathy for the feelings, viewpoints, and problems of other members of society. Teachers who use sociodramas successfully find they are most useful when working to help students achieve various affective domain objectives. Typical of such objectives might be the following.

You will be able to:

1. Identify and explain the cause for your reaction to the statement, "Homosexuality is normal."
2. Add or eliminate at least one rationale used to defend your attitude about abortion.

To conduct a sociodrama successfully, the teacher must make certain that all students understand that participants will be acting out roles as they believe people would actually behave. Participants, therefore, theoretically do not act out their *own* feelings, but what they perceive the feelings of others to be. It is made clear that the sociodrama will be stopped if students step out of their roles or begin to get too emotionally involved.

Once the ground rules are understood, the class proceeds to identify a situation in which two or more people interact and the specific roles and "positions" of the participants. After this is done students are encouraged to volunteer to play each of the roles. No one should be forced to participate.

Participants are allowed to confer briefly about how they intend to act out the situation (not to rehearse) and should then act it out. Usually two or three minutes is sufficient for students to decide how they intend to present the situation and another ten minutes for the actual sociodrama.

Before any discussion of the sociodrama takes place, it is sometimes worthwhile to have a second set of students confer and act out the same situation. After the second sociodrama, students can compare and contrast pertinent points in the dramatizations. No effort is made to evaluate the performance level of students. The focus of the discussion after a sociodrama is on the differing perceptions of the roles by the participants and nonparticipants, on an attempt to understand the probable feelings and beliefs of the person(s) in the real situation, and on an examination of personal rationales for values held.

Field Trips

The logical extension of bringing part of the world into the classroom is taking the class into the "real" world. Field trips are useful not only because they give students firsthand knowledge and enable them to see how a number of skills and processes blend into a whole, but also because they can be used to provide students with cultural experiences available in no other way. Many students, for example, would never get to see the printing of a newspaper from start to finish unless they saw it on a school field trip. Similarly, many students never go to an art museum, concert, or professional play unless they are introduced to them on a field trip.

Field trips should be related directly to an ongoing unit of work. When possible, it is desirable to capitalize on a perceived student need for a field trip, but if long-range planning is a necessity for a particular trip, the teacher should take the initiative. Once it has been decided that a field trip is useful or desirable, specific objectives to be achieved by the trip can be shared with, or generated by, the class. Of course, the teacher may have determined beforehand that such a trip is an instructional experience that can help to achieve some of the objectives on the list handed out at the beginning of the term. In either case, the objectives can be used as a springboard to produce specific questions to be answered by students while they are on the field trip or upon their return. During a trip many activities and new experiences will be competing for the students' attention, and the questions will help focus their attention on the most important activities and experiences.

Student involvement during each step of planning a field trip helps generate interest and make the trip more worthwhile. For example, while some students are building questions that focus attention on important aspects, others may gather information about the facilities at the site of the field trip. This latter group may wish to write for information on the availability of guided tours, admission costs, dates and times the facility is open, specific clothing requirements, and the availability of eating facilities. Still another group may obtain information about transportation. Even though you will probably be familiar with bus use, it is instructive to students to discover for themselves whether school district regulations allow classes to use school buses for field trips and whether this use is dependent upon the buses being returned before they are needed to transport students home from school at the end of the day; whether the distance is such that students will have to leave particularly early or get back after school hours; how to charter a bus if necessary; and the importance of school insurance policies that cover field trips and their ramifications for the use of private automobiles.

If chartered transportation is needed, it must be paid for, which may be an inhibiting factor. Depending on the student population, it may be unfair to expect parents to contribute enough money to cover both the incidental expenses of their children and transportation costs. If such is the case, the class may decide to raise the necessary money. Regardless of how the money is raised or collected, it is important to keep accurate and public records. The procedures adopted should coincide exactly with those advocated by the school.

Most schools require that the parents or guardians of students going on a field trip sign permission slips. These slips are *not* legal documents meant to protect schools and teachers from a lawsuit; they are simply devices to assure the school that parents know where the students will be going that day and approve of the trip. The teachers can extend the utility of permission slips by including on them details parents would wish to know, such as departure and arrival times, whether students are to bring food with them or purchase it, and special clothing requirements.

All these considerations are influenced by board and administrative policies. Teachers must cooperate with the school administration to ensure that policies are followed concerning absences from other classes, providing for students who are unwilling or unable to go, securing sufficient chaperonage, special cases such as financially or physically handicapped students or students with particular religious or dietary restrictions. There may also be regulations concerning taking along a first-aid kit or extra cash. Students, of course, should be asked to demonstrate that they know where the bus will be waiting for the group should they get separated, and what time it is scheduled to leave the field trip site.

Proper follow-up activities are particularly important with respect to field trips. Unlike other instructional activities, field trips involve staff members outside of the class. If, after disturbing the instructional plans of other teachers and perhaps keeping students from attending other classes, the field trip does not yield worthwhile results, the sponsoring teacher may find it difficult to secure permission for other trips. This possibility, coupled with financial problems, has caused many boards of education to prohibit field trips completely. When the field trip has focused on specific objectives and students are given adequate preparation, follow-up discussions and evaluations do not prove difficult. General and ambiguous reactions to the trip, while perhaps of passing interest, are not the main concern. This experience should be evaluated primarily on the basis of how well the instructional objective was achieved, how well the newly acquired information was related to previously learned information, and how well the experience can serve as the basis for future instructional experiences.

School-community relations tend to improve as interaction between the two increases. Field trips and the use of outside speakers both provide interaction and thus help to improve school-community relations.

SMALL-GROUP ACTIVITIES

Small-group activities are well suited to a number of instructional situations. Such activities are useful for increasing social interaction and thereby maximizing social development. They make efficient use of limited materials and resources; they allow complex problems and tasks to be divided into less complex components; they provide opportunities for peer-to-peer tutoring; and they enable students to take more responsibility for planning and carrying out educational tasks.

Depending upon the situation, any one of several procedures may be used to determine group makeup. Simple random assignment or alphabetical arrangement is useful when no homogeneity is desired. Social development is maximized by such grouping since students will interact with other people with whom they may or may not have much in common.

Another procedure for the grouping of students is on the basis of friendship. When students are motivated, an advantage to this grouping pattern is that since the students are already on a friendly basis they tend to get to work more quickly. Digression, when not purposefully motivated, however, is a potential hazard.

Groups can also be formed on the basis of interest. The main advantage to this pattern is that productivity is usually high since students are intrinsically motivated, and the motivation of each reinforces the motivation of the group.

A fourth grouping pattern is by achievement. In this pattern, no one individual overshadows all the rest and the work load can be divided equally. Progress is usually rapid because the group is not held back by one or two members who work at a different pace. This type of grouping is useful if a few slower students seem to be on the fringe of the class activities. Grouping these students together and providing them with special help makes it possible for them to make a significant contribution to the class and to build up their own self-esteem.

Still another way to group students is heterogeneously. By deliberately putting students with varying abilities and interests in the same group, the teacher can increase social interaction and development and provide opportunities for slower students to receive spontaneous help from brighter students. It is crucial, however, to consider very carefully the personalities of the students in the group, to be sure the slower students will be helped and not ridiculed.

Once the group is formed, the teacher must ensure that the group realizes how their work will fit into the ongoing class activities. The teacher should stress that each of the four, five, or six members will have a specific job to do by prearranged deadlines if the class as a whole is to accomplish its task. The students may be encouraged to write out an operating plan.

When the small-group activities are completed, the results are brought to the attention of the entire class. This not only enables the class to benefit from the work of the small groups, but it also provides the teacher with an opportunity to commend publicly the members of the groups for their efforts. Frequently panel discussions or modified debates provide appropriate vehicles for the dissemination of the results of such efforts.

The teacher should be aware of groups in which one or two members are being "carried" by the rest. Assisting in decisions about what each member is to do helps to minimize this problem, but evaluation of individual contributions is still difficult, especially when students of differing abilities and interests are assigned to the same group.

OUT-OF-CLASS ASSIGNMENTS

Among the possible instructional procedures available, the use of individual or whole-class homework assignments creates more than its share of controversy. The opponents of such assignments point out that many students have neither the time nor the environment in which to complete such assignments. They point out, too, that once students leave the classroom there is no assurance that they will be the ones actually doing the assignment. Friends, relatives, or parents may do the actual work and the students may then pass it in as their own. Finally, many question the justification of asking students to continue doing formal schoolwork on their own time.

Proponents of out-of-class assignments, on the other hand, point out that a student's chief responsibility should be to schoolwork, that formal learning should not be restricted to particular school hours, and that many valuable instructional experiences cannot easily be engaged in within the four walls of the classroom or within the usual class meetings. For these reasons, the proponents claim that out-of-class assignments are absolutely necessary.

As with most controversial issues concerning education, there is no one right or wrong position that is valid for all situations. If a teacher attempts to eliminate mundane out-of-class assignments, the probability of other assignments being completed, and being completed properly, increases. As with any other instructional procedure, overuse is counterproductive.

Some of the purposes appropriate for out-of-class assignments include the following.

1. *Helping students acquire new information.* When teachers assign a section of a textbook to be read as a basis for a future discussion, or ask students to view a particular TV program or listen to a particular tape-slide sequence, they are asking students to acquire new information. These new data will be dealt with in class, but they are to be acquired outside of class.

2. *Providing practice in particular skills.* Some skills, such as typing or solving mathematical problems can be polished by repeated practice. Since teachers may be reluctant to use class time for extended periods of such practice, they ask students to engage in such practice out of class.

3. *Giving students practice in long-term planning.* Some assignments, such as term papers and correspondence-type projects, require a good deal of student planning. The fact that students must allocate time to achieve the long-term objective is, in itself, a valuable experience that teachers may consider sufficient justification for such assignments. In this case the process and the product are of equal, or nearly equal, importance.

4. *Providing for student creativity and particular student needs.* In-class activities generally force students to be one of a group and leave little opportunity for them to demonstrate skills unique to them as individuals or to engage in instructional activities they feel are of particular interest to them personally. By working with individuals in planning out-of-class assignments, teachers can do much to make school relevant and interesting.

For whatever reasons teachers may make out-of-class assignments, certain steps help to make those assignments more effective and valuable. If the assignment is one in which all students are going to engage, the teacher must ensure that all students understand the exact nature of the assignment. Such assurance can be gained by writing the assignment on the board or duplicating it and handing it to each student. A verbal explanation may accompany the written directions, and questions concerning the assignment may be elicited from the students. If the assignment is one designed to help students acquire new information, guided questions may be utilized profitably. If the assignment is one in which a product is generated, students should have a clear idea of the qualities necessary for minimum acceptability of that product. If the assignment is long-term in nature, a final deadline should be determined, and students should be encouraged to bring in drafts, partially completed work, and so forth for periodic appraisal. If the assignment is individualized, the teacher should make sure there is agreement on exactly what is to be done and what the final product is to be. The teacher can facilitate student accomplishment of out-of-class assignments by making sure that required instructional materials are available. Placing needed books, magazines, film strips, and so forth on reserve in the library is one step in this direction; providing worksheets is another.

If an assignment is worth making, it is worthy of careful evaluation and student feedback. If students perceive that their work is being ignored or dealt with lightly, a large incentive for continuing such efforts will be lost. In addition, the teacher loses an excellent opportunity to detect students' problems and determine the effectiveness of instruction. With rare exceptions, an assignment should be corrected and returned to students before a second assignment is made.

One useful out-of-class assignment procedure is the self-instructional package. Self-instructional packages can be used for any of the purposes mentioned earlier and have a number of advantages. They are built around specific instructional objectives, all the information or sources the student needs to achieve the objective have been included or specified, preassessment and self-assessment instruments are included, and practice exercises are provided. Even more important, self-instructional packages can be self-paced and are designed with this goal in mind. This means that students receive the benefit of a carefully sequenced set of learning activities and are at the same time being given the freedom to learn at their own rates. Self-instructional packages constitute an ideal intermediary between whole-class, teacher-dominated experiences such as lectures and questioning, and experiences such as individual projects in which individual students design and carry out instructional projects reflecting their own needs and desires with guidance from the teacher only when the student seeks it.

SUMMARY

Preassessment means the assessment of students' abilities before instruction begins. The results of preassessment can tell a teacher if students possess the skills and knowledge necessary to proceed with instruction, whether they have already mastered the skills and knowledge to be taught, and the extent to which they can use the language. Teachers who find that most of the students are either well below or well above the expected level of competence should seek administrative approval before making major changes in the objectives already approved for the course.

One source of preassessment data is the cumulative file, which typically contains data such as test scores, attendance records, and anecdotal comments. Some teachers choose not to examine such files because they feel that knowing about a student's past performance might influence their assessments of current performance. Few teachers today are willing to add anecdotal comments to a student's file because such comments might be difficult to defend in a court of law.

The one situation in which most teachers welcome as much preassessment data as they can get involves mainstreamed students. With the passage of Public Law 94-142 in 1975, handicapped students were placed in the "least restrictive environment," which, in most cases, meant that they were placed in regular classrooms. In order to provide the individualized educational plans required for such students, most teachers find it useful to examine cumulative files and to discuss the student's needs with counselors and special education teachers. Although not all teachers have mainstreamed students in their classrooms, all teachers can benefit from preassessing the abilities of their students.

Instructional activities can be divided into two broad classes, teacher-directed and student-directed. Teacher-directed activities (such as lectures, questioning, demonstrations, and guest speakers) are useful for conveying information quickly. Typically these activities are used to help students achieve low-level cognitive objectives. Student-directed activities (such as discussions, debates, field trips, and projects) are useful for enabling students to practice the skills and information that they have acquired. Typically these activities are used to help students achieve higher-level objectives.

As teachers go about the task of selecting instructional procedures, they should keep in mind that the basic idea is to move students from teacher-directed to student-directed activities and from low-level to high-level skills. The more responsibility and control that students have, the more responsible they become. By analogy, if a person is to learn to ride a bicycle, the teacher eventually has to let go of the bike. In the classroom, the teacher must provide the skills and information that students need and then provide opportunities for students to use what they have learned.

STUDY QUESTIONS

1. Preassessment usually focuses on academic or psychological readiness. What specific factors would be most relevant in your own discipline? Why?
2. What are the three main provisions of the Education for All Handicapped Children Act (Public Law 94-142)?
3. How are typical four-step instructional models and such skills as the Stanford skills similar in purpose?
4. What specific kinds of instructional activities would most help students achieve higher-level cognitive objectives? Why would they be particularly helpful?
5. What are two of the main reasons for inviting guest speakers into the classroom?
6. Explain at least two advantages and two disadvantages of using small group activities.

NOTE

1. Robert F. Schuck, "The Effect of Set Induction upon Pupil Achievement, Retention and Assessment of Effective Teaching in a Unit on Respiration in the BSCS Curricula," *Educational Leadership Research Supplement* 2, no. 5 (May 1969): 785–793.

—5—

Selecting Instructional Media

INTRODUCTION

For many educators, it is somehow unsettling to realize that in a technologically advanced country such as ours, much instruction is still conducted in the same manner it was twenty-four hundred years ago. When Socrates, Plato, and Aristotle were helping students to learn at about 400 B.C., they did so by asking questions, by telling, and by discussing. Most students today learn in school in the same way. While it is not the intention of the authors to downgrade the value of lectures or discussions, it is important that the teacher recognizes the unique and valuable contributions to the teaching-learning process that can be made by alternative instructional forms.

There is an ancient proverb that says, "A picture is worth a thousand words." One wonders then what the "exchange rate" would be for a time-lapse motion picture that enables students to watch a rosebud as it unfolds into full bloom or a motion picture that gives students an idea of the drama and mindless passions aroused by one of Hitler's torchlight parades. How does one calculate an "exchange rate" when a student experiences an accident in an auto simulator rather than in a real car? Without the use of mediated instruction, many valuable and interesting learning experiences would be either impossible or impractical, and the students' education would be that much poorer.

Since virtually all teachers find themselves using mediated instruction at one time or another (with varying degrees of effectiveness), this chapter will be devoted to discussing a variety of alternative instructional forms. Teachers who are familiar with the alternatives are more likely to use them intelligently to enhance and enrich students' learning experiences.

SAMPLE OBJECTIVES

When you complete this chapter, you will be able, in writing, to:

1. List three forms of mediated instruction (knowledge).
2. Describe six steps that lead to effective utilization of instructional media (comprehension).
3. Develop a lesson plan for a 20-minute micro-lesson in which a form of mediated instruction plays a central role (synthesis).
4. Take a position for or against the use of mediated instruction in your particular subject-area and defend that position, in no more than two pages, by citing specific facts or by the use of logical reasoning (evaluation).

GENERAL UTILIZATION FACTORS

Mediated instruction, by definition, includes any instruction that makes use of some device (mechanical or otherwise) to facilitate learning.

Although there is tremendous variety in the forms of mediated instruction available to teachers, some utilization procedures are generally applicable to all forms. Among these are the following.

1. *Select mediated instruction for specific instructional objectives.* To be of maximum effectiveness, mediated instruction should be an integral part of the instructional procedures; its use should not be an afterthought. Familiarity with a variety of forms of instruction enhances learning by enabling the teacher to:

    a. Obtain an overview of the types of mediated instruction you intend to use and thus provide for greater variety.
    b. Order materials well in advance.
    c. Use material effectively.

When mediated instruction is used on the spur of the moment, without relationship to specific objectives, students will realize that it is being misused, probably as a time-filler or diversion. If the medium contains a message, do not let the message be, "I did not have anything else planned, so we will try this."

2. *Become familiar with the material or device prior to using it with students.* Depending on the form of mediated instruction being considered, the teacher should read it, view it, handle it, and otherwise use it prior to exposing students to it. This procedure not only provides assurance that the instructional aid is exactly what was expected, but it also enables the teacher to estimate how much time to allow for correct use and to pinpoint specific strengths and weaknesses and thus better prepare students. When mechanical devices are involved, the teacher will become more proficient in the operation of the device and thus avoid the potential loss of attention that accompanies the misuse of equipment.

3. *Prepare the students.* If students are to derive the full benefit of mediated instruction, they should be given some idea of its general content or purpose before-

hand so they will know what to emphasize. Usually a brief description is sufficient to orient students, but some teachers find it useful to formulate a set of guide questions for students to answer. This helps further to focus student attention on important points.

4. *Use the mediated instruction correctly.* There is little value in attempting to use a form of mediated instruction if there is insufficient time for its proper use or if other conditions are not appropriate. While most forms of mediated instruction have utilization factors unique to them, common sense will dictate acceptable procedures. For example, if the device being used has a volume control, remember that it controls only the machine's volume, not the students'. If students are noisy, raising the volume on the device will not necessarily cause them to quiet down; in fact it may have just the opposite effect. Establishing the proper motivational set is a function of preparation of activities, and it is often difficult to use the mediated instruction itself for this purpose.

Among other common-sense considerations is the problem of light. In most classrooms there is sufficient light control for all activities, but many teachers find it difficult to get their rooms dark enough to use some forms of mediated instruction, particularly film projectors and opaque projectors. Light control should be checked before materials are ordered.

5. *Conduct follow-up activities.* Follow-up activities provide an opportunity to clarify confusing points, answer questions, discuss interesting points, and integrate the new information with previous learning. The need for follow-up activities varies with the form of mediated instruction being used, but it is most crucial when aids such as films or broadcasts have been used. Since it is inconvenient or impossible to interrupt these types of aids while they are in use, students may misinterpret some point or miss subtle points altogether because of lack of teacher emphasis. Follow-up activities enable the teacher to correct misconceptions and tie up loose ends. As with all instruction, follow-up activities should be planned in advance and ensure student participation.

6. *Evaluate the mediated instruction.* After using any form of mediated instruction, it is helpful to write a short evaluation of how effectively it helped students achieve the specified objectives. As these evaluations accumulate, they can be used to help select the most appropriate and effective form of mediated instruction for each type of objective.

READING MATERIALS

Textbooks (Traditional)

Ever since the mid-1400s, when Johann Gutenberg developed movable type, educators have made increasing use of books as instructional aids. Today books are by far the most common aid to instruction available to teachers and, surprisingly, they can be one of the most powerful.

Textbooks have a number of sometimes forgotten advantages. Most people, for example, can read and comprehend at least twice as fast as they can listen and comprehend. Students without reading problems can acquire information from texts quickly and efficiently. Textbooks also provide students with a common body of information arranged in some logical order. It is possible to base discussions on commonly available data and to help students perceive cause-effect relationships. Most texts also include chapter summaries, questions to be answered, and associated learning activities that provide guides for studying the information. Considering that most textbooks can be used repeatedly and that many contain pictures, charts, graphs, and maps, they are relatively inexpensive. Finally, textbooks can be adapted to individualization and self-pacing if the teacher chooses to use them in this way.

As with any instructional aid, textbooks can be misused, and most of the disadvantages associated with them stem from such misuses. Perhaps the greatest single misuse of texts is allowing them to dictate what will be taught. While textbook authors may be specialists in their fields, they are unlikely to be familiar with a particular group of students or with a teacher's particular instructional objectives. In some cases, especially in those that involve older texts, the information may not be up to date.

Often teachers are guilty of using the "chapter a week" approach; sometimes teachers assume that because they are using a text they must teach the contents from cover to cover before the last day of school. Teachers who adopt this approach tend to find the slower readers in the class falling farther and farther behind as the rest of the class members lockstep their way through the material. This in itself will cause problems, but more important, more emphasis is being placed on how many pages are being turned than on how much is being learned. Such an approach also stifles the creativity of both teacher and students and can discourage full utilization of some of the text's built-in features.

The often-neglected first step in using a textbook is for the teacher to review it. Though the teacher has a grasp of the material to be taught, the approach of the text may be unique. Textbook authors include what they feel is important and exclude whatever they feel is less important. A careful perusal of the text will enable the teacher to capitalize on the author's particular insights.

The next step is to help students acquire an overview of the text. Many teachers have found that students at all levels can benefit from a short lesson on using the textbook. Good teachers will often include a survey of the table of contents with comments concerning what will and will not be emphasized, a discussion of the author's intent, an explanation of how the index is organized, and a survey of a representative chapter.

When surveying the representative chapter, it is helpful to encourage students to convert the chapter title and headings to questions and then read to find the answers. Encouraging students to look at the chapter summary and the questions at the end of the chapter before reading it is profitable. Perusing boldface type, italics, maps, charts, and so forth will help later in locating major points. Some teachers find it useful to teach students the skill of skimming, with particular emphasis on the importance of introductory and culminating sentences. Still others find it useful to encourage students to write out answers to teacher-posed questions pertaining to and reinforcing important points in the chapter.

Textbooks (Programmed)

Programmed instruction began as an attempt to make learning more efficient by applying what was known about reinforcement and animal behavior to the teaching-learning process. Programmed instruction did not gain broad attention, however, until 1954, when B. F. Skinner published an article entitled "The Science of Learning and the Art of Teaching."[1] This article gave major impetus to the programmed learning movement.

Programmed instruction presents information to students in a series of very carefully planned sequential steps. As students move from step to step, they receive immediate feedback concerning learning progress and in some programs, are "branched" to review remedial or enrichment information depending on the response made to a given question. Active student participation in the learning process (students are forced to construct or select a response) makes up one of the major differences between programmed and traditional texts and instruction. A second difference is that the formation of misconceptions is reduced (or eliminated entirely) because the sequential nature of the program carefully relates each new piece of information to the one immediately preceding it.

There are two basic kinds of strategies for all programmed materials whether they are presented through the use of programmed texts, teaching machines, or computers. These are linear and nonlinear strategies.

Linear Programs. Linear programs are most closely associated with B. F. Skinner.[2] The following are some of the characteristics most closely associated with such programs:

1. Each student is required to go through *an identical sequence* of small steps.
2. Each student *constructs responses,* usually by writing a word or a number, from recalled information.
3. Via the *liberal use of cues* such as boldface type, italics, and underlining, an attempt is made to keep each student's performance as error-free as possible. Usually an error rate of less than 5 percent is sought by authors of programmed materials.
4. *No remedial steps are taken when a student makes an error.* Except with slightly modified, quasi-linear programs, the student simply sees the correct response and moves on.

Nonlinear Programs. Nonlinear (or branching, or intrinsic) programs are associated most closely with Norman Crowder.[3] The following are some of the characteristics most closely associated with such programs.

1. Each student *selects* responses to multiple-choice questions and those responses determine the *unique path* that student will follow through the material, that is, whether the student goes on to new material or is given review or enrichment material.

2. *Little, if any, use of cues* is made since errors are anticipated and remedial instruction is provided to deal with the specific weakness disclosed by the student's choice of response.

Another kind of "programming" has been advocated by Sidney L. Pressey.[4] It was Pressey's work in 1924 that served as a basis for the later development of sophisticated teaching machines, but although he himself was a strong advocate of programmed learning, he saw it as an adjunct to more traditional kinds of instruction. He felt that information should first be acquired in some traditional manner and then reinforced via programmed techniques. The term "adjunct programming" is therefore sometimes used to label Pressey's view.

It is not likely, however, that students of the future will find themselves following a programmed text as the exclusive learning mode.[5] Most programmed texts available today deal with basic, concrete facts, and this situation is not likely to change in the near future. By its very nature, noncomputerized programmed instruction virtually eliminates student creativity. All acceptable responses are already programmed, and divergent thinking is, in terms of the program, incorrect thinking. There are many who believe that for basic, sequential kinds of material, programmed materials will eventually replace traditional kinds of instruction and that it is in the integration and application of knowledge that human teachers are most needed.

Since the use of texts, whether programmed or not, requires students to read, their use must be limited to students who exhibit this skill with a competence commensurate with the materials used. This limitation inhibits their use.

All the forms of mediated instruction surveyed in the balance of this chapter are useful as adjuncts to more traditional kinds of instruction.

AUDIO AIDS

Radios, Record Players, and Tape Recorders

Radios, record players, and audio tape recorders all utilize a single input sense, that of sound. With the advent of films, television, and videotapes, purely auditory devices are being used less frequently, but they still have their place.

Radios, for example, are still a convenient means for getting up-to-the-minute news reports for class analysis. Record players make it possible to listen conveniently to plays, operas, concerts, and speeches, while tape recorders make it possible to record broadcast material or live performances of guest speakers, class debates, and so forth for later use and analysis. These forms of mediated instruction are also used extensively as audio models for students, and the audio tape recorder provides an added dimension by enabling students to record and then listen to their own voices for diagnostic, developmental, or remedial purposes.

As young people have increased their leisure-time use of films and television, they have become accustomed to having a visual point on which to focus their attention. When using audio aids, students may literally not know what to look at. The teacher may take the position that learning to use straight audio inputs is a skill that needs development or that appropriate visual aids (pictures, maps, etc.) that relate to what the students are listening to, and that can serve as visual focal points, should be supplied.

Research in the area of listening is enlightening. It is estimated, for example, that approximately 45 percent of the average adult's working day is spent listening and that this figure rises to 60 percent for elementary school students and to 90 percent for high school and college students.[6] Unfortunately, the research also shows that, even if students are concentrating on what they hear, they will retain only about 50 percent and within two months will be able to recall less than half of that.[7] Obviously students can use additional practice in the frequently overlooked skill of effective listening. Radios, record players, and audio tape recorders can be used to provide that practice.

Telephones

Telephones represent yet another purely auditory form of mediated instruction. Although the telephone was invented in 1876 and the radio in 1895, the telephone's nineteen-year advantage has not been reflected in its significantly greater use by educators. This is unfortunate because the telephone companies have much to offer and they are generally quite willing to work with educators.

One unique application of telephone technology is the "teleinterview." Upon request, most telephone companies will rent to schools equipment that makes it possible to set up two-way communication between a whole class and a speaker at some distant point. The equipment is relatively inexpensive (especially when compared with the costs of bringing the speaker physically to the class), yet it has many of the advantages of actually having the speaker there. All students can listen at the same time, ask questions, and receive answers.

Although student preparation is important with all forms of mediated instruction, it is particularly important when teleinterviews are used, since the charges are calculated according to the time for which the telephone line is in use. Adequate preparation in this case would include preparing the speaker by involving him or her in the objectives of the telelecture. Preparation of the students should include the formulation of specific questions to ask the speaker.

In 1971 the American Telephone & Telegraph Company developed a device called a Variable Speech Control (VSC). The purpose of the VSC is to change the rate at which speech can be understood by omitting pauses and shortening vowel sounds. The practical applications of the device include enabling blind people to listen to, and comprehend, spoken words nearly as quickly as sighted people can read and comprehend written words, and enabling teachers and students to make greater use of taped materials by allowing them to listen to extensive recorded tapes in shorter periods of time.

VISUAL AIDS

Pictures

Still pictures, whether in the form of paintings, magazine clippings, photographs, slides, or filmstrips, have unique properties that make them extremely valuable as instructional aids. Among these properties is their ability to convey abstractions powerfully without depending on verbal descriptions, their ability to focus attention on a characteristic situation or on a particular step in a process, and their ability to allow students to study an image at length, to refer back to it conveniently, and to make side-by-side comparisons. The combination of these properties is not available in many other forms of mediated instruction.

Pictures, such as those available from magazines, travel bureaus, and commercial concerns, represent one of the easiest to acquire and least expensive forms of mediated instruction available to teachers. The teacher can increase the instructional value of pictures if common-sense principles are followed. For instance, the picture selected must be appropriate for the students who will see it. Very complex pictures, for example, are not well suited for younger students, regardless of how attractive they may be otherwise. Colored pictures can usually attract and hold students' attention better than can black-and-white pictures, and all pictures must be large enough to be seen easily. Ensuring that the picture is relevant to what will be studied and that it does not present a biased view (unless such a view is intended) is important.

Opaque Projectors

It sometimes happens that a picture is of particular benefit but is too small to be seen by the entire class at one time. In such instances, the opaque projector may be useful. The "opaque" will project and enlarge any flat picture whether it is a single sheet or a page bound in a book. Furthermore, most opaque projectors come equipped with a built-in light arrow, which can be used to draw students' attention to particular points on the projected image. Many teachers have also found the "opaque" useful for projecting images on chalkboards so they can be traced.

Opaque projectors make use of a large and powerful bulb as a light source, and this bulb gets hot. Most "opaques," therefore, include a built-in, heat-absorbing glass plate between the bulb and the projection stage. In spite of this precaution, thin materials sometimes curl or scorch. Proper use would then include checking prior to using an "opaque" to make sure there is a heat-absorbing glass plate and checking material periodically during use.

Although opaque projectors generate a lot of heat, they do not project a lot of light. Opaque projectors use a reflected light source rather than a direct light source such as that found in film projectors. Less light reaches the screen than with other kinds of projectors, and unless the room is reasonably dark students may have difficulty seeing the projection. Check to see if the room can be darkened sufficiently before using the "opaque" with students. Because the room must be darkened, students may be unable to take notes. For this reason most teachers do not use opaque projectors for extended periods of time.

Slides and Filmstrips

Slides and filmstrips have all the advantages of pictures and the added advantage of increased realism. Because slides are actual photographs and are shown via a bright light source, the scenes they portray appear more "real" than printed pictures and the colors appear more brilliant. These factors appeal to students. In addition, it is much easier to store a set of slides than to store a set of large, mounted pictures.

A more significant advantage associated with slides is the opportunity they provide for the teacher to create instructional aids. Many teachers make it a point to take along a camera and slide film (rather than print film) when encountering circumstances pertinent to their teaching area, and many have thus compiled an impressive set of slides that are useful in stimulating and maintaining students' interest. Many teachers have also initiated class projects wherein students organize a slide program complete with an accompanying tape recording. Such projects have the dual advantages of being useful, interesting learning activities, and increasing the teacher's store of instructional aids.

A filmstrip is essentially a series of connected slides. Most filmstrips are prepared commercially and many have brief captions printed on each frame. A recent development is the sprocketless filmstrip projector, which should result in longer life for a filmstrip. As the filmstrip is advanced and each frame is discussed by the teacher, various procedures may be used to enrich the experience. Besides a basic approach, such as asking students to read the captions out loud, teachers have discovered that teacher and student comments and discussion are possible and profitable while the filmstrip is being shown as well as afterward.

Bulletin Boards

Bulletin boards are ideally suited for the display of visual materials such as pictures, cartoons, postcards, newspaper clippings, outstanding papers, and student-made collages and montages. Common sense will dictate procedures for the use of bulletin boards. For instance, bulletin boards promote learning best when they concern a single idea or topic. They should also be neat and uncluttered, make use of bright colors and attention-getting materials such as colored yarn and plastics, and they should be oriented pictorially rather than verbally. The instructional value of bulletin boards can be increased further by building into the display participation devices, such as manipulative devices or questions with the answers covered by flaps.

A bulletin board's instructional value lasts a relatively short time, in some cases not more than a few days. Having gone to the trouble of constructing an exceptional bulletin board, the teacher may be reluctant to take it down. There is certainly no reason to take down a display that students still find useful, but once students stop paying attention to the display or the class moves on to some other topic, the bulletin board display needs replacement.

Teachers have found that some groups of students enjoy the responsibility for putting up new displays periodically throughout the year. This helps to increase students' interest in the display and can lead to increased learning as groups find that research in the area will assist in developing an attractive and interesting display. The teacher can provide advice and assistance in the form of suggesting sources for and providing actual materials.

Maps and Globes, Charts and Graphs

Maps, globes, charts, and graphs are grouped together because each of these forms of mediated instruction may require increased student preparation. Students may have difficulty interpreting maps, globes, charts, and graphs unless the teacher makes a special effort to help them.

Maps and globes are used to show portions of the earth's surface in a less than life-sized scale. Cartographers have constructed maps and globes to emphasize political, geographic, and climatic divisions and have developed a number of different map projections. The teacher will find it useful to draw students' attention to the particular kind of projection being used and to discuss the way it distorts the real size and shape of particular geographic features. Without an understanding of projection, students may have misconceptions about maps.

Efforts to draw students' attention to the legend of the map or globe will reap dividends. It is here that the cartographer explains the meanings of the symbols used on the map or globe, gives the scale to which features are drawn, and provides additional information such as the meanings of particular colors.

The teacher should study maps and globes before using them. Political divisions, particularly boundaries and names, change more often than is suspected, and it is not uncommon for a map or globe in a classroom to be out of date. If so, this fact should be made known to students and, if possible, transparencies and overlays should be used to emphasize the changes.

Charts differ from graphs and diagrams in that they may include a wider variety of pictorial forms. Graphs and diagrams generally have only simple lines or bars. The most common kinds of charts are flow charts (showing sequential steps), process charts (showing some process from start to finish), and time charts (showing developments over a period of time). The instructional value of charts is maximized when the teacher takes the time to make sure students can read and interpret the data presented. A special lesson devoted to reading all types of charts is time well invested.

Graphs are used primarily to condense and convey numerical data in visual form. The most common kinds are the circle or pie graph (useful for showing the relationship of parts to the whole), bar graphs (useful for showing comparative data such as the changes in unemployment from year to year), and line graphs (useful for plotting profiles of patterns).

Although students should be given special instruction in the use of maps, globes, charts, and graphs, teachers should obtain the least complicated aid that will serve their immediate purpose. Trying to select an aid that can be used in a variety of lessons will be a false economy if students have difficulty interpreting the aid or are confused by it.

Chalkboards

Chalkboards are available in almost every classroom and most teachers use them frequently. Chalkboards are used to display instructions, diagrams, examples, and other information that is subject to frequent change. Board work also gives students the chance to demonstrate their abilities and allows active student participation.

There are a number of ways the teacher can utilize chalkboards to make them more valuable to students. One way is not to talk to the board. Students may have difficulty hearing teachers who insist on trying to face the board and talk to students at the same time. Teachers who make frequent use of the board often construct, or invest in, templates to facilitate the drawing of frequently used shapes. This not only saves time, but allows more consistency. An inexpensive form of template can be made by simply tracing a design and punching holes along the traced lines. Brushing a dusty chalk eraser across the template while it is held to the board will create a dotted outline. As was mentioned earlier, pictures can also be traced on the board from projected images.

When using the chalkboard, the teacher should avoid cluttering. Once an item written on the board has served its purpose, it is best to erase it so students will not be distracted by it. Certain types of colored chalk are intended for use on paper, not on chalkboards. If the wrong kind of chalk is used, it may stain the chalkboard permanently. Finally, lettering must be large enough to be seen easily. Usually letters that are about two and a half inches high can be seen easily from a distance up to thirty feet.

Overhead Projectors

Of the types of projectors available to teachers, overhead projectors are easily the most common. Overhead projectors can project any material that is drawn, written, or printed on transparent film. They are often used instead of the chalkboard because they allow a teacher to write and at the same time face the students. Being able to maintain eye contact with students is one of the greatest advantages of the overhead. Another advantage is being able to use the machine without darkening the room, which facilitates note-taking and, more important, student interaction.

The use of overlays with base transparencies is a particularly effective instructional tool. A typical overlay package might contain a base map of the United States, a transparency to go over the base outline to show major river systems, a third transparency to depict major cities and to show their relationship to rivers, and a fourth transparency to show railroad development.

Using an overhead projector as an "electric chalkboard" requires only a sheet of clear plastic (usually acetate, but cellophane or even a commercial plastic wrap will do) to protect the glass projection plate and a grease pencil, china marker, crayon, or felt-tipped pen. Grease pencils are usually filled with a wax-based material and generally project black lines. Grease pencils can project colors, but if color is desired (and it does make the projections more attractive), felt-tipped pens are less expensive and work just as well. Crayons and china markers will project black lines regardless of their color, but they have the advantage, along with grease pencils, of being erased by light rubbing with a soft cloth or tissue. To remove transparent ink it is often necessary to use a cleaner or even a solvent, depending on the kind of ink in the pen. Some overheads come equipped with a roll of acetate. The teacher writes on the acetate and then simply rolls up the used surface to expose an unused portion, thus temporarily eliminating the need to erase. The teacher may construct transparencies by simply drawing them, but if better quality or permanency is desired, one of a number of heat processes, or an ammonia process known as "diazo," may be used. Most school librarians have sources of information concerning these processes, or the audiovisual department in the school or a nearby college or university may offer assistance.

While becoming experienced in the making of transparencies and overlays, the teacher will find that the use of color can add interest and emphasis, that printed (manuscript) characters are easier to form and read than are cursive characters, and that typing (especially when done with a primary typewriter)—one that types characters 1/4 to 1/2 inch high—adds to the neatness and legibility of the finished product. Including too much on one transparency can inhibit use by learners; about twenty lines seem to be optimum. Typewriters with pica or elite type are not commonly used for transparency work since the projected image is usually too small to be read easily.

It is often possible to acquire commercially prepared transparencies and overlays made by experts with a wealth of materials to work with, and thus, are usually more polished than teacher-made materials. But they may also involve more expense.[8]

Most overhead projectors have a thermostatically controlled switch that permits the fan to continue operating until the interior of the projector is cool. Do not be upset if the machine does not stop when it is turned off, and do not pull the plug. It will stop automatically when it has cooled down.

Realia

The term "realia" refers to any specimens, models, mock-ups, or artifacts that can be used to help students learn. Depending on what is being taught, teachers and students may display living animals, coin collections, insects, or dozens of other objects. The list is as limitless and as varied as there are real things in the world that may be displayed without danger or great expense. Modified representations of real things, such as cut-away or "exploded" models, are also helpful. In the latter, the whole is broken into segments and each segment is held apart from the others, while the pieces still maintain the same relative positions as in the unexploded model. Other good teaching tools are models that students can assemble and disassemble, and dioramas, which are three-dimensional scenes that students can construct.

AUDIOVISUAL COMBINATIONS

Multimedia Kits

As an increasing number of schools adopt a systems approach to education, many educators are finding multimedia kits helpful. Multimedia kits are compilations of instructional materials that include a variety of mediated instruction forms designed to help students achieve a specific instructional objective by exposing them to different types of closely integrated educational experiences.

A typical multimedia kit may contain, for example, booklets, filmstrips, a loop film, audio tapes, and artifacts. All the components are selected with a single purpose in mind—to generate and maintain students' interest in a particular topic or subject while at the same time providing them with as much pertinent information as possible.

Multimedia kits can be used with excellent results for groups, but perhaps their greatest utilization is found when they are used as self-instructional devices for students to use at their own convenience and at their own rate. As with most other forms of mediated instruction, multimedia kits may be prepared by teachers themselves or can be purchased ready made.[9]

Films and Television

Films and television provide students with more of a "you are there" feeling than do most other forms of mediated instruction. They also enable students to view demonstrations (both scientific and social), experiments, natural phenomena, and other events that would be too difficult, dangerous, or even impossible to view otherwise (for instance, moon walks and erupting volcanoes).

Techniques such as time-lapse photography, microphotography, long-range photography, animation, and slow-motion projection offer unique approaches for students' exploration. Students may watch as a flower unfolds into full bloom or as a single cell divides. They can see the earth as an astronaut would see it or gain an understanding of the phenomenon of nuclear fission. Infrared photography, "zoom-ins," and even X-ray photography are also possible through films and television.

Proper preparation of students and good planning in the use of films can enhance learning. One researcher has found that students who are well prepared for a film (by being given such things as questions to be answered, study guides, and explanations of new or difficult words) experience a learning gain 20 percent greater than do students who are not so prepared.[10] Other researchers have found that periodically stopping a film to provide time for active student participation, or splicing into the film questions for discussion, can also increase student learning.[11]

Teachers are often pleasantly surprised at the ease with which films can be borrowed. Most universities and state departments of education maintain extensive film libraries, as do many businesses and public utilities. A check with the audiovisual department in any public school or with a school librarian can result in the acquisition of good sources of free or inexpensive films.[12]

In addition to 16mm films, educators are also finding that 8mm, single-concept or single-skill continuous-loop films are very useful. Like the larger 16mm films, 8mm films can be used for large groups, but they are especially well suited for individual use and can thus play an important part in individualization and self-pacing of instruction. Most 8mm loop films are silent, but that has not detracted from their popularity.

An advantage of television over film is that of immediacy. Via television, students can watch events as they are actually happening. In effect they are seeing for themselves, but the TV camera can even improve on personal presence by providing each student with a clear, unobstructed, and close-up view.

Television has been used effectively in a variety of ways. The first and most common is the use of commercial programs. Although often thought of only in terms of its entertainment value, commercial television frequently broadcasts special programs and documentaries that have significant instructional value.

Another type of broadcast television is educational television, or ETV. ETV broadcasts are primarily instructional but they are aimed at a broad, public audience and, therefore, attempt to meet a variety of needs. Typical ETV programs include discussions with industrial, political, and social leaders, "how-to-do-it" courses, and nonviolent children's programs. One of the most famous of the ETV children's programs is *Sesame Street*.

A third type of broadcast television is instructional television, or ITV. The distinctions between ETV and ITV are considered to be both in programming intent and in program financing. ETV programs, such as *Sesame Street*, are not intended for specific and formal instruction; ITV programs generally are. ETV programs are frequently sponsored by commercial concerns, whereas ITV programs are financed most often by governmental grants, private foundations, individual school systems, and colleges and universities.

Closed-circuit television represents a fourth way to use the medium. In closed-circuit television, only TV sets connected directly to a transmitter, or adapted to receive the 2500 mHz (megaHertz) wavelength reserved for closed-circuit television, can receive the programs. Closed-circuit television is most often used on an "in-house" basis to televise meetings and debates, demonstrations and experiments, and even regular classes. Because it is an in-house operation, students can participate in the actual program development and televising, thus adding yet another dimension to their educational experience.

A fifth way to use television is via video cassette recorders or VCRs. VCRs are directly analogous to audio tape recorders, with the obvious difference that the former provides a visual, as well as an audio, record. More and more schools are acquiring VCR equipment, not only for taping and saving lectures, demonstrations, and theatrical presentations, but also for use in everyday teaching situations. As a way of enabling both teachers and students to see themselves as others see them, VCR equipment has found increasing use. Coaches, for instance, have found VCR equipment invaluable for instant feedback of student psychomotor skills.

COMPUTERS AS TOOLS FOR LEARNING

Computers were originally designed to facilitate the work of scientists and engineers; later, business people began using them. Although the machines were not designed to be instructional tools, their suitability for this application quickly became apparent. The major strength of computer-assisted instruction (CAI) is that it is interactive. Other forms of mediated instruction—books, films, and television—are one-way communicators: information goes from them to students. Computers, on the other hand, are two-way communicators. Information, questions, and other stimuli go from them to students, but then the students can provide input that shapes the next output from the computer. This interaction makes it possible for computers to approximate some of the individualization typically associated with tutoring.

In the 1960s, when CAI was first provided to students in some large school districts, it prompted predictions of dramatic improvements in the instructional process. Students would be able to work at their own rates, overworked teachers would be able to devote more of their time to helping those students who most needed that help, and students would be more actively engaged in learning since they had the "teacher's" full attention.

These projections grew even rosier with the advent of microcomputers in 1975 because then the relatively low cost of the hardware made computer power available to virtually all schools. A report by the congressional Office of Technology Assessment indicates that between the years 1977 and 1987, schools spent approximately $2 billion on computer hardware. That money purchased between 1.2 million and 1.7 million computers and, as of 1987, more than 95 percent of our schools have computers for instructional use. The number of computers in schools may seem large, but given the number of students to be served, there is only one computer for every 30 students. Further, those students with access to computers typically get to use them for only about one hour per week.[13]

With the dramatic increase in computer availability since 1978, one might expect to see some of the projected improvements in education. Few of them have materialized. The reasons are not difficult to understand and they will be examined before looking at how teachers *can* make effective use of computers.

Problems in Using Computers in Schools

The most basic problem hindering the effective use of computers in schools is the fact that most schools are set up to provide group instruction, not individual instruction. While most teachers try to work with individuals as much as possible, the main thrust of their planning, teaching, and evaluating is geared to working with groups. Computers, however, like pens, pencils, and hand-held calculators, are tools best used by individuals as they work at their own rates. Computers simply do not fit very well into a system set up for group instruction.

The basic problem generates other problems. For example, lesson planning is complicated because teachers plan lessons for whole classes. If some students engage in activities other than those planned for the class, teachers must have separate plans for those students. The plans might not be as extensive as complete lesson plans but if, for example, some students are going to be working at computers, the teacher should be able to explain to a parent or to a principal how the computer work will help those students achieve specific course objectives. Many teachers find that they do not have enough time or energy to make additional plans, so they avoid activities that require such plans. To the extent that computers cause teachers extra work, many teachers are reluctant to use them.

Aside from the problem of extra planning, a related problem is that while students are using computers they are missing all or part of the planned lesson. When it comes time for students to be tested, those students who were using the computers will have missed some of the instruction. It is unfair to test students on material that was covered when they were told to do something else. Some adjustment in evaluating students will have to be made and this means, again, more work for the teacher.

Another problem hindering the use of computers in schools is the fact that few teachers are adequately trained to use computers. In most teacher education programs, students spend more time talking about computers than they do actually using them to acquire skills or knowledge. Many prospective teachers have moved into the computer age by learning how to use a word processor. This familiarity with the technology will make it easier for them to explore other instructional uses of computers. Those who have not yet discovered what a benefit word processing can be are urged to find out. Computers are here to stay. The sooner teachers become comfortable with them, the sooner they will be able to use this tool to help themselves and their students.

Advantages to Using Computers in Schools

The most important advantage to using computers is that they can help students learn. A second advantage is that computers can help students learn to learn, and a third advantage is that computers can help students integrate knowledge. To substantiate these claims, various classes of software packages will be examined along with ways in which they can be used with students. A software package includes the program (usually on a disk) and the documentation (the written instructions that explain how the program should be used).

Drill-and-Practice Programs. As the name implies, drill-and-practice programs provide drill and practice over skills and knowledge already learned. Due to their purpose, most drill-and-practice programs focus on low-level skills. These programs can help students succeed because: (1) each student is able to progress at his or her own rate, (2) such programs often adjust the complexity of the content so that it is commensurate with the abilities of the student, and (3) the interaction is fast so the learner is directly involved with the work all the time.

There is some evidence that indicates that students gain the most from the use of drill and practice programs during the first 15 minutes of use. After that, the fast interaction seems to tire students, resulting in diminishing returns.[14] The most appropriate use of drill and practice programs is to provide an alternative to seat-work drill and practice and for remediation.

Tutorial Programs. The primary purpose of tutorial programs is to teach something for the first time—to provide primary instruction. Typically these programs provide some information and then ask the student to respond to a question. The student's response determines whether the program presents new information or goes back to help the student correct his or her thinking about the information just presented. This branching is what prompted the name "tutorial" program: the program acts somewhat like a tutor. These programs typically focus on low-level skills.

Tutorial programs can help students succeed by providing remediation or enrichment. Remediation is called for when a student either misses a lesson or does not understand a lesson. An appropriate tutorial program may provide the additional help such a student needs to progress. Enrichment is called for when a student already possesses the skills and knowledge to be taught. Such a student should be encouraged to acquire new skills or knowledge and for this, the use of a tutorial program might be appropriate.

Usually, tutorial programs are *not* appropriate to use in teaching a whole class a particular skill or piece of information. In the hundreds of studies that have compared CAI with non–computer-assisted instruction, the vast majority showed no significant differences in student achievement. This evidence leads to the conclusion that, for the most part, people teach people at least as well as machines teach people. Therefore, for whole-class instruction, teachers would be wise to do the job themselves.

Simulation Programs. The purpose of simulation programs is to present to students approximations of real-life situations. A student may become the ruler of a country or a chemist with a laboratory full of dangerous chemicals, but in all cases, the student is in charge. Simulation programs can help students because they remove the danger or inconvenience of the real-life situations, but they still require the student to make a decision about what to do next. This, in turn, causes the student to begin considering the logical consequences of his or her actions, and this kind of thinking is essential to the maturation process. Therefore, simulation programs can be said to help students mature.

Further, such programs help students integrate knowledge and to learn from mistakes. These features combine to make simulation programs among the most valuable that students can use. They enable students to engage in an activity that may be impossible, impractical, or too dangerous to engage in without computers.

Application Programs.   The previously discussed classes of programs were clearly CAI programs in that they helped students learn skills or information for specific subject areas. Application programs differ in that they are more clearly tools. Such programs include word processors that are to typewriters what typewriters are to pens and pencils, gradebook programs that can save teachers hours of calculation time and enable them to give students more frequent and complete progress reports, and databases that enable teachers to build, maintain, and easily manipulate banks of test items. Some of these tools, such as word processing and database management, are now frequently taught to students. A prospective teacher's ability to use such tools will be a point in his or her favor in a job interview.

Developments in CAI

When microcomputers became popular in the early 1980s, thousands of instructional programs were put on the market. Most of those programs were (and most new programs still are) stand-alone programs. They stand alone in that they focus on isolated skills or information. They are not designed to relate to other programs or to units of study. This makes it difficult for teachers to integrate them into instructional plans.

Some vendors responded to this problem by marketing sequences of programs that built upon each other (dealing with nouns, pronouns, and other parts of speech), or had some common element, typically a record-keeping system that kept track of students' achievements as they went from program to program. Programs of this type are somewhat easier to build into a curriculum because they can help students develop a sequence of skills. Further, because they typically keep track of the student's performance through more than one program, they enable the teacher to see if any performance pattern is evident that might point to particular areas of strength or weakness.

The most recent, and potent, form of CAI is the integrated computer curriculum. An integrated computer curriculum is one in which some subject-area such as math or reading is dealt with through a series of grade levels such as K–6 or K–12. The most sophisticated of these integrated computer curriculums include a series of precise instructional objectives, a variety of program types (tutorial, drill and practice, and simulation) to help each student achieve the objectives, and a sophisticated record-keeping system that tracks each student. Three companies that market such integrated computer curriculums are the Computer Curriculum Corporation, Educational Technology Systems, and Wicat.

Another new CAI development is interactive video. This technology links the interactive capability of computers with material stored on videotape or -disks. Instead of calling up just words or pictures, the computer can start a videotape or -disk player and make use of any material such as a segment of a political speech or an actual demonstration. This technology mates two of the most sophisticated learning tools we have, computers and television.

Regardless of type, computer-assisted instruction is here to stay. Teachers do not have to use computers all of the time, but they will be able to help more of their students more of the time if they know how and when to use the tool.[15]

SUMMARY

Two of the main reasons instructional media are used are to: (1) help vary the stimuli by which students learn, thus helping to capture and maintain interest, and (2) expose students to stimuli and experiences that might not otherwise be available, safe, or practical. Regardless of the kind of media being considered, there are certain steps that a teacher can take to help ensure that the media are selected and used properly. These steps include: (1) selecting media that will help students achieve specific instructional objectives; (2) becoming familiar with the content of the material or the operation of the device before using it with students; (3) preparing the students so they can focus on specific elements or ideas; (4) maximizing the utility of the media by properly adjusting volume, brightness, size, or clarity; (4) conducting follow-up activities in order to clarify confusing points and to bring about closure; and (5) evaluate the experience to determine to what extent it contributed to students' achievement of the specified objective.

Many forms of mediated instruction are available to teachers, including older forms such as textbooks, film and filmstrip projectors, overhead projectors, maps and charts, bulletin boards, realia, and audio tape recorders, and newer forms, such as television, VCRs, computers, and interactive video. Although each form of media has specific advantages and disadvantages, only computers and interactive video have the advantage of being two-way communicators. The ability to respond to the input of individual students makes these two forms of media among the most powerful that a teacher can use.

The expansion of computer utilization in the schools makes it possible for teachers to help students acquire skills that are highly relevant to our increasingly technological society. Two of these skills are the ability to use computers for word processing and to use them to search large databases for specific information. Computers and interactive video are also used to provide different forms of computer-assisted instruction, including drill and practice, tutorials, and simulations.

In order to capitalize on computer technology, teachers will have to be prepared in teacher-education programs to use computers for instruction, and the number of computers in schools will have to increase so the ratio is more nearly one computer for each student. The ratio in 1987, with between 1.2 and 1.7 million computers in the schools, was about one computer for every 30 students. Changes will also have to be made in the structure of public education if computer use is to be maximized. Public education is currently set up to provide group instruction. Computers are best used by individuals. This basic conflict generates problems for teachers with respect to planning and teaching and is hindering the infusion of computers into the curriculum. The problem will have to be resolved if computers are to be used for more than word processing, database searches, and occasional instruction.

STUDY QUESTIONS

1. What are the six steps, in sequence, that lead to the effective utilization of instructional media?
2. What kinds of media are videotapes likely to replace? Why?
3. Describe at least three instances in which the use of an overhead projector would be appropriate.
4. What are some of the major factors inhibiting the integration of computers into many curriculums?
5. Why do many educators consider simulation programs to be the most useful kind of CAI?
6. How does interactive video differ from computer-assisted instruction?

NOTES

1. B. F. Skinner, "The Science of Learning and the Art of Teaching," *The Harvard Educational Review* 24 (Spring 1954): 86–97.
2. B. F. Skinner, *The Technology of Teaching* (Englewood Cliffs, N.J.: Prentice-Hall, 1968).
3. Norman A. Crowder, "Automatic Tutoring by Means of Intrinsic Programming," in *Automatic Teaching: The State of the Art,* ed., Eugene Gatanter (New York: John Wiley, 1959), pp. 109–110.
4. Sidney L. Pressey, "A Machine for Automatic Teaching of Drill Material," *School and Society* 25, no. 645 (May 7, 1927): 549–592.
5. See Leslie J. Briggs, Peggy L. Campeau, Robert M. Gagné, and Mark A. May, *Instructional Media: A Procedure for the Design of Multi-Media Instruction, A Critical Review of Research, and Suggestions for Future Research* (Pittsburgh, Pa.: American Institutes for Research, 1967), p. 116, for further discussion.
6. James W. Brown, Richard B. Lewis, and Fred F. Harcleroad, *A. V. Instruction—Media and Methods,* 3rd ed. (New York: McGraw-Hill, 1969), p. 327.
7. Ibid.
8. Among the many sources of commercially prepared transparencies are the following: Encyclopaedia Britannica Educational Corp., 425 North Michigan Ave., Chicago, Ill. 60611; Instructo Products Co./McGraw-Hill, 18 Great Valley Park-

way, Malvern, Pa. 19355; 3M Audio Visual, Bldg. 225-3NE, 3M Center, St. Paul, Minn. 55144.

9. Perhaps the single best source of information about films, filmstrips, videotapes, and other forms of audiovisual materials is the National Information Center for Educational Media [NICEM], PO Box 40130, Albuquerque, N. M. 87196.

10. Briggs et al., *Instructional Media*, p. 112.

11. Ibid., p. 114.

12. Some excellent sources include the local telephone company; American Iron and Steel Institute, 1000 16th St. N.W., Washington, D.C. 20036; and General Motors Corp., General Motors Building, Detroit, Mich. 48202.

13. "Study: Schools Lack Computers," *The Daily Pantagraph* [Bloomington, Ill.], Sept. 13, 1988, p. C2.

14. Gloria Poulson and Elizabeth Macken, *Evaluation Studies of CCC Elementary School Curriculums, 1975–1977* [Palo Alto, Calif.: Computer Curriculum Corp., 1978], p. 2.

15. For further information concerning the most recent work concerning computers in schools it is recommended that the reader turn to periodicals such as *Electronic Learning,* P.O. Box 2041, Mahopac, New York 10541, and *The Computing Teacher,* 1787 Agate St., Eugene, Oregon 97403, or *T.H.E. Journal* (Technical Horizons in Education), 2626 S. Pullman, Santa Ana, California 92705-0126; write for information to corporations such as Computer Curriculum Corporation, P.O. Box 10080, 700 Hansen Way, Palo Alto, California 94304-1016; Education Systems Corporation, 6170 Cornerstone Court East, San Diego, California 92121; and MECC, 3490 Lexington Avenue North, St. Paul, Minnesota 55126; or visit local outlets of major computer corporations such as the local Radio Shack store or Tandy Computer Center.

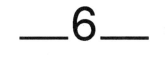

—6—

Planning Instructional Units

INTRODUCTION

So far, we have examined the structure, classification and use of instructional objectives, a variety of learning activities, and forms of mediated instruction. These are the tools with which teachers work. In this chapter we will examine a process for organizing instruction so that those tools can be used to maximize learning. Basic to this chapter is the idea that one of the main goals of instruction is to help students move from low-level, teacher-directed activities to higher-level, student-directed activities. In all subject areas, teachers are trying to help students become self-directed learners who are able to integrate knowledge and who know how to learn. They are trying to help students acquire information and convert it into useful knowledge. Planning can help make that happen.

The chapter begins with an examination of the components and use of a knowledge structure and its associated rationale and objectives. The difference between knowledge structures and content outlines are examined next, and the chapter concludes with an examination of the elements of instructional units.

SAMPLE OBJECTIVES

When you complete this chapter, you will be able, in writing, to:

1. Explain the function of each of the three major concepts in a Waimon knowledge structure.
2. Explain at least two ways in which a knowledge structure differs from a content outline.

3. Construct an instructional unit for a given length of time in your teaching field, including a rationale, precise instructional objectives, suitable content and instructional activities, and optional activities.

ORGANIZING CONTENT

There is no doubt that people would rather be successful than unsuccessful. Every student would rather get A's than C's or D's, and every teacher would like to help make students' lives happier and more productive. Why then are so many students and teachers less successful than they would like to be? The reason may well be that sometimes neither the teachers nor the students see the utility or relevance of the information to be taught or learned. If the utility and relevance of the information is not clear, it is difficult to be enthusiastic about teaching or learning it. The following discussion will focus on ways to organize information so that its utility and relevance will be more apparent to students and so they will find it easier to learn, remember, and use the information.

Structures of Disciplines

In *The Process of Education,* Jerome S. Bruner puts forth the idea that every discipline has an inherent structure, and he contends that effective teaching and learning depends upon understanding that structure. "Grasping the structure of a subject is understanding it in a way that permits many other things to be related to it meaningfully. To learn structure, in short, is to learn how things are related."[1] This relatedness of ideas within a discipline and between disciplines is the key to making the information useful. By organizing the fundamental concepts and principles of a discipline so that their interrelatedness is emphasized, Bruner argues that: (1) the subject will become more comprehensible, (2) important information will be easier to remember, and (3) the information will be easier to apply to other areas. As an example of how fundamentals can help make a subject more comprehensible, he cites an example from social studies.

> Once one has grasped the fundamental idea that a nation must trade in order to live, then such a presumably special phenomenon as the Triangular Trade of the American colonies becomes altogether simpler to understand as something more than commerce in molasses, sugar cane, rum, and slaves in an atmosphere of violation of British trade regulations.[2]

In explaining how structure can help students remember information, Bruner cites over a century of research that demonstrates that "unless detail is placed into a structured pattern, it is rapidly forgotten" (p. 24). As an example, he cites the fact that we often remember how to perform the specific steps in making a calculation by remembering the appropriate formula. By remembering the essence, we can recreate the details.

Bruner goes on to further explain the idea of knowledge structures, and to discuss the ideas of readiness, intuitive and analytic thinking, motives for learning, and aids for teaching. The purpose here is not to review *The Process of Education,* though teachers would find it thought-provoking. Our task here is to try to capitalize on the idea of structuring knowledge to emphasize its utility.

Time-Frames

Bruner talked of knowledge structures in terms of whole disciplines. That may be a bit ambitious at this point. Instead of dealing with a whole discipline, we will work with knowledge structures in the context of four-week units of work. Why four-week units? Because during the eight months that teachers are typically with students, they are expected to cover a great deal of information. Unless the information is divided into reasonable blocks, it is possible that so much time will be spent on one or two units that not enough time will be left to do an adequate job with other units. A quick check of the tables of contents of typical texts will show that publishers are aware of this danger. The books are usually divided into seven or eight major units of work, each consisting of about four or five chapters. This results in seven or eight four-week units. There is nothing magic about four weeks; it is merely a guideline.

Concepts

Now that we have a time-frame within which to work, we must define a central term: *concept.* (We defined the term earlier, but a repetition here might be helpful.) As we will use the term, a concept is a group of things, either concrete or abstract, that have enough characteristics in common to make them a unique set. An example of a concrete concept would be *tree.* The word "tree" calls up thoughts of a pine tree, a maple, or a giant sequoia, but it will not call up thoughts of a rose or a dandelion. Trees, as a group, have enough characteristics in common to differentiate them from other kinds of plants, and therefore we can refer to the concept of trees. An example of an abstract concept is *democracy.* Here, the word may call up thoughts of the Athenian Assembly or New England town meetings, but it would not call up thoughts of Nazi Germany or Czarist Russia except possibly as negative examples.

Now we are ready to think about what concepts to put into the four-week unit. Dr. Morton D. Waimon (Professor of Education at Illinois State University) has built upon Bruner's idea of structuring knowledge. Dr. Waimon agrees that the concepts basic to a discipline should be exemplified in the knowledge structure so that both the interrelatedness of the concepts and their utility are made clear. He goes on to suggest that one way to do this is to develop a sequence of concepts that focus on the intellectual, personal, and social significance of the information.

WAIMON KNOWLEDGE STRUCTURES

A Waimon knowledge structure is constructed in an outline format. Roman numeral I should consist of the most basic and powerful concept of the unit. Think of this concept as the umbrella that will cover all the other concepts in the unit. It is the concept that experts in the area would agree to be true and to be most central to the whole unit. For example, a high school earth science teacher might teach a unit about the formation of the earth's crust. Roman numeral I for this knowledge structure might be:

> I. The earth's surface is affected by many dynamic forces and processes, such as internal heat, solar radiation, meteorite impact, and human activity, all of which continually change its appearance.

In a more advanced class, such as a college-level geology class, the teacher might focus an entire unit on just the effects of the earth's internal heat upon surface formations, so Roman numeral I for that knowledge structure might be:

> I. The heat trapped in the earth's core and mantle when the earth was formed is now thought to be the primary cause of volcanoes and the movement of tectonic plates.

Under the major concept, the teacher would list a number of minor concepts that expand upon but do not duplicate the information in the major concept. In the earth science knowledge structure about the formation of the earth's crust, the minor concepts might be:

> A. Internal heat affects the surface by causing volcanism, plate tectonics, mountain building, and earthquakes.
> B. Solar radiation, acting on the atmosphere and surface of the earth, causes erosion by wind, water, and ice.
> C. Human activities, particularly the expansion of agriculture and urban areas and the retrieval of natural resources, have accelerated many changes in the earth's surface.

The function of the first major concept and its associated minor concepts is to present the substance of the unit: the basic facts and information. Most of this information will be available in textbooks, although the teacher will probably have to refer to texts at levels more advanced than the one being used for the course. The nature of the next two major concepts is different.

Bruner emphasized and common sense reinforces the idea that students are more likely to learn, remember, and be able to use information if its utility is made clear. That is the function of the second major concept. Here, the teacher needs to focus on how individuals can use the information. Going back to the example about the earth's crust, a second major concept might be:

> II. Individuals can do relatively little to alter the natural factors that shape the land but, via conservation efforts, they can help to preserve or improve landforms, and

by increasing their understanding of the formation of landforms they can better understand the interactions between the land and the people.

This concept flows logically from the last minor concept (I. C) because it builds upon the link between people and landforms. It also focuses attention on the fact that information about landforms can be put to practical use. Minor concepts that expand upon this second major concept might be:

A. Homes that are built or landscaped to capitalize on natural features are generally more comfortable and less costly to live in than homes not so built or landscaped.
B. Farmers who practice conservation tillage tend to preserve the topsoil on their property while decreasing their expenditures for fuel and chemicals.
C. By better understanding the relationship between the kind of land on which people live and how those people live, we may gain a better understanding of the interactions among the peoples of the world.

Having established the intellectual basis for the unit and at least begun to address ways in which individuals can make use of the information, the next task is to establish the fact that this topic is relevant to current concerns of society as a whole. One way of developing this concept is to check recent periodicals for articles relating to the topic of the knowledge structure. Citing such articles to students will help establish the ongoing, real-world concern that exists about the topic they are studying and help them to more clearly see the relevance of their studies. A major concept that addresses this need for the unit on landforms might be:

III. Advancements in technology have enabled us to make significant changes in the earth's topography and therefore we need to consider the long-term and global effects that these changes might produce.

Again, the major concept follows logically from the last minor concept by linking interactions among people of the world, with changes in the earth's topography made by relatively few people. Minor concepts that expand upon this major concept might be:

A. High levels of emissions from factories and motor vehicles are posing problems ranging from an increase in average temperatures worldwide (due to the "greenhouse" effect) to the accelerated erosion of priceless artifacts.
B. Harnessing natural power sources, such as wind, water, nuclear energy, and the sun, will result in the conservation of fossil fuels and the preservation of the land surrounding them.
C. Large-scale earthmoving projects, such as damming or changing the direction of rivers, can affect people thousands of miles from the site of the project, so their needs, too, should be taken into consideration before the project is begun.

Just as there was no magic in designating four weeks as a useful length of time for a unit, there is no magic in having three major concepts, each of which is followed by three minor concepts. The format does seem to fit the need fairly well, but it is quite possible to have other formats. The key point to keep in mind is that the major concepts must address the intellectual, personal, and social significance of the unit. This is not a simple task because there may be many good ways to structure knowledge for a given unit. You may have already thought of good alternatives to the examples shown. Look now at the difference between a knowledge structure and a topical outline.

TOPICAL OUTLINES

Topical outlines usually arrange information so that each section logically follows the one before it. If the unit about the earth's surface were arranged topically, the major points might look like this:

    I.   The earth's surface is affected by many dynamic forces and processes, such as internal heat, solar radiation, meteorite impact, and human activity, all of which continually change its appearance.

    II.   Heat from the earth's hot core is a major cause of surface formations, not only because that heat causes volcanoes, but because the heat keeps the rock supporting the crustal plates molten, enabling them to drift into, over, and under one another, forming mountains and causing earthquakes.

    III.   Solar radiation powers the water cycle and the air circulation process, two of the major causes of erosion of the earth's surface.

    IV.   The impact of large meteorites is relatively rare due to the earth's thick atmosphere, which, via friction, destroys most things falling through it, but when such impacts do occur they can cause massive cratering and destruction.

The topical outline could easily be continued, but one point should be clear. While the outline does permit the logical presentation of information, it does not address the basic question of the utility of the information. If that utility is not clear, students may view the information as irrelevant to their lives and see little reason to learn it. Take the time to demonstrate to students how the knowledge can be of practical use.

RATIONALES

In developing the knowledge structure, the teacher expresses the intellectual, personal, and social significance of the unit in the three major concepts. This activity has its reward in facilitating the development of appropriate instructional objectives (the concepts are not the objectives). There is, however, one other thing that a teacher can do to help establish the relevancy of the material. The teacher can develop a rationale that has as its sole purpose the "selling" of the topic to a hypothetical reluctant learner. In developing this rationale, the teacher must directly address a student who is either neutral about learning the information in the unit or even reluctant (for any number of reasons) to do so. The task is to demonstrate to the student that the information is both interesting and useful.

Note how this step differs from developing the knowledge structure. There, the teacher develops concepts that could lead to lesson plans. Here, the teacher must persuade students to learn. It is useful to make students feel involved. One way this can be done is by frequently using the word "you." Here is an example of a possible rationale for a unit on the formation of the earth's crust.

> As you travel along highways and pass through areas where the road cuts through a hill or mountain, have you ever wondered about the way the rock is layered in the walls of the hill or mountain? In this unit you will learn not only about how the rock was layered, but also about how the hill or mountain came to be and what is likely to happen to it.

It is much easier to build a convincing rationale if the teacher sees the relevance of the material. If the teacher starts thinking, "You need to know this information in order to graduate," or "You will be tested on this information, so pay attention," that teacher is on the wrong track. What the teacher is saying might be accurate, but it is far less convincing to a student than demonstrating how the information can be used, preferably in the very near future.

It may be that a teacher will never need to answer a student's direct question about why he or she has to learn a particular body of information. However, if the need arises, perhaps because the expressions on students' faces suggest that they are thinking about such a question, it is good to have a substantive answer at hand. The rationale is that answer, so give it careful thought. Teachers should not assume that because they want to teach something or are expected to do so that their students will automatically want to learn it. In a sense, teachers are salespeople. If they want the student/customer to buy, then they need to present legitimate and convincing reasons for them to do so.

It might be useful to study the sample knowledge structure, rationale, and objectives in Chapter Appendix A. Look for ways to improve upon these samples and then do so in a new knowledge structure and rationale.

UNIT PLANNING

The first step in planning an instructional unit is determining the major concepts to be covered. The next step is determining how students can use the information and how the relevance of that information can be demonstrated. The teacher then writes a rationale that highlights, for the student, the immediate and long-term benefits of learning the information. Following this, the teacher organizes objectives that cover a range of cognitive abilities. With these components in place, the last step is to actually write the plan for the unit.

What Is a Unit Plan?

A unit plan is a document that describes how a teacher intends to deal with a specific block of content during a specific block of time. A unit plan usually begins with an overview, which describes the general focus of the unit. This is typically followed by a rationale, a set of precise instructional objectives, the actual content needed to achieve the objectives, teaching-learning activities appropriate to the content and the objectives, optional learning activities, and a list of needed materials. A unit plan typically ends with an evaluation instrument. A unit plan represents a teacher's most complete idea of what students will accomplish in a given block of time and how it will be accomplished.

The construction of a unit plan takes time, but the resulting benefits are great. First, by looking at the instructional unit as a whole, the teacher can ensure that the unit provides a sequence of activities that helps students move from low-level, teacher-directed activities to higher-level, student-directed activities. The activities planned can also be designed to help students integrate knowledge from other subject-areas. Further, once the teacher does the necessary gathering and organization of information and materials, that work will be useful from year to year. Though the information and materials are likely to need occasional updating, the teacher will not have to start from scratch each time the unit is taught. It pays, therefore, to do the job well the first time.

The Herbartian Unit

The idea of unit planning is not new. Johann Herbart (1776–1841) was an educator who believed that the teaching-learning process was amenable to analysis and improvement. He set forth a series of steps that defined instructional planning in terms of function. In his view, instruction, of whatever duration, should include at least the five following steps.

1. *Preparation.* Developing an appropriate learning environment by gathering and organizing appropriate materials and by helping students recall ideas that were learned earlier and that relate to the new information.
2. *Presentation.* Communicating the skills and information as clearly as possible and with the abundant use of examples relevant to the students.
3. *Association.* Helping students clarify their thinking by bringing out similarities and differences between old and new ideas.
4. *Generalization.* Helping students broaden their understanding of ideas by bringing out the interrelationships and applicability of ideas in various contexts.
5. *Application.* Providing opportunities for students to use the information and skills that they learned. Knowledge not used is knowledge lost.

These steps have become the essence of the "Herbartian Unit." Today, most educators agree that Herbart's five steps facilitate effective teaching and learning. The following discussion uses the Herbartian plan as the basis for developing instructional units, but additional steps have been added to build on what has already been discussed.

Components of a Unit Plan

The first component of a unit plan, the overview or introduction, briefly familiarizes students with what the unit will be about. It gives them the big picture. The second part, the rationale, we have already discussed. Here the teacher is answering the asked or unasked question, "Why do we have to learn this?" It is not much of an overstatement to say that the extent to which students will cooperate with a teacher is directly dependent upon the extent to which this question is satisfactorily answered. We have already examined the structure and classification of instructional objectives, but this is where the teacher isolates the specific objectives relevant to this particular unit and lists them in the sequence in which they will be addressed.

Selecting Content.   The bulk of the unit consists of the actual information to be presented. This information, in outline form, should include but go beyond the information in the students' text and should correlate with the objectives of the unit. Since unit plans are generally made well in advance of the time they are used, the teacher should take time to sift through a great deal of material. As teachers select the most important and/or interesting content for inclusion in the unit, they frequently discover relationships among facts and concepts that previously eluded them.

Taking the time to acquire content from a number of different sources has advantages. A variety of sources act as an internal accuracy check, ensuring that information is correct, the examples appropriate, and the anecdotes relevant. This kind of preparation tends to increase self-confidence. This self-confidence, in turn, tells students that the teacher is well prepared, knows what he or she is doing, and is convinced the material is worth learning.

There are many sources to which teachers can turn for supplemental content for unit plans. Among the obvious sources are college texts and notes, personal experiences, and the school library. Many of the sources in the library have low reading levels, and teachers can skim them relatively quickly and extract relevant information with a minimum of effort. The librarian may have suggestions for other possible aids.

One of the best sources of information for unit plans are compilations called *resource units.* Many public schools, state departments of education, and university instructional materials centers maintain resource units on a wide variety of topics. These compilations often contain such items as lists of possible instructional objectives, rationales, subject-matter outlines, suggested instructional experiences, optional experiences, instructional aids, bibliographies, and even sample tests. The wealth of material available in most resource units can tempt teachers to build their own units solely from this material, but resource unit material should be supplemented not only with the most current material available but also with whatever other material is needed to meet the specific objectives.

The subject-matter outline for the unit should cover all the information students will need to achieve the objectives. The outline should be complete enough to be used without the need for supplemental sources (which may not be available when needed) or "remembered" material (which may be forgotten when needed). A helpful rule to follow is that, if the content is important to students (or if it will help students learn or remember something), it should be written into the outline, including not only facts, figures, definitions, diagrams, and explanations but also supplemental information, such as examples and anecdotes.

The primary advantage to building a comprehensive subject-matter outline is the elimination of last-minute research or attempts to find appropriate examples. Everything perceived as needed should be built into the unit while the teacher has the time and the resources to be selective and thorough. A second advantage is that the teacher will become familiar with the "big picture." Knowing the exact nature of the material to be presented in the future, the teacher can refer to points yet to be made (thus cueing the students) and can more readily refer to points previously made (thus appropriately reinforcing prior learning).

Selecting Instructional Experiences.   Each instructional experience, like each portion of content and each use of mediated instruction, should be selected on the basis of how well it will help students achieve the precise instructional objectives. The objectives themselves will suggest appropriate instructional experiences. For example, a low-level cognitive objective such as, "You will describe, in writing, at least two examples of natural landforms," could easily be facilitated by a teacher presentation or a film. A higher-level cognitive objective such as, "Given a series of facts and fallacies concerning pollution, you will underline each of the facts," might be better achieved in a guided practice session accompanied by student discussion.

When selecting instructional experiences, effective teachers consider the types of analogous (practice of skills similar to, but not the same as, the final skill) and equivalent practice (practice of a skill virtually identical to the final skill called for) that students will need as preparation for the demonstration of the instructional objective. For the objective cited earlier concerning facts and fallacies about pollution, a teacher may wish to plan one lesson that would provide analogous practice (such as listing fallacies on the board and briefly discussing why they are fallacies) and another lesson that would provide equivalent practice (such as examining articles containing both facts and fallacies about pollution and identifying the specific facts and fallacies).

Selecting Instructional Media.   When some part of a particular unit will be learned through the use of mediated instruction, unit planning allows for long-range planning. The long-range view made possible by good unit planning enables the teacher to order films, books, videotapes, models, and other instructional aids early enough to assure delivery when needed. Early delivery will ensure sufficient time to preview material, test equipment, and still make alternate plans if either the material or the equipment is unavailable or unsuitable.

To get information about films and filmstrips, teachers often find it helpful to survey film and filmstrip catalogs available in the school library, the audiovisual department, or the film and filmstrip libraries maintained by nearby colleges and universities. Additional sources include the state department of education, many public utilities, the local telephone company, large corporations, and national organizations.

The following types of information concerning films and filmstrips are helpful if included in the unit plan.

1. The exact title of the film or filmstrip.
2. The name of the company that produced the aid (sometimes needed in ordering).
3. The length of the aid in minutes or frames. (Make sure there is time in available time modules to use the aid effectively.)
4. Whether color or black and white.
5. The address from which the aid can be obtained.
6. The cost.
7. Rental or loan conditions. Of particular importance are the deadline for ordering to ensure delivery when needed (two weeks in advance, six months in advance, etc.), and the length of time the aid can be retained.

In addition to films and filmstrips, teachers should take advantage of other forms of mediated instruction. As a general rule, the more variety in instructional experiences, the more chance students will become genuinely involved in the material.

ORGANIZING THE PARTS OF A UNIT:
AN ABBREVIATED MODEL

The preceding unit plan components can be arranged in many ways. A simple outline form is one way, as exemplified in the abbreviated model in Chapter Appendix B. A full model is included as the book appendix.

Another procedure for organizing unit plans is to write out separate lesson plans for each of the objectives. Since the objectives, subject matter, instructional experiences, and materials have already been selected (or, in the case of instructional experiences, at least seriously considered), the writing of separate lesson plans is greatly facilitated. The advantage to such an organizational pattern is that extremely little preparation is needed once the unit is under way. The disadvantage is that the lesson plans may impose too rigid a structure on the progress of the class, thus discouraging deviations from the plans even when such deviations would be worthwhile.

Still another way of organizing unit plans is by subject matter and experiences that are to be used. The teacher may decide, for example, to use certain subject matter or certain instructional experiences to stimulate interest in the unit. Other blocks of subject matter and other experiences may be designated for use in developing understanding and general instruction, while still others may be earmarked for concluding activities such as summarizations and reinforcement. If unit plans are organized according to introductory, developmental, and concluding categories, the pattern can be used in conjunction with either of the patterns described earlier.

DECIDING ON OPTIONAL ACTIVITIES

There are two major categories of optional activities that can be considered for unit plan inclusion. The first includes any that students may be interested in. For example, activities such as constructing a bulletin board, model, or diorama; participating as a panel member in a panel discussion; or engaging in an independent study project potentially appealing to a wide variety of students.

A second category includes those designed for exceptional students. Perhaps the most common experience found in this category is a carefully selected special reading opportunity. While gathering and selecting content for units, the teacher will encounter numerous sources of information written at differing levels of difficulty and representing various points of view. By building a file of short, annotated bibliography cards on such sources, the teacher will have a ready-made pool of sources to which students with varying abilities can be directed. In this way slower students can be given material written at a lower level so they do not fall behind, whereas brighter students can be directed to more challenging material, such as special readings, reports, and interviews. The key is to gear optional activities to the specific abilities of the students in the class.

The optional activities section is an excellent place to place experimental experiences. Since the teacher is likely to generate some innovative and creative instructional possibilities while planning units, these untried experiences may be listed in the optional activities section and attempted on a voluntary basis by students. If the activities prove fruitful, they may become part of the regular instructional activities.

PLANNING FOR EVALUATION AND FUTURE USE

The final step in planning a unit is to construct the instrument(s) needed to determine whether the objectives have been achieved. The objectives of the unit dictate the types of evaluation instruments needed. At the same time that the evaluations are constructed, the teacher may wish to construct answer keys or appropriate models. If skill tests are to be used, appropriate checklists should be constructed.

The experienced teacher has written objectives that require students to synthesize a number of subsidiary skills in the process of demonstrating competence in the objective. Such objectives enable the teacher to develop evaluation procedures that communicate to students the applicability of the content more clearly than traditional evaluation procedures. Objective and essay tests have important roles, but it is desirable to supplement them with other forms of evaluation whenever possible. (See Chapter 8 for other suggestions for evaluation.)

After the unit plan has been constructed and the components are in polished form and suitably organized, it is useful to make an expanded title page, which includes the title of the unit, the name of the course for which the unit was written (such as American History, Home Economics I), the type of student and grade level for which the unit was designed (such as general—freshmen; college preparatory—juniors), a brief overview of the unit (four or five lines describing the main points covered), a brief statement describing the unit preceding or following the unit (to help place the unit in a logical sequence), and a close estimation of the time frame needed for the unit.

This information will save time when instructional programs are being planned for future classes and the use of a previously written unit is being considered. Such concise data also facilitate the sharing of unit plans among teachers if such arrangements can be made.

SUMMARY

Jerome S. Bruner, in *The Process of Education,* presented the idea that the interrelatedness of the basic concepts of a discipline constitutes a structure that, if taught to students, can help them learn, remember, and use information. Morton Waimon, building upon this idea, recommended that one way to do this and to focus attention on the utility of the information to be learned was to build a three-part knowledge structure. In this kind of knowledge structure, the first major concept focuses on the intellectual basis for the unit. This underlying and powerful concept is like an umbrella, which covers all other concepts in the unit.

The second major concept focuses on the utility of the information to students. Here the teacher develops concepts that could make a difference in the lives of the students. This section should not be confused with the rationale. The knowledge structure deals with concepts. The rationale deals with reasons.

The third major concept would focus on the relevance of the information to society as a whole. Here the teacher would develop concepts that focus on the impact the information has on the decisions made by society as a whole, by governments, or by governmental agencies.

Following each of the three major concepts are three minor concepts that expand upon but do not duplicate the major concept. Ideally, the third of these minor concepts builds a bridge to the major concept that follows.

A teacher can help ensure success of the unit by taking the time to build a rationale. A rationale should take the form of a monolog to a student and should present facts and ideas that the targeted student would be likely to find interesting and convincing. The rationale is, in essence, the teacher's best attempt to persuade students that the unit will be worth their time and effort.

Once this conceptualization has been completed, the teacher can prepare an instructional unit. A typical unit plan has a title page indicating the title of the unit, an estimation of time required for the unit, the name of the course for which the unit was designed, and the academic grade level for which the unit was designed. The next page typically consists of a brief overview that describes the concepts and facts to be presented and a brief description of preceding and following units (to place the unit in the overall structure of the course). Next, the teacher includes a rationale to explain, from the viewpoint of the student, what benefits will be gained (this will probably be the same rationale that the teacher put together while developing the knowledge structure). Following this is a list of the precise instructional objectives of the unit; the teacher should make sure that they reflect a variety of cognitive or psychomotor levels.

The bulk of the unit will consist of the facts, definitions, examples, explanations, and anecdotes, in outline format, that students will need to achieve the objectives. These should be gleaned from a variety of sources, including the text for the course, college texts, and similar resources. Most teachers continually update the content sections of unit plans, so they find it useful to cite the sources of their information. These sources should be cited either in a bibliography intended for student use or in a bibliography intended for the teacher's use.

The next section of the unit plan typically consists of the instructional activities. These might be organized in a general outline; in separate lesson plans; in broad categories such as introductory, developmental, and concluding; or—in keeping with the knowledge structure—in terms of database development, utility, and social significance. The unit should also include appropriate ordering information for mediated instructional aids.

The next section should include optional activities. These should take the form of either remedial activities intended for students who are having difficulty with the regular instruction or enrichment activities intended for students who are more advanced than the bulk of the students. The enrichment activities can help the student move ahead of the class, perhaps into a new unit or into a unit that the rest of the class will not have time for (vertical growth) or help them learn more about the content of the unit being worked on (horizontal growth).

The last section of the unit consists of the evaluation instruments that will be used to determine the extent to which the objectives have been achieved. Those instruments should include the actual answer keys, model answers, or checklists that will be used.

CHAPTER APPENDIX A

Sample Knowledge Structure

Lovett, Kenneth D.
Sept. 28, 1988
Knowledge Structure

FORMING THE EARTH'S CRUST

I. The earth's surface is affected by many dynamic forces and processes, such as internal heat, solar radiation, meteorite impact, and human activity, all of which continually change its appearance.
    A. Internal heat affects the surface by causing volcanism, plate tectonics, mountain building, and earthquakes.
    B. Solar radiation, acting on the atmosphere and surface of the earth, causes erosion by wind, water, and ice.
    C. Human activities, particularly the expansion of agriculture and urban areas and the retrieval of natural resources, have accelerated many changes in the earth's surface.
II. Individuals can do relatively little to alter the natural factors that shape the land but, via conservation efforts, they can help to preserve or improve landforms, and by increasing their understanding of the formation of landforms they can better understand the interactions between the land and the people.
    A. Homes that are built or landscaped to capitalize upon natural features are generally more comfortable and less costly to live in than homes not so built or landscaped.
    B. Farmers who practice conservation tillage tend to preserve the topsoil on their property while decreasing their expenditures for fuel and herbicides.
    C. By better understanding the relationship between the kind of land on which people live and how those people live, we may gain a better understanding of the interactions among the peoples of the world.
III. Advancements in technology have enabled us to make significant changes in the earth's topography and, therefore, we need to consider the long-term and global effects these changes might produce.
    A. High levels of emissions from factories and motor vehicles are posing problems ranging from an increase in average temperatures worldwide (due to the "greenhouse" effect) to the accelerated erosion of priceless artifacts.
    B. Harnessing natural power sources, such as wind, water, nuclear energy, and the sun, will result in the conservation of fossil fuels and the preservation of the land surrounding them.
    C. Large-scale earthmoving projects, such as damming or changing the direction of rivers, can affect people thousands of miles from the site of the project, so their needs, too, should be taken into consideration before the project is begun.

CHAPTER APPENDIX B

Abbreviated Unit Model

SHAPING THE EARTH'S SURFACE

I.   Overview
     This unit will discuss the natural and man-made processes and forces that shape
     the earth's surface as seen today.

II. Rationale
     Ever wonder why there are no mountains in the Midwest or why there are
     volcanoes in Hawaii and on the west coast but none on the east coast? These are
     just some of the topics to be discussed in this unit.

III. Objectives
     Upon successful completion of this unit, the student will be able to:
     1.   List the major physical features of the earth's surface, how they were
          formed, and what effect these features have on mankind (comprehension,
          analysis).
     2.   Describe how modern technology has influenced the ongoing changes of the
          earth's surface (analysis).
     3.   Defend various positions pertaining to what mankind can do to utilize the
          earth's surface more efficiently (evaluation).

IV. Subject Matter
     A.   Dynamic forces of the earth
          1.   Plate tectonics has been continually changing the surface of the earth
               for millions of years
               a.   Evidence supporting this phenomenon
                    (1) Mid-oceanic ridge
                    (2) Fossil remains
                    (3) Matching continental coastlines
               b.   Physical features created by this process
                    (1) Deep ocean trenches
                    (2) Continental margin mountain ranges
          2.   Volcanism and mountain building processes are continually increasing
               the elevation of the surface of the earth
               a.   Volcanic activity can result in two types of eruptions
                    (1) Explosive
                    (2) Nonexplosive
               b.   The type of eruption determines the shape of the resulting cone
                    (1) Cinder cone
                    (2) Shield
                    (3) Composite
     B.   Human influences on the earth's surface
          1.   Changes brought on by agricultural processes
               a.   Removal of natural vegetation
               b.   Increase of erosional processes
          2.   Changes brought on by urban expansion
               a.   Alteration of land by construction
               b.   Changes in wind patterns due to high-rise buildings

V. Materials and Experiences
  A. Dynamic forces of the earth
    1. Materials
      a. Overhead and slide projectors
      b. Transparencies of tectonic forces and plates
      c. Slides of different types of volcanoes and mountains
    2. Experiences
      a. Use lecture and discussion to communicate content
      b. Use overhead projector and transparencies to explain concepts
      c. Use photographs and slides to provide illustrations

STUDY QUESTIONS

1. How does a teacher decide on approximate lengths of instructional units?
2. What is the focus of each of the three major concepts in a Waimon knowledge structure?
3. How does a knowledge structure differ from a content outline and from a traditional unit plan?
4. What is the purpose of writing a rationale for an instructional unit?
5. What are the steps in a Herbartian plan?
6. What similarities exist, if any, between the focus of the concepts in a Waimon knowledge structure and the steps in a Herbartian plan?

NOTES

1. Jerome S. Bruner, *The Process of Education* (New York: Vintage, 1960), p. 7.
2. Ibid., pp. 23–24.

__7__

Planning Daily Lessons

INTRODUCTION

A unit plan is a powerful instructional tool because it enables teachers to plan instruction on a large scale and to incorporate in those plans a variety of learning experiences. Lesson plans are equally powerful tools because they enable teachers to take the overall instructional strategy exemplified in a unit plan and divide it into segments that can be completed (conveniently and logically) in single class periods.

    This chapter will examine some of the arguments for and against lesson plans, some of the components included in typical lesson plans, steps for writing lesson plans, and some lesson plan models.

SAMPLE OBJECTIVES

When you complete this chapter, you will be able, in writing, to:

1. List at least three components of a lesson plan (knowledge).
2. In a paper of no more than two pages, explain at least two possible advantages and two possible disadvantages associated with lesson plans (comprehension).
3. Given a precise instructional objective, describe at least two possible teaching-learning activities that are logical outgrowths of the objective and explain how these activities will help students achieve the stated objective (application).
4. Observe a peer-taught, 20-minute lesson and, using a copy of the plan for that lesson, write down all instances of differences between the lesson as planned and the lesson as taught (analysis).
5. Construct a one-page lesson plan so the instructional objective, the content, and

the teaching-learning activities are directly related to one another in such a way that, if the plan were followed exactly, it would be logical to expect students to achieve the stated objective (synthesis).

6. Given a sample lesson plan for a hypothetical teaching situation, judge whether it is a good or bad lesson plan, writing at least five reasons for that judgment (evaluation).

PROS AND CONS OF LESSON PLANNING

Teachers have been debating the pros and cons of lesson planning for years. The main reason no agreement has been reached is that both sides are able to support their positions with convincing arguments. Those teachers who favor lesson plans, for example, include the following points among their arguments:

1. Lesson plans specify the instructional objective of the lesson and thus help keep the main purpose of the lesson clearly in focus.
2. By containing all the important content, lesson plans help ensure that no crucial points will be inadvertently omitted.
3. Lesson plans include teaching-learning activities that were determined to be most likely to help students achieve the instructional objective(s), thus eliminating or at least decreasing the need for improvisation.
4. Lesson plans provide a basis for determining how effective particular teaching-learning activities were in helping students achieve particular objectives and thus provide a basis for modifying instructional methods.
5. Lesson plans facilitate long-range planning by providing a record of what was taught during each lesson, thus assisting in maintaining continuity.
6. Lesson plans are essential if a substitute teacher is to do more than conduct a supervised study period in the teacher's absence.

Opponents of lesson plans have an arsenal of arguments to support their position:

1. Lesson plans are largely unnecessary since most teachers already know what and how they are going to teach.
2. Once teachers go to the trouble to write a lesson plan, they may tend to follow that plan as closely as possible, rather than feel free to capitalize upon immediate student interests.
3. Planning lessons takes an inordinate amount of time, and this time could be better spent doing content-area research or gathering instructional material.
4. The presence of a lesson plan can cause complications when a teacher chooses to deviate from the plan and an administrator expects the plan to be followed.
5. Once a series of lesson plans is written, if any lesson goes much more quickly or slowly than was anticipated, subsequent plans must be modified or scrapped, thus wasting time and effort.

Obviously, both sides have some sound arguments. There are, however, three other points that teachers should keep in mind. The first is that, since it is generally not possible to individualize all instruction, some group instruction will be necessary.

Second, there is little doubt that lesson plans help beginning teachers to feel more at ease and confident in the classroom and therefore help them to be effective. Third, many school systems and individual principals require their teachers to prepare written lesson plans, and some go so far as to require that those plans be approved before they are implemented.

LESSON PLAN COMPONENTS

Objectives

Teachers write lesson plans primarily to increase their effectiveness in helping students to learn or, to be more precise, to increase their effectiveness in helping students to achieve specific instructional objectives. It follows, therefore, that a crucial component of a lesson plan is the instructional objective. It is the objective that states exactly what students will do at the end of the lesson.

The prime source of objectives for lesson plans is the master list of objectives generated for the course or unit. If, when these original objectives were written, the teacher wrote them so they could be achieved within single class periods, no difficulty is encountered when transferring objectives from the master list to the lesson plans. Certainly low-level cognitive objectives such as, "You will be able to list, in writing, at least three components of a lesson plan," are amenable to such transfer, since students can achieve them within a single class period, but unit and course objectives frequently reflect final behaviors and thus must be broken down into sub-objectives before they can be used in daily lesson plans. It may be possible to use the complex objectives as they are and have the lessons carry over to another day, but it is more likely that the teacher will divide the complex objectives into a number of less complex, enabling or en-route objectives, each of which becomes an objective for an individual lesson plan.

There are at least three reasons for trying to avoid carrying a lesson over to a second day. The first is that the longer the wait between the use of particular teaching-learning activities and the assessment of student performance resulting from those activities, the less sure the teacher can be that the lesson resulted in student learning. Waiting even one day, for example, can enable numerous variables to affect student performance. Without accurate information concerning the effectiveness of instructional methods, the teacher is less able to modify, and thus to improve, those methods.

The second reason is that stopping properly in mid-lesson is easier said than done. Under ideal circumstances, lesson closure includes summarization, review, student demonstrations of competence, and a report to students concerning their progress. This kind of closure provides students with a feeling of accomplishment and serves as an impetus to further learning. Some elements of the ideal closure will have to be omitted or at least modified if the lesson is carried over to a second day. The degree to which students achieve a feeling of accomplishment and are able to continue the lesson on the following day depends greatly upon what kind of closure is provided. If the teacher anticipated the problem and built into the lesson plan a series of possible stopping points (which is tantamount to writing a series of mini-lesson plans), and also kept track of the time, he or she could provide for summarization and review and lay the groundwork for the next day's lesson. A teacher who does not plan for this contingency may end up trying to make one last point after the class should be over and half the students are out the door. In this case the value of the time and effort committed to the lesson may be in jeopardy.

The third reason concerns effective time utilization. When a lesson is carried over to a second day, it is difficult to determine how much time will be needed to complete the old lesson and how much time will be available for new work. Teachers who continually find themselves with awkward blocks of time left at the end of class periods and are unable to improvise or plan activities for those blocks (for example, by giving individual help to students) will have to deal with growing student boredom and its attendant problems. (Interestingly, the problems of excess time and student boredom sometimes result from the use of instructional objectives that are too simple or too easily achieved.) It is best to avoid carrying lessons over to a second day and instead to break complex objectives into less complex enabling or en-route objectives. One example of such a subdivision is provided now.

Suppose a college instructor saw value in developing the ability to analyze lessons on the basis of what actually took place in comparison with what the teacher had *intended* to take place. An objective reflecting this ability might be, "You will observe a full-period lesson and, using a copy of the plan for that lesson, write an in-class paper that cites each instance of difference between the lesson as taught and the lesson as planned."

While this objective may seem reasonable at first glance, a second look reveals that if the student teachers are to observe carefully what is going on in the class and compare that with the plan for that lesson, they will miss some differences while they write down their observations. The problem could be avoided by dividing the original objective into two subobjectives:

1. You will observe a lesson taught within a single class period and take sufficient notes to enable you to compare the observed lesson with the plan for that lesson with respect to objective, content, and teaching-learning activities.
2. You will, using your notes, write a paper of no more than four pages comparing the observed lesson with the plan for that lesson, citing specific instances of differences between what was observed and what was planned with respect to objectives, content, and teaching-learning activities.

These two enabling objectives provide sufficient time for students to demonstrate the desired competencies and are therefore suitable (at least in that respect) for use on individual lesson plans.

One source for objectives for impromptu lesson plans is unexpected events. Although the vast majority of lessons will be planned before they are taught, events sometimes occur that should rightfully preempt planned lessons. When these events occur, it is the teacher's responsibility to devise and share instructional objectives so that the efforts of the class to capitalize upon the learning potential of the interrupting event are focused on some clearly understood goal. The teacher's proficiency in this skill makes the difference between an unexpected event causing confusion in the classroom and the same event becoming the basis of an interesting and profitable learning experience.

Content

The content of a lesson plan is dictated by the objective and consists of the actual information (the facts, definitions, and explanations) that students will need to achieve competency. Teachers should not try to write into the content every single thing that will be covered, nor should they try to rely on the content portions of a lesson plan for information with which they are not familiar. The functions of the content component are to help assure that in the midst of a hectic or complex lesson teachers do not unintentionally omit crucial points and to provide a means of ensuring the relevancy of the content with respect to the objective.

The *form* of the plan will depend upon the teaching-learning activities selected. A lecture, for example, is facilitated best by a word or phrase outline of factual information. A discussion moves most smoothly if the plan consists of key statements, examples, and pivotal questions with possible answers. Activities such as demonstrations or experiments can progress according to plan with a content component consisting of procedural steps and descriptions, whereas art lessons might require limited verbal but extensive visual content, such as slides or pictures. Regardless of the form of the content, it should still contain the minimum data students will need to achieve the objective.

Some instructional objectives require that students demonstrate a skill that is not dependent upon specific content. Once the basic information concerning that skill has been conveyed, other lessons may provide students with practice in that skill, although the "content" for these lessons may have little or nothing to do with the original objective. For example, examine the following objective: "You will write a computer program that will use at least two input statements, will run in less than two minutes, and will result in an accurate printout." Aside from the technical information necessary, the content on the program could consist of anything from information about a company's payroll requirements to an airline's flight schedule. Trying to concoct hypothetical content on the moment as a vehicle to develop a skill can be a nerve-wracking experience, and because this procedure is prone to error, it can seriously weaken an otherwise strong lesson. Depending upon the objective, basic factual information or practice data may be needed.

Instructional Activities

The instructional activities are those in which the teacher and students engage during a particular lesson to facilitate achievement of the lesson plan's objective.

Often instructional activities will be implied by the instructional objective. In most instances the teacher selects activities that will provide students with either analogous practice or equivalent practice, or both.

For example, if an instructional objective was, "You will describe, in one paragraph each, at least four ways information can be fed into a computer," appropriate activities might include a short demonstration or filmstrip concerning input modes (to provide basic information), a discussion during which students could suggest examples, a review period to allow students to review main points orally (analogous practice), a time during which students would actually write short explanations of input modes (demonstration of the stated competence), and a short session in which students receive feedback through a discussion of selected student responses.

Five separate instructional activities were included in this single lesson. By selecting a variety of activities, the teacher provides for a "change of pace," thereby reducing the possibility of students becoming bored. Of course, in the hands of the proficient teacher one activity may be used consistently without boredom and in the hands of an inexperienced teacher all the activities described may become deadly. It is a good idea, however, to look back periodically through lesson plans to see if there has been too much reliance on just one or two types of activities.

Materials

Occasionally teachers will wish to use instructional materials that are not readily available in classrooms. A delineation of these items (such as films, projectors, models, collections, etc.) in the lesson plan serves to remind teachers to make sure the required materials are available when they are needed. Since not all lessons require special materials or equipment, it is not necessary to include this component in every lesson.

Evaluation

In the description of instructional activities, one activity listed was student demonstration of the stated competence. Since the point of the lesson plan is to help students achieve a particular competence, it is obvious that it is essential to have planned the demonstration of that competence as the basis for evaluating the lesson. Ideally, this demonstration should be a part of the lesson on that day, but it may take place at a later time.

The evaluation component should contain space for the teacher to write comments relative to student achievement of the objective, the reaction of the class to particular activities, and possible ways in which the lesson could have been improved.

Time

Since teachers must work within certain time limitations, it is a good idea to assign approximate lengths of time to each of the planned activities. This procedure is particularly helpful for beginning teachers, since they often have a great many details requiring their attention and sometimes lose track of time. It can be a shock to hear the dismissal bell ring or to be informed by a student that the time is gone and realize that the lesson is only partially completed.

Miscellaneous Components

Since lesson plans reflect the needs of the particular teachers who write them, not all plans have the same components. Most lesson plans provide for an instructional objective, content, and instructional activities, and many contain sections for materials, evaluation, and time estimations. Other components are often included, however, that are not as common. Because they are largely self-explanatory, they are listed here with no discussion: homework assignments, date, title of course and/or subject, grade level, title of the unit, special announcements, preassessments, and preliminary tasks. Additional components may be added at the teacher's discretion.

SAMPLE LESSON PLANS

Having examined typical lesson plan components, we will look next at how they might be combined into a lesson plan. The target population is a group of high-school freshmen enrolled in a beginning computer science course. Keep in mind that the following plan is a sample. Other, equally effective approaches might be taken to help students achieve the same objective. The comments in parentheses are included to help explain the various components. They would not be included in an actual lesson plan.

SAMPLE 1: CONCEPT LESSON, ONE PERIOD

UNIT: Computer Input, Output, and Storage Devices

LESSON: Input Devices

OBJECTIVE: You will be able to orally describe how two computer input devices operate to enter data into a computer (comprehension).

CONTENT
Input devices and modes include at least the following:

1. *Punched cards.* Either a beam of light activating a photoelectric cell or a metal brush is used to detect the presence or absence of a hole at each predetermined spot on a card. These data are then converted to an electrical impulse and "read."
2. *Punched paper tape.* Analogous to a continuous punched card; however, the metal brush cannot be used for reading because of the inherent weakness of the material.

3. *Magnetic tape.* Spaces on a strip of magnetic tape are magnetized or demagnetized. These spaces are then "read" by a device sensitive to magnetic fields.

4. *Light pens.* A light-sensitive penlike device is held against a cathode ray tube and used to indicate certain areas to the computer. Light pens are often used in conjunction with more conventional terminals.

5. *Terminals.* Typewriterlike devices that can be used to code data directly into a computer via either direct electrical hook-ups or indirect hook-ups such as acoustic couplers.

6. *Consoles.* Analogous to terminals but usually connected directly to the central processing unit.

7. *Electron pens.* Analogous to light pens, but utilizing a stream of electrons on either a CRT display or an electric table. Specific spots are activated by the electron stream.

8. *Magnetic ink.* A magnetically sensitive device compares configurations as characters printed in ink containing a ferromagnetic substance with a series of precoded configurations. When a match occurs, the computer "recognizes" the character and converts its value into a series of electrical impulses. Magnetic ink is used extensively on checks.

9. *Optical scanners.* Marks made in pencil at small but specific spots on a sheet of paper are "read" via reflected light and converted to a series of electrical impulses. Optical scanners are used extensively to machine score tests.

10. *Profile scanners.* Still in the experimental stage, they will use a TV-like device to convey images to a computer for comparison against a series of precoded images. When matches occur the data are acted upon. Have been used to enable robots to move about freely and for crude personnel identification.

INSTRUCTIONAL ACTIVITIES

1. Begin by showing students a mark-sensing form and asking if anyone knows how information gets from it into a computer. Briefly discuss students' responses and, if no one knows, explain that a beam of light is reflected off the shiny graphite marks at specific locations and is converted into electrical signals to the computer. 2 min

   (It is not likely that many students would know how information is taken from a mark-sensing form, so their interest might well be stimulated and their answers would provide active involvement. Another idea would be to show students a blank check and one that had cleared the bank and ask them about the difference in the number of magnetic ink characters at the bottom of the check.)

2. Explain the objective and ask one or two students to paraphrase it to verify students' understanding. 1 min.

   (To be reasonably sure that students understand the purpose of the lesson, a teacher should ask specific questions about the objective. Simply stating the objective and then asking if there are any questions is not usually effective because not many students will admit to being confused.)

3. Ask students to list devices that are used to enter data into a computer and list these on the board as they are mentioned. 2 min.

   (To the extent that students can list devices they will be actively involved, and they may also list some devices that the teacher had not included.)

4. Ask students to explain the operation of listed devices. If they are not sure how the devices work, provide the needed information. When the explanations are complete, erase the board. 5 min.

   (Students might not be able to explain the operation of the devices that they listed, but some might be able to do so. Giving them the opportunity to demonstrate their knowledge will help build their self-concepts. If students name a device with which the teacher is unfamiliar, the teacher should acknowledge the fact and tell the class that he or she will find out how that device works. Be sure then that this is done and that the information is shared with the class. This can be a very useful experience for students since it demonstrates that even teachers continually learn.)

5. Show a transparency listing the input devices included in the content section and check off those already discussed. 1 min.

6. Use transparencies to explain each of the remaining devices included in the content section. 15 min.

   (The operation of each device listed in the content section should be described on a separate transparency. This will make it easy to use only those that have not already been discussed.)

7. After the operation of each device has been explained, turn off the overhead projector and review by asking students to recall the main points. Provide corrective feedback as needed and praise all reasonable responses. 5 min.

8. Close by explaining that new input devices are continually being developed to meet new needs, but that in all cases, it is necessary to convert information into electrical signals so that they can be processed by computers. 3 min.

9. For evaluation, ask for volunteers to name a computer input device and to explain how it is operated to enter data into a computer. Get at least six devices listed. Provide corrective feedback as needed and praise all reasonable answers. 6 min.

   (The length of this lesson, as planned, would be about 40 minutes. The times allocated for each activity are only estimates, since students' questions or comments may take more or less time than planned. Nevertheless, it is a good idea for beginning teachers to estimate the length of time for each component to help avoid grossly miscalculating the time required for the lesson.)

MATERIALS: Overhead projector and transparencies

> (List only those materials that are not ordinarily in the classroom. Do not list materials such as chalkboards or chalk unless there is a specific reason to do so.)

SAMPLE 2: CONCEPT LESSON TO BE CARRIED OVER TO THE FOLLOWING DAY

UNIT: Romantic Literature

LESSON: Characteristics of Romanticism

OBJECTIVE: You will be able, orally, to explain at least two characteristics of Romanticism (comprehension).

CONTENT

1. Definition: Romanticism is a way of looking at life and at oneself with a state of mind centered around emotions.
2. Major characteristics of Romanticism
   a. A return to "nature"
   b. Sympathy for rural life and its activities
   c. Sentimental contemplation
   d. Predominance of imagination over reason
   e. Idealization of the past
   f. Concern for all that is aesthetically beautiful in the ideal sense
   g. Praising of childhood
   h. Idealization of women
   i. A wish to explore the personal inner world of dreams and desires (soul searching)

INSTRUCTIONAL ACTIVITIES

1. Begin by showing students pictures of a jackhammer and a sunset and asking what thoughts each picture brings to mind. Briefly discuss answers. 1 min.
2. Ask two students to paraphrase the objective that is written on the board. 2 min.
3. Explain, exemplify, and discuss the term "Romanticism." 5 min.
4. Show a five-minute videotape segment of an original *Star Trek* episode featuring the emotionless Mr. Spock. 7 min.
5. Lead class discussion of the value of emotions and introduce the various points listed in the content section if they are not brought out by students. List the points on the overhead as they are made. 10 min.
6. Divide the class into groups of four or five students and tell them to prepare a three-minute skit for presentation the following day. As-

sign some groups to prepare skits portraying people as they normally are, and other groups to prepare skits portraying people as
very machine-like and emotionless. Allow time for skit preparation to
begin. 5 min.

7. Review by asking students for the major characteristics of Romanticism. 5 min.

8. Close by explaining that the next day, the three-minute skits will be
presented and the feelings they arouse will be discussed as a way of
further exploring the idea of Romanticism. 3 min.

9. For evaluation, ask students to cite characteristics of Romanticism.
2 min.

The next plans are for a sequence of three 20-minute micro-lessons. The first
two plans are for concept lessons intended to help students understand a concept. The
third plan is for an analysis lesson intended to enable students to engage in higher-
order thinking and to use the information they learned.

*SAMPLE 3: CONCEPT LESSON ONE (20-MINUTE
MICRO-LESSON)*

UNIT: Organizing the Elements of a News Story

LESSON: The Lead

OBJECTIVE: You will be able to orally describe the function of any of the five
W's (who, what, when, where, and why) that are typically in a news story lead
(comprehension).

CONTENT

1. The first paragraph of a news story is called the lead.
2. The lead tells *who* did it, *what* happened, *when* and *where* it happened, and perhaps *why* it happened.
3. Good reporters find the answers to each of these questions, determine the most important fact (key thought) answered by these
questions, and build the lead around this key fact.
   a. *Who?* Should be answered first when a person is the most
   important or interesting factor in the story.
   b. *What?* Should be answered first when the thing that happened
   is the most important/interesting factor in the story.
   c. *When?* Should be answered first when the time of the occurrence is the most important/interesting factor in the story.
   d. *Where?* Should be answered first when the place of occurrence
   is the most important/interesting factor in the story.
   e. *Why?* Should be answered first when the reason for the action
   will attract the attention of the greatest number of readers.

4. When the reader has finished the first paragraph, all essential facts should have emerged.

INSTRUCTIONAL ACTIVITIES

1. Begin by showing two sentences on the overhead projector and asking students which one they think is the most interesting and why. Briefly discuss responses. 1 min.
2. Explain the objective and ask a student to paraphrase it. 1 min.
3. With the aid of a transparency, define and discuss the elements used to build a news story lead. 4 min.
4. Show two news leads via a transparency and ask students to identify differences and similarities between them. 2 min.
5. Distribute handout that explains when each of the five W's should be used as the first key item in the lead. Discuss each of the general rules and provide examples on overhead transparencies. 5 min.
6. Review by asking students to provide one hypothetical example for each of the five key-thought leads discussed. An example of a "where" key thought lead is: The Jefferson High School Gymnasium will be the site for the boys' basketball final playoff next March. 3 min.
7. Close by returning to the first transparency used in the lesson and discussing the reasons why one of the two examples is clearly a more effective lead for a news story. 1 min.
8. Evaluate by asking students, at random, to describe the function of one of the five W's. 3 min.

MATERIALS: Transparencies and handout

SAMPLE 4: CONCEPT LESSON TWO (20-MINUTE MICRO-LESSON)

UNIT: Organizing the Elements of a News Story

LESSON: The Body

OBJECTIVE: You will be able to orally describe at least two characteristics of a well-organized news story.

CONTENT

1. Organizing the body of a straight news story requires that the reporter weigh each factual element related to a story and determine its news value to the story.
2. The lead is the most newsworthy idea in the story and should, therefore, be explained first. In the paragraphs immediately following the lead, the reporter should amplify and expand upon the key thought in the lead.

3. In the paragraphs following the appropriate explanation of the key thought, the reporter should arrange the details/facts in order of descending importance.
4. Having the broadest, most important part of the story at the top, with facts of lesser importance beneath, is called the inverted-pyramid style.
5. Each paragraph should contain information about a single detail or fact.
6. Paragraphs should be organized so that specific information is presented first and secondary detail (amplification) is presented later.

INSTRUCTIONAL ACTIVITIES

1. Read a short news story to the class and then ask students to choose which of four symbols drawn on the chalkboard best represents the organization of the information contained in the story. Briefly discuss responses. 2 min.
2. Ask two students to paraphrase the lesson's objective that is written on the board. 1 min.
3. With the aid of a transparency, discuss the characteristics of a well-written inverted-pyramid news story. 3 min.
4. Distribute handout that diagrams the inverted-pyramid approach to organizing the elements of a news story. Discuss the order of descending news value in each paragraph. 4 min.
5. Show students transparencies of short news stories with paragraphs in random order. Provide practice by asking students to place the paragraphs into descending order of importance. 4 min.
6. Review by asking students to list, in order, the characteristics of a well-written inverted-pyramid news story. 1 min.
7. Close by explaining that the organization of the elements in a news story is a natural extension of logic, i.e., gather the facts and determine the relative importance of each fact. 2 min.
8. Evaluate by asking students, at random, to describe elements of a well-organized news story. 2 min.

MATERIALS: Transparencies (5), handout

The next sample differs from the previous examples in two important ways. First, it is intended to immediately follow the preceding lesson (sample 4) and secondly, it is an analysis lesson. Note the difference in the structure of the content section. It consists of questions that will be used, as needed, to focus students' attention on critical points. Ideally, cueing questions will be used to lead students to discover, on their own, the key questions that they should ask themselves in order to organize the key elements of a news story.

It is important to keep in mind the fact that students should do the analyzing. It is easy to deprive students of the opportunity to think for themselves by telling them too much during an analysis lesson. The point of the lesson is not to show students how easily the teacher can make the analysis. The point is to help students learn which questions to ask themselves so that *they* will know how to make similar analyses on their own. Do not tell. Ask cueing questions—questions that lead students to discover important points for themselves. This helps students learn to learn.

SAMPLE 5: ANALYSIS LESSON (20-MINUTE MICRO-LESSON)

UNIT: Organizing Elements of a News Story

LESSON: Analyzing the Elements of the Inverted-Pyramid Style News Story

OBJECTIVE: Given two brief news stories to analyze, organize the elements of at least one of the stories into a perfect inverted-pyramid style (analysis).

CONTENT

1. Does the lead clearly and concisely answer the questions asked by the five W's (who, what, when, where, and why)?
2. Does the lead accurately focus on the key thought (the most important fact) answered by the five W's?
3. Is the key thought adequately explained in the paragraph(s) following the lead?
4. Are the secondary facts/details of the story organized in order of descending importance?
5. Does each paragraph contain information about a single detail or fact?
6. Could the story stand on its own if the final two or three paragraphs were deleted?

INSTRUCTIONAL ACTIVITIES

1. Begin by showing two brief news stories via a transparency and asking students which would be best to submit to the news editor of the local newspaper. Discuss students' reasons for choosing one over the other and write some of the reasons on the board. 3 min.
2. Explain the objective and ask a student to paraphrase it. 1 min.
3. With the aid of transparencies, lead students into a guided discussion during which *they* will identify the elements of two news stories, place the elements into an inverted pyramid style, and decide how well each element fulfills its purpose. Provide cues leading to the questions in the content section, as needed. 7 min.
4. Review by asking students to provide the characteristics exemplified in the inverted-pyramid style news story. 3 min.

5. Close by pointing out that the key to writing cogent news stories is first understanding the reasoning for organizing the elements in the inverted-pyramid style. 2 min.
6. Evaluate by showing students two brief news stories and asking them to organize the elements of at least one of them into an inverted-pyramid style. 4 min.

MATERIALS: Transparencies

SUMMARY

Appropriate preparation is one of the most important components of effective teaching. Lesson plans demonstrate that planning. The following checklist embodies many of the ideas discussed in this chapter. The checklist may be useful in developing or checking lesson plans.

1. Objective:
   a. Clearly specifies an observable, terminal behavior and a minimum acceptable standard.
   b. Can be classified at a specific and appropriate cognitive or psychomotor level.
   c. If at the analysis level, specifies what is to be analyzed.
   d. Is relevant to students and seems to be worth achieving because it has some practical or long-term usefulness.
2. Content:
   a. Contains accurate and up-to-date information and, where appropriate, examples and anecdotes.
   b. Is complete enough to enable students to achieve the objective and for a reasonably competent substitute teacher to teach the lesson.
   c. Is complex enough for the target population.
   d. Is appropriate for the length of the lesson.
3. Learning activities provide for:
   a. An appropriate set induction and the communication of the objective.
   b. Stimulus variation with respect to modes of presentation (lecture, discussion, etc.) and the appropriate use of media.
   c. Assessment of students' achievement of the objective.
4. Materials: Category includes all materials needed for the lesson except those that are normally in the classroom.
5. Ideally, the plan should be no longer than one page in length.

STUDY QUESTIONS

1. What is the prime source of ideas for lesson plans?
2. Explain at least three ways in which lesson plans can be used to improve the teaching-learning process.
3. What are two advantages in planning lessons that can be completed in a single class period?

4. What are the characteristics of a good content section for a concept-level plan? How do they differ from the characteristics of the content section of a typical analysis-level plan?

5. What is meant by "change of pace"? How might it be accomplished during a lesson?

6. Name two factors that should be evaluated following each lesson.

___8___

Measurement and Evaluation

INTRODUCTION

The main reason teachers evaluate students is to determine the extent to which those students have achieved specific instructional objectives. This information helps students identify areas of strength and weakness and gives them a basis for comparing their abilities to those of other students. The information also provides a basis upon which teachers can assess the effectiveness of particular instructional procedures and materials. Further, the data are used by students, parents, other teachers, admissions officers, and employers to make decisions about educational and vocational options. For all of these reasons, evaluation that is as accurate and unbiased as possible is needed.

This chapter begins with an examination of some of the basic principles and terminology related to measurement and evaluation. This is followed by a discussion concerning the construction of different kinds of objective tests, examples of test items at specific levels of the cognitive domain, and ways of organizing the test and preparing students. A similar section focusing on essay tests follows. The remaining major sections deal with standardized tests, alternate evaluation procedures, analyzing tests, calculating and reporting grades and, finally, teacher evaluation.

SAMPLE OBJECTIVES

When you complete this chapter, you will be able, in writing, to:

1. Define terms such as measurement, evaluation, reliability, validity, and objective and essay tests (comprehension).

2. Explain how criterion-referenced and norm-referenced evaluation differ and cite at least one example of how each could be used in your subject-area (comprehension).

3. Construct a six-item multiple-choice test for a given topic, with at least two of the items being at the analysis level (synthesis).

4. Given a set of scores, a preset level scale, and a standard-deviation cutoff scale, properly assign letter grades to the scores using each of the scales (application).

BASIC PRINCIPLES AND TERMINOLOGY

There is a difference between measurement and evaluation. Measurement has to do with quantifying something by assigning numbers to it; an example is measuring height or weight. Unfortunately, we cannot measure skills and knowledge quite so easily. The tests, papers, and projects that students complete do not yield measures as precise as those yielded by yardsticks and scales. Further, educators are usually trying to assess a complex mix of skills and knowledge. This means that we more often engage in evaluation than in measurement.

Evaluation means making a value judgment. To be as accurate as possible, a value judgment should be based, in part, on whatever measurement data are available, but it should go beyond that data to include assessments about such factors as the student's ability to write and speak effectively, to organize ideas clearly, and similar qualities that defy simple quantification. Evaluations are more wholistic assessments than are measurements. What follows are some basic principles that can help increase the accuracy of evaluations.

Obtain Enough Samples

Students need feedback in order to identify strengths and weaknesses. The more feedback that is provided, the more students are able to correct mistakes and achieve objectives. On the other hand, it is not practical to test every day; even if it were, too much testing sends the wrong message to students. It tells them that grades, per se, are all-important. A balance is needed.

Students should not have to go more than a week without feedback concerning their progress. This feedback may take the form of grades on a formal test or paper, comments written on homework assignments, or comments made to individuals during class discussions. The behaviors called for in the objectives dictate the kinds of activities in which students will need to engage and the most appropriate forms of feedback about progress. Since the purpose of the feedback is to help students form or shape their abilities in order to demonstrate specific objectives, evaluations carried out during instruction are known as formative evaluations.

There is another advantage to frequent assessments: They make it possible to drop a low grade. Most teachers recognize that tests only sample skills or knowledge, and they also recognize that the results can be flawed by factors such as less-than-perfect test items or a student's health when the test was taken. If a teacher has ten or more samples of each student's skills and knowledge, it makes good sense to drop the lowest grade. Dropping the lowest grade will not seriously distort a student's achievement pattern, but it will help minimize the effects of a poor grade, regardless of the reason for that grade. Further, knowledge that the lowest grade will be dropped acts as an incentive for students to continue to work even though they may get a low grade on a test or a paper. Their averages can always be improved.

Obtain Different Kinds of Samples

At the end of each grading period and at the end of each semester or year teachers are expected to give each student a grade—a single letter to represent the achievements of weeks and weeks of work. That grade should reflect the student's achievements as accurately as possible. Some of the achievements, particularly those embodied in low-level cognitive objectives, might be assessed via objective tests such as true-false, multiple-choice, and matching tests. Other objectives, particularly higher-level objectives, will require students to use skills and knowledge in more creative and wholistic ways. To assess achievement of these objectives, teachers use essay tests or projects of one kind or another. The point is that the accurate assessment of students' achievements requires the use of a variety of assessment techniques.

Another reason to vary assessment techniques is that students respond to assessment instruments in different ways. For example, some students take objective tests well; others freeze up on such tests. Some students write well; others are more adept at demonstrating their knowledge orally. Still others are better at completing projects that require the utilization of knowledge (such as constructing a tape-slide sequence or manipulating a hypothetical stock portfolio). If only one or two assessment techniques are used, the real extent to which students have mastered skills and knowledge may be masked by their reaction to the assessment mode itself. A variety of assessment techniques is needed.

Check for Validity

Validity refers to how accurately an instrument measures whatever it is supposed to measure. There are at least three kinds of validity to consider. Content or face validity reflects the extent to which a test covers what was taught—that the test accurately reflects the instruction. Teachers sometimes construct tests that seem to cover the content taught but in fact do not. For example, if the instruction focused on developing understanding of trends and issues, the test should give students the opportunity to demonstrate their understanding of those trends and issues. If the test focuses on specific names and dates or the grammatical correctness of responses, its content validity would be low.

Predictive validity is a measure of how well performance on one measure or task reflects probable performance on some other measure or task. For example, college entrance exams are given because they provide some insight into the probable success of students in college. Performance on the test is used to predict performance in college. Preassessment tests sometimes have high predictive validity.

Construct validity has to do with the ability of a test to assess psychological constructs such as honesty or tolerance. Teachers do not usually deal with construct validity, but it is useful to know the term because some standardized tests assess psychological constructs.

Assess Student Effort

The issue of student effort is one that troubles many teachers. On one hand, it is necessary to have students' grades reflect their actual achievements. On the other hand, it seems inhumane to ignore the efforts that many students make even though they may not achieve well. One way of reflecting factors such as effort, attitude, and attendance is to report them in supplementary comments. This may help a student's morale, but it will not help his or her grade.

Another technique is to provide a way for students to earn points by demonstrating effort. For this technique to work, students must be able to demonstrate extra effort as opposed to extra work or greater ability. One way to do this is to announce that extra points, perhaps five, will be awarded for every paper that is turned in with no spelling, punctuation, or grammatical errors. These errors frequently reflect carelessness rather than lack of ability, so students could earn the extra points by simply taking the time to carefully proofread their work.

In order to keep achievement and effort points separate, the points for effort should not be added to the grade for the paper. They should be reflected in a separate notation on the paper. A student might get only 50 points out of 100 for achievement, but might get the full five points for effort. The grade might appear as 50/100 +5. A separate area of the grade book should be used to keep track of the extra points each student accumulates. Since all students have the same opportunity to acquire the extra credit points, the total number of points that each student earns is a fair measure of demonstrated effort.

By providing a way to fairly assess effort, in addition to fairly assessing achievement, teachers give themselves greater peace of mind and increase the validity of their grades. Valid grades give students, parents, and all others who base decisions upon them the kind of information they need to make sound decisions. Invalid grades may lead to decisions that result in much wasted time and in needless frustration and disappointment. Teachers should make certain that the grades they record are valid.

Check for Reliability

Reliability refers to how consistently an instrument measures whatever it measures. To the extent that a test is reliable, the relative positions of scores will remain the same on repeated administrations of the test or upon the administration of an equivalent form of the test. Students who score high on one form will score high on an equivalent form. If the test is not reliable, students who score high on one form may score low on an equivalent form.

The degree to which a test is reliable is expressed as a decimal known as a reliability coefficient. These coefficients range from the highest degree of reliability (1.00), to the lowest (.00). It is also possible for a test to have a negative reliability coefficient, possibly as low as −1.00. This would indicate that those students who scored highest on one measure, scored lowest on the other. Reliability coefficients of .65 and higher are desirable.

Generally, longer tests are more reliable than shorter tests. For example, commercially available tests, such as college entrance exams and standardized achievement tests, frequently have hundreds of items and require hours to complete. Their length contributes to their reliability because so many questions are asked that it is unlikely that large areas of skills or knowledge that the student possesses will be missed. This means that if the student took the test again, the same skills and abilities would be assessed, and the score would be close to the previous score unless new skills or abilities were acquired between the test administrations.

Because teachers prefer not to use their limited instruction time for testing, their tests usually do not consist of hundreds of items. A test of about fifty items is generally long enough to yield reliable results and is not too long for students to complete within a class period. When planning a multiple-choice test, teachers should allow about thirty seconds for each four-choice item. A fifty-item test would take about twenty-five minutes to complete. Since time is needed to take attendance, make announcements, and distribute and collect the test, more time is needed. In order to allow students as much time as possible to recall and apply their skills and knowledge, a full class period should be used for a major test.

Just as teachers want to construct reliable tests, they also want to be sure that their semester grades are reliable. They do this by basing those grades upon a variety of samples such as tests, papers, and projects. Just as the reliability of tests tends to increase with the number of test items, the more samples of students' abilities that are used to determine the semester grade, the more reliable that grade will be.

Criterion-Referenced Evaluation

Criterion-referencing means that the grade reflects performance relative to some preset standard. A passing grade means that the standard has been met; a failing grade means that the standard has not been met. For example, the minimum acceptable standard of a precise instructional objective spells out precisely what constitutes an acceptable demonstration of a particular ability. If the standard is met, the demonstration is acceptable and the student has achieved the objective. If the standard is not met, the demonstration is not acceptable and the student has not achieved the objective. The grade is either pass or fail. A driving test is an example of a criterion-referenced test.

Since the scores on a criterion-referenced test are either pass or fail, all the items should be about equally difficult. Differences in difficulty levels would be necessary only if a spread among scores was needed, but none is needed. Students either pass or fail the test, and, if the instruction was successful, many more students will pass than will fail. Beyond knowing if a score was above or below the minimum passing grade, the exact score does not matter.

As it happens, there are relatively few uses for criterion-referencing in education. The most common applications of criterion-referencing are those in which cut-off scores are established for such things as competence tests and entrance tests. A certain score must be obtained in order to move on or to be considered for admission. Most other forms of evaluation are norm-referenced.

Norm-Referenced Evaluation

Norm-referencing means that the grade reflects performance relative to the performance of some norming group. A norming group is a group of people who have some relevant characteristic in common, such as grade level or age. The students in a class constitute a small norming group, whereas all high school seniors who take a college entrance examination constitute a large norming group.

Since our society is basically competitive, teachers need data that allows them to rank-order students according to abilities. It is not enough to separate students according to those who can and those who cannot do something. Finer distinctions are needed, and norm-referenced tests provide them. In order to rank-order students in terms of demonstrated abilities, the teacher must create test items of varying difficulty levels so that differing ability levels can be assessed.

Although norm-referenced tests require items of varying levels of difficulty, they do not require trick questions or questions that deal with trivial points. Most students prefer to do well, rather than poorly, on tests and are willing to study to do so. Their desire to do well will be lessened if the instruction focuses on important skills and ideas but the test includes questions that focus on relatively unimportant points. Students can make a serious attempt to learn important skills and information, but they cannot learn every possible bit of information. What follows are some ideas and techniques that can help teachers develop effective tests.

TEACHER-MADE TESTS

Pencil-and-paper tests are not the only kind of assessment instruments that teachers should use, but they will probably be the most common. There are three basic reasons for this. First, pencil-and-paper tests present the same questions to all students under the same test conditions. This means that the test results provide a reasonable basis for comparison. Second, pencil-and-paper tests generate products (students' responses) that are easily stored. This means that the tests and the results can be kept readily accessible for analysis or review either to improve the test or to explain to students or parents how a grade was determined. Finally, pencil-and-paper tests can be used equally well to broadly sample students' knowledge or to probe deeply into a more narrow area.

Objective Tests

Questions that require true-false, multiple-choice, matching, or completion answers are all examples of a basic test form that requires students to select or construct responses from a given or very limited range of options. These "objective" tests are objective only in the sense that there is no need to make value judgments about the quality of the answers. They are clearly either right or wrong. There are, however, many value judgments made while objective tests are being constructed. It is the teacher who decides which questions to ask, how many questions to ask, and what vocabulary to use. These judgments are largely value or subjective judgments.

Objective tests are popular for a number of reasons. First, such tests are intended to sample broadly but not deeply. Rather than asking one or two questions which might be the "wrong" questions for some students, objective tests ask many questions about different aspects of the topic, thus sampling students' knowledge more broadly. Further, objective tests are easy to score and they lend themselves well to item analyses, so that teachers can continually improve items and develop a test bank of valid and reliable questions.

There are also a number of disadvantages associated with objective tests. Some educators point out that objective tests can emphasize the memorization of bits and pieces of information. They claim that students often do very well on the basis of memorizing and recognizing these bits and pieces, even though they may have little idea of the relationship of the parts to a larger whole. In addition, constructing items for objective tests is time-consuming, and even teachers who work hard to construct good items may find that some questions still confuse students.

Considering all the pros and cons, many teachers have concluded that their own objective tests meet some of their evaluation needs better than any other means, especially when they wish to sample students' general knowledge about some topic. Typical objectives for objective tests might include the following:

1. You will recall and apply information about the steel industry, from mining through smelting and product production, well enough to achieve a score of at least 80 percent on a multiple-choice test dealing with this information.
2. You will, given a wiring diagram containing numbered connections, place a check before the numbers of all incorrect or superfluous connections.

Important general rules can be followed that will help teachers to build and administer valid and reliable objective tests.[1]

A. *Keep the language simple.* Unless the purpose of the test is to survey the extent of students' vocabularies, there is no point in using words that are unfamiliar to students or in phrasing questions so they are difficult to understand. Students will be justifiably angry and frustrated if they get answers wrong because they could not understand what was being asked rather than because they did not know the right answer. Compare the following two examples:

1. The physical relationship between most petroleum products and most purely aqueous solutions is generally such that physical interaction and diffusion of the two is severely limited. (a) True, (b) False.
2. As a general rule, oil and water do not mix. (a) True, (b) False.

The only justifiable reason for using example 1 is if the teacher was attempting to check students' vocabulary. Ask questions as simply and concisely as possible to help ensure valid and reliable test results.

B. *Ask students to apply, rather than simply to recall, information.* If students can apply the information they learned, it is a safe bet they have committed it to memory. It does not follow, however, that simply because students have memorized information they can also apply it. This being the case, it is better to aim questions at application rather than simple recall. Consider the following two examples:

3. The area of a rectangle is found by multiplying the length by the width. (a) True, (b) False.
4. A rectangle 2' × 4' has an area of 8 square feet. (a) True, (b) False.

The computation involved in example 2 is not difficult, yet it enables students to apply what they learned and thus emphasizes learning for the sake of practical application rather than learning for the sake of passing tests.

C. *Make sure that each item is independent.* Check questions to be sure that one question does not provide a clue to some other question or that the answer to one question is not crucial to the answer of another. Both situations decrease the reliability of the test results. For example,

5. The number of square feet in a room nine feet long and twelve feet wide is:

    a. 3
    b. 21
    c. 81
    d. 108
    e. 144

6. At $2.00 per square foot, what would it cost to carpet the room described in question number 5?

    a. $ 6.00
    b. $ 42.00
    c. $162.00
    d. $216.00
    e. $288.00

Given these two questions, any student who missed 5 would almost certainly miss 6. Other than having the student miss two items instead of just one, nothing was gained by linking the questions. It would have been more advantageous if questions 5 and 6 had been combined, for example, "How much would it cost to carpet a room 9′ × 12′ if carpeting costs $2 a square foot?" and the extra space used for a separate and distinct item.

D. *Do not establish or follow a pattern for correct responses.* Regardless of how clever an answer pattern is, some student will eventually discover it and compromise the test results. The problems involved with detecting compromised tests and doing something about them are far greater than any possible advantage to patterning responses.

E. *Do not include trick or trivial questions.* Sometimes teachers are tempted to ask questions that require extended effort for correct interpretation or that deal with unimportant points. This temptation may stem from being unable to build items as quickly as one would like or from a desire to assure a wide spread among test scores. Trick or trivial questions not only reduce the validity and reliability of tests, but they may have a powerful negative effect if they antagonize students.

F. *Do not answer questions after the test has started unless it is done publicly.* Sometimes individual students will seek further clarification of a question as they work through the test. If additional information is provided to that student, the test results may be biased, since that student will have had access to direct help when others did not. It is wise to make a general announcement prior to each test concerning your reluctance to answer questions during a test. This, plus careful proofreading of tests prior to their administration, should forestall most questions. If it does become necessary to answer a question about some test item, assume that other students may be equally confused about it and call everyone's attention to the clarification. Remember, however, that interrupting students during a test destroys their train of thought and thus should be avoided whenever possible.

In addition to these few general rules, other considerations relevant to the construction of specific kinds of objective test items are presented in the paragraphs that follow.

Multiple-Choice Items

Multiple-choice items are particularly useful because they can be used easily to sample cognitive skills ranging from simple recall through analysis. The following examples illustrate several levels of cognition:

Knowledge Level. The purpose of knowledge-level questions is to have students recall information. Be sure that the information to be recalled is worth knowing. If students are asked to recall information that they perceive as relevant and useful, they are more likely to take the teacher and the course seriously. Here is a sample of a knowledge-level question.

7. Which of the following domains described in Bloom's taxonomy is most concerned with the acquisition and manipulation of factual information?

   a. Cognitive
   b. Intellectual
   c. Affective
   d. Empirical
   e. Psychomotor

Comprehension Level. The purpose of comprehension-level questions is to have students translate from one symbol system to another, to interpret (put into their own words), or to extrapolate (go beyond the data given). Here is an example of a comprehension-level question.[2]

8. "Milton! Thou shouldst be living at this hour; England hath need of thee; she is a fen of stagnant waters"—Wordsworth.

   The metaphor, "She is a fen of stagnant waters," indicates that Wordsworth felt England was:

   a. largely swampy land.
   b. in a state of turmoil and unrest.
   c. making no progress.
   d. in a generally corrupt condition.

Application Level. The purpose of application-level questions is to have students apply skills and knowledge to problems and situations that are new to them. Here is an example of an application-level question.

9. The scores on a test were 95, 90, 90, 85, 70, 60, and 0. What is the mode?

   a. 90
   b. 85
   c. 81.66
   d. 70
   e. 47.50

Analysis Level. The purpose of analysis-level questions is to have the student engage in higher-order thinking. This can be done by having the student examine a whole, looking for its constituent elements, for relationships between and among elements, or for organizational patterns. Depending upon the objective, the "whole" could be a poem, a musical excerpt, an editorial, a hypothetical situation, or even a rock sample, but it is necessary that students be given something to examine that requires careful analysis. Finding the obvious does not usually demonstrate higher-order thinking. Here is an example of an analysis-level question.

10. The Education for All Handicapped Children Act of 1975 (Public Law 94-142) requires not only that all handicapped children be educated, but

that they be educated in the least restrictive environment. Which of the following was the most critical assumption made by the drafters of the legislation?

   a.   That all students would be willing to be in the "least restrictive environment" in order to be in compliance with the law.
   <u>b</u>.   That regular classroom teachers could provide for the needs of handicapped students about as well as could the special education teachers.
   c.   That sufficient funds would be available since special education students frequently need special materials.
   d.   That special education teachers were not doing a very good job with their students so the students should be placed in regular classrooms whenever possible.

Since writing questions at the analysis level is more difficult than writing them at lower levels, a second example may be useful. This example illustrates how a question can require a student to demonstrate that he knows what the true state of affairs is, and why it is so.

   11.   The animal shown below has been found outside the school.

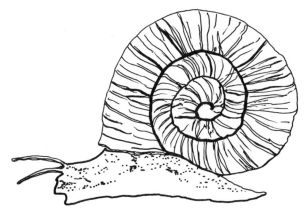

An analysis should demonstrate that this animal is:

   a.   an arthropod because it has an exoskeleton.
   b.   an arthropod because it has antennae.
   <u>c</u>.   not an arthropod because it lacks jointed legs.
   d.   not an arthropod because it exhibits bilateral symmetry.

Principles for Building Multiple-Choice Items

   A.   *Put as much of the item as possible into the stem.* The "stem" of a multiple-choice question is that part that asks the question or states the problem. If the stem does its job properly, it gives the student an idea of what is sought before reading the options. Consider the following two examples.

12. John Adams was:

 a. the second president of the United States.
 b. the third president of the United States.
 c. the fourth president of the United States.
 d. none of the above.

13. The second president of the United States was:

 a. John Adams.
 b. Thomas Jefferson.
 c. James Madison.
 d. none of the above.

In example 12 the students do not know what is sought until they have read the options. Further, because it is necessary to repeat the same words in each option, the student must spend more time reading. Both points make for inefficient testing.

In example 13, the options are shorter than the stem (which is, in itself, a good guide), the stem clearly and concisely asks the question, and it provides sufficient data to help the student start thinking about the correct answer.

B. *Make options reasonable.* In norm-referenced tests, the teacher attempts to discriminate among students. This discrimination process is facilitated by ensuring that all options seem reasonable to someone who is unsure of the exact information. Option d in examples 12 and 13, for instance, may not be very useful since most students are aware that John Adams was one of our early presidents. Even though students may not be sure just which president Adams was, they could still eliminate option d and thus increase the chance of guessing correctly from among the remaining options. One way to construct good options is based on the type of error students are most likely to make. In the application sample on page 153, for instance, the second option is the median, the third is the mean of the three middle scores, the fourth is the mean, and the fifth is the mean of the highest and lowest scores. To someone who was unclear about measures of central tendency, any of these options might seem reasonable. The advantage to this tactic is that the student's *incorrect* response can be used to diagnose the source of difficulties.

C. *Make sure that unintentional clues are not provided.* Sometimes a student can eliminate an option simply because it is grammatically incorrect. For example, if a question ends with "an," the correct option must begin with a vowel. If the question ends with "a," the correct option must begin with a consonant. Ending the question with "a(n)" avoids the problem. Incorrect tenses or forms of words can provide clues, as can correct options that are consistently longer or shorter than incorrect options. The use of "always" and "never" is usually a giveaway, as is the use of "all of the above," and "none of the above."

D. *Check for correct spelling and punctuation.* Proofread each question and its choices to eliminate errors and to make each item as easy to read as possible. If the stem is a complete question, it should end with a question mark; for example, "How many ounces are in a pound?" In that case, the choices would begin with capital letters but would not end with periods unless they were complete sentences. If the stem is part of a statement that will be completed by one of the choices, it should end with a colon—colons precede lists and the choices constitute a list. If the choices complete a statement, each should begin with a lower-case letter and end with a period because the stem plus the choice will form a complete sentence.

E. *Check the format.* Skip a line between the stem and the choices to make it easier for students to visually separate those components. Keep entire questions (stem and choices) together on a single page. If there is not enough room on a page for the question and all the choices, move the entire question to the following page. Look at the following example and identify the six format, grammatical, and punctuation errors that it contains.

14. The recall of specific facts is best checked through the use of an
   a. Objective test
   b. Essay test
   c. Subjective test
   d. Application test

The first error is the use of "an" at the end of the stem. Since the grammatically correct choice must begin with a vowel, students could eliminate option "c" even if they knew nothing about testing for recall. The second error is failure to include a colon at the end of the stem. The colon precedes a list and the choices constitute a list. The third error is failure to skip a line between the stem and the options. The skipped line makes it easier for students to visually separate the choices from the stem. The fourth error is beginning each choice with a capital letter. Since the choices complete the statement, they are part of the statement and should begin with lower-case letters. The fifth error is including the word "test" in each choice. Items should be worded so that students will spend as little time as possible reading. If the choices include words that could have been included in the stem, students must read those words repeatedly rather than just once. This takes time that could be used for thinking. The sixth error is failure to include a period at the end of each choice. Since the choice will complete a statement, it should have appropriate punctuation.

True-False Items

True-false items are often singled out as prime examples of the superficiality of objective testing, and often they stand justly accused. Because true-false items seem so easy to write, many teachers rely heavily upon them and forget that they are most appropriate for the lower-level cognitive skills. Keep in mind that a student who has no idea of the correct answer still has a 50:50 chance of guessing correctly. Although true-false items are often misused, it is possible to exercise the needed care to construct true-false items that sample cognitive skills as high as the analysis level. Consider the following examples.

Knowledge Level

15. In the United States, BASIC is one of the most common computer programming languages. (a) True, (b) False.

Application Level

16. A man earning $250 a week would earn $13,000 a year if he worked every week. (a) True, (b) False.

Analysis Level

17. If every teacher were given his or her own computer, the most difficult problems currently limiting wider use of computer-assisted instruction would be solved. (a) True, (b) False.

Even though it is possible to write true-false items at various levels of the cognitive domain, it is still questionable whether the time required to write such items is well spent considering that other kinds of items could sample the same cognitive levels without requiring as much preparation time. Here are a few points to keep in mind when writing true-false items.

1. *Be sure that every item is wholly true or wholly false.*
2. *Whenever possible, avoid such terms as "generally" and "usually."* These terms, while not as obvious giveaways as "always" and "never," are still open to varying interpretations.
3. *Be sure that items are not dependent upon insignificant facts.* Make sure that each item asks something of importance and worth remembering.
4. *Be sure that correct items are not consistently longer or shorter than incorrect items.*
5. *Avoid the use of double negatives, but if you use any negative at all, call attention to it by underlining or capitalizing it.*

Matching Items

Matching items are used most easily to measure low-level cognitive skills such as recall and comprehension. A typical matching test might ask students to link people with events or dates. Variations include asking students to match terms with numbers on a diagram or to match labels for a chart, graph, or map in which such labels have been replaced by letters or numbers. Guidelines for the construction of matching items follow.

1. *Keep the number of items to be matched short.* If students are required to search through more than ten or so items as they respond to each question, they will spend valuable time just searching. Their time would be better spent responding to another series of items in another question.

2. *Make sure that all items concern one topic.* Unless all items are concerned with one topic, students can simply eliminate some options as being irrelevant to some questions. This reduces the reliability of the test.

3. *Include more possible answers than questions or stipulate that some answers can be used more than once.* These steps will also help prevent students from getting right answers purely by eliminating some options.

4. *Arrange the options in some logical order such as chronological or alphabetical order.* This will make it easier for students to search through the options and will help avoid providing unintentional clues.

Completion Items

Completion items depend almost entirely upon the student's ability to recall a key word or phrase. Since most secondary school teachers are after more than rote memorization, generally completion items are not used as frequently as are other kinds of objective test items. Here are some points to keep in mind if completion items are written.

1. *Write items that can be completed with a single word or a short phrase.* There is a difference between a completion item and an essay exam. When students are required to "fill in" more than a few words, the grading of the item is complicated, and it ceases to be a completion item.

2. *Be sure that only one word or phrase can correctly complete the sentence.* In a phrase such as, "The first World War began in _____" either a date or the name of a country could correctly be used. Guard against this common error by trying different words or phrases to see if there are correct alternatives. Revise each item until only the one word or phrase sought can be used correctly.

3. *Put the blanks near the end of the sentence so the student is guided toward the correct response.*

4. *Make all the blanks the same length.* Sometimes unintentional clues are provided when teachers try to make the size of the blanks correspond to the size of the word or phrase to be inserted. The items should be clear enough to make this kind of clue unnecessary.

5. *Do not put more than two blanks in any item.* The more blanks in the item, the greater the chance the student will be unable to determine just what is sought.

Although there is considerable overlap, Table 8.1 helps to illustrate the types of test items that are usually most appropriate with specific types of precise instructional objectives. Keep in mind that the overlap exists because different kinds of test items *can* be written to sample almost any behavior. Table 8.1 is simply illustrative.

TABLE 8.1

OBJECTIVE	POSSIBLE TEST ITEM
1. List, in writing, two distinguishing characteristics of a republic. (Knowledge)	1. Two distinguishing characteristics of a republic are (a)_____, (b)_____.
2. Given a graph and a series of statements relating to the data presented, label all the incorrect statements. (Comprehension)	2. According to graph A, the greatest production of thingamagigs occurred in 1783. (a) True, (b) False.
3. Given word problems involving the derivation of cost per yard, label the correct solution to at least 80 percent of the problems. (Application)	3. At $10 per square yard, how much will it cost to carpet a room 9' × 9'? (a) $810 (b) $90 (c) $890 (d) $270
4. Given a wiring diagram with various circuits shown in specific colors, match the outcome of power input to any given circuit and its result. (Analysis)	4. Power input in this circuit (input column) will cause this output (output column).

Input	Output
red	ring bell
blue	blow horn
green	light bulb
yellow	turn on fan, start motor

Preparing the Test and the Students

Regardless of the type of objective test used, there are three things that teachers should do to help students succeed. The first is to organize the test questions in the same general order that the information was covered in class. People tend to remember sequences better than isolated facts, so if the test questions follow the same sequence as the original instruction, students will find it easier to remember specifics than if questions about those specifics appear randomly throughout the test.

Second, arrange the test items into specific blocks so that, for example, Part 1 of the test deals with topic A, Part 2 with topic B, and so forth. This arrangement helps the teacher ascertain that the test reflects the major topics covered and that the number of questions per topic is in correct proportion to the amount of time spent on that topic in class.

Finally, the teacher should conduct a formal review session a day or two before the test, with the test in hand. The review session serves two purposes. First, it helps the students focus on the ideas and information that will be tested. They should be told what each part of the test will cover, how many questions will be in each section, the type of questions that will be included (multiple-choice, true-false, etc.), and the total number of items on the test. They should also be told how many points the test will be worth, how much time they will have for the test, and that they should bring pencils and work to do if they complete the test early. Second, as the teacher reviews with students by going over the information included in each item or in blocks of items, they have the opportunity to proofread the test again and to be certain that there are no questions on the test that have not been covered in class or in assigned readings. These steps will help students to be successful.

Essay Tests

Essay tests represent a second kind of teacher-made evaluation device. The greatest single advantage of essay tests is that they require students to synthesize a response and, in so doing, to demonstrate not only their understanding of the relationships among bits and pieces of information but also their understanding of the body of information as a whole. Essays call upon students to interpret, evaluate, and organize data; draw conclusions; make inferences; and express their thoughts coherently. This makes the essay test useful in assessing higher-level cognitive skills such as synthesis and evaluation.

Offsetting these strong points are a number of disadvantages.

1. Teacher fatigue, subconscious biases, and other extraneous variables can affect students' grades.
2. Essay tests are inherently biased in favor of those students who can write quickly, neatly, and effectively.
3. Essay tests are often low in reliability and validity since only a few questions are asked and a student may, by chance, be asked questions about which he or she happens to know a great deal (or very little).
4. Essay tests take a longer time to grade than do other types of evaluations.

Other problems, particularly those concerning reliable grading, can be avoided or minimized by following definite procedures in the construction and grading of the tests.[3]

A. *Be definite about what is expected from students.* As test items are formulated, keep in mind the types of thought processes in which students are to engage, and the types of points that should be included in their responses. Consider the following two examples.

18. Describe the "water cycle," including the cause-effect relationships among the various phases.
19. Identify three problems associated with mandatory public education and explain how these problems might be eliminated or lessened.

Example 18 requires more precise information than does example 19 and may only be checking student comprehension. It may be more efficient to check student comprehension by an objective test.

In example 18, students are expected to demonstrate greater originality than in example 19, so this item is better suited for an essay test.

B. *Describe the task clearly.* Examples 18 and 19 describe clearly what the student is to do. They provide sufficient direction so that if the student has the necessary information he or she would be able to formulate acceptable answers. Compare the preceding two examples with the following two examples.

20. Discuss the effects of World War II.
21. State your opinion concerning East-West détente.

Example 20 provides so little direction that students would not be able to formulate precise answers. Some students might concentrate upon the military effects, others on the social effects, others on the technological effects. The structure of the question is too broad. Depending upon the teacher's intent, some students would find they had included some of the appropriate information while others would find they had not—even though all might have been able to formulate acceptable answers had they known more precisely what the teacher wished.

Example 21 presents a similar problem. Unless the exact grading criteria were specified before the test, the teacher should give full credit for any given answer. How can it be argued, for example, that a student's answer did not represent an opinion? The teacher who asks general questions must be prepared to accept general answers.

Specifying grading criteria is a good idea. To do this, the teacher should make a list of the important points expected in the best responses. The teacher should share these points with students as they review for the test. This review should take the form of examining possible essay questions that might be asked and going over the important points that should be included in responding to each. Students will not know which question or questions will be asked on the test, but they will have a better basis for studying than if no such review is provided. Further, the criteria described in the review session should be the basis for determining the quality of the students' responses, thus helping to make the grading more objective. To facilitate grading, criteria should be arranged from the most to the least obvious. Those points that everyone should know and include should be listed first. These are the D level criteria. Then, increasingly sophisticated criteria should be listed, ending with the points that only the best students would include in their answers (the A criteria).

C. *Make sure that students have sufficient time and materials to do the job.* One strength of essay tests is the opportunity they provide to students to analyze relationships among points within a topic or problem and then formulate responses by synthesizing the information they possess. This process is much more time-consuming than responding to objective test items, and students must have sufficient time to analyze the items, perhaps outline their answer, and then write it legibly. If students are unduly pressed for time, their responses may not be as true a reflection of their abilities as they might otherwise have been.

A practical way to estimate the amount of time to allow students for each item is for the teacher to write an acceptable response to see how long it takes. The teacher should allow students additional time. This procedure provides not only a good estimate of how many items to which students can reasonably be expected to respond but also a model response against which student responses can be compared.

Many teachers find it easier to read responses that are written in ink on lined paper. Other teachers prefer to have students write their answers on the sheet containing the questions.

D. *Grade papers anonymously.* Sometimes, when evaluators know the author of a paper, it can bias the evaluation. Conscientious teachers, for example, may often be able to identify many students from handwriting samples. This possibility can be minimized by using procedures that make it possible to ignore the names on the papers, one of which is to use code numbers on papers rather than names.

E. *Compare each response with a model answer.* There is a tendency, after grading a few responses, to begin comparing those read later with those read previously. This tendency can be offset by making frequent reference to the model answer(s) that were prepared in order to estimate the time students would need to write their answers.

F. *When possible, use more than one evaluator and then average the grades.* Greater reliability can be achieved if more than one evaluator is used and the separate evaluations are averaged.

G. *Avoid mixing essay items and objective test items on the same test.* The intellectual operations required to synthesize a response to an essay item are significantly different from those required to select a response to an objective test item, and to expect students to demonstrate both kinds of cognitive skills within a single class period may be expecting too much.

QUICK REFERENCE GUIDELINES

OBJECTIVE TESTS
I. Advantages
    A. Provide a broad sampling of students' knowledge.
    B. Present the same problems and the same alternatives to each student.
    C. Minimize the chance of student bluffing.
    D. Permit rapid scoring with little or no need for subjective decisions.
    E. Permit items to be improved on the basis of item analysis.
    F. Permit increased reliability through item improvement.

II. Disadvantages
    A. Present difficulties in assessing some cognitive skills, such as synthesis and creativity.
    B. Increase the possibility of guessing.
    C. Require a relatively long time to construct items.
III. Utilization Factors
    A. Construction and administration
        1. Keep the language simple.
        2. Ask students to apply rather than simply recall information.
        3. Make sure that each item is independent.
        4. Do not establish or follow a pattern for correct responses.
        5. Do not include trick or trivial questions.
        6. Do not answer questions after the test has started unless you do so publicly.
    B. Multiple-choice items
        1. Put as much of the item as possible into the stem.
        2. Make all options reasonable.
        3. Do not provide unintentional clues.
        4. Avoid the use of all-inclusive or all-exclusive terms.
    C. True-false items
        1. Be sure that each item is wholly true or wholly false.
        2. Avoid the use of all-inclusive or all-exclusive terms.
        3. Be sure that items are not dependent upon insignificant facts.
        4. Be sure that true items are not consistently longer or shorter than false items.
        5. Avoid the use of double negatives and call attention to single negatives by underlining or capitalizing the negative word.
    D. Matching items
        1. Limit the number of items to be matched to ten or less.
        2. Make sure that all items concern one topic.
        3. Have more answers than questions or stipulate that some answers can be used more than once or not at all.
        4. Arrange options in some logical order.
    E. Completion items
        1. Write items that can be completed with a single word or a short phrase.
        2. Be sure that only one word or phrase can correctly complete the sentence.
        3. Put the blanks near the end of the sentences.
        4. Make all blanks the same length.
        5. Do not put more than two blanks in any one item.

ESSAY TESTS

I. Advantages
    A. Emphasize high-level cognitive skills, such as synthesis and evaluation.
    B. Provide an in-depth sampling of students' knowledge of a specific topic.
    C. Allow for student creativity, analysis, and synthesis skill assessment.
    D. Easier to construct than objective tests.
II. Disadvantages
    A. Reduce reliability and validity compared with objective tests.
    B. Create bias in favor of those students who write well.
    C. Make grading time-consuming.
    D. Increase possibility of bluffing.

III. Utilization Factors
  A. Be definitive about what you expect from students.
  B. Make sure that students have sufficient time and materials to do the job.
  C. Grade papers as anonymously as possible.
  D. Compare each response with a model response or a list of crucial points.
  E. When possible, have tests checked by more than one evaluator and average the grades.
  F. Do not mix essay items and objective items on the same test.

Validity and Use of Teacher-Made Tests

Teacher-made essay and objective tests deserve emphasis because the classroom teacher, better than anyone else, knows what the instructional objectives were and what kinds of questions need to be asked to determine whether the objectives have been achieved. Hence, the teacher determines whether content validity of the evaluation exists. Because teachers know exactly what they have taught, they can construct tests for their students that will have a higher degree of content validity than virtually any standardized test.

Both essay tests and objective tests can be used prior to instruction (to determine students' existing abilities), during instruction (to check on progress and determine areas of strengths and weaknesses), and after instruction (to determine final achievement). Well-constructed teacher-made tests, if tailored to precise needs, can be a key tool to help improve the teaching-learning process.

STANDARDIZED TESTS

Standardized tests are usually constructed by commercial test producers. Each item that appears on a standardized test has generally been checked carefully to assure that it (1) is appropriate in difficulty for a particular, described population, (2) has high discrimination power (spreads the scores), (3) has a high reliability index, and (4) has a good biserial correlation (students who score well on the test tend to get any given item correct, and students who score low tend to get any given item wrong). Standardized tests usually come with a detailed set of instructions for administration and can often be machine scored.

Appropriate "norms" are included to facilitate the interpretation of scores. Test norms are averages against which individual scores can be compared. In the case of most standardized tests, these norms are derived by averaging the scores of a wide sampling of students all having in common some characteristic such as age or grade level. The large size of the norming groups helps eliminate gross distortions caused by extreme scores, thus making the norms rather stable measures. Additional information relevant to the norms (such as the test's standard error, standard deviation, and standard scores) also help make score interpretation more valid.

For test manufacturers to stay in business, they must produce tests that are not only reliable but also attractive to large numbers of prospective users. One characteristic of standardized tests that contributes to their reliability and attractiveness is their generality. Most standardized tests concern themselves with general kinds of skills and knowledge, thereby enabling measurement experts to construct items that provide a reliable survey of that skill or topic as a whole.

Since standardized tests are *general* measures, they are often not appropriate for use in measuring achievement of specific instructional objectives. It is unlikely that a standardized test will emphasize the exact content a teacher is emphasizing, and therefore the test's content validity may be questioned. A teacher would be foolish to assume that his or her efforts were wasted simply because students did not do well on a standardized test. To determine whether students achieved stated objectives, it is usually necessary to use teacher-made, not standardized, tests. The former are specific measures, the latter, general ones. When the purpose of the test is to compare the student with a large population in a broad content area, standardized tests may be in order.

Standardized tests usually measure general intelligence, achievement, aptitude, or interest. A brief description of each follows.

Intelligence Tests. Intelligence is an ambiguous term often defined by phrases such as "mental abilities," "capacity to learn," and "the ability to cope successfully with new situations." Most intelligence tests require the person being tested to solve a series of previously unseen problems by manipulating factual information, perceiving relationships, making generalizations, and applying other cognitive skills.

Intelligence tests can be administered on either an individual or a group basis. Individual tests, such as the *Stanford–Binet Intelligence Scale* and the *Wechsler Intelligence Scales,* tend to be more reliable than the group tests, but because they require one test administrator for every person being tested, they also tend to be more expensive and more time consuming.[4] Group tests, such as the *Otis Quick-Scoring Mental Ability Test* and the *Lorge–Thorndike Intelligence Tests,* while somewhat less reliable than the individual tests, still have good predictive validity and are much more commonly used.

When looking at an individual's IQ score, the teacher should remember that (1) "intelligence" has no precise definition and therefore cannot be measured precisely, (2) most intelligence tests are verbally oriented and culturally biased, and (3) they cannot be interpreted without understanding a statistic called a "standard error" included in score interpretation data. The standard error is intended to be used to construct an interval into which the student's "true" score would be likely to fall. For example, if a student's IQ score is 100 and the standard error is 10, it is commonly interpreted to mean that there are about two chances in three that the student's IQ is between 90 and 110. This is considerably different from stating that the IQ is exactly 100.

Achievement Tests. Achievement tests are focused more narrowly than are intelligence tests. Intelligence tests function by posing problems and giving individuals the freedom to integrate whatever skills and knowledge they have at their command to solve those problems. Little effort is made to test the individuals' abilities in any specific subject area. The intention of the achievement test is somewhat different. Achievement tests specify particular subject areas (such as mathematics, reading, and language) and then test students' abilities in each of those areas by providing appropriate subtests.

Test manufacturers intend their tests to evaluate content achievement, but they are faced with the complex problem of attaining reliability, discrimination, and good biserial correlations and consequently are in a peculiar position. The more precise and detailed the questions that are asked, the farther the test may get from a particular school's instructional objectives, the lower the content validity will become, and the less likely will be the purchase of the test by large numbers of schools. On the other hand, if the manufacturers use a minimum of detailed facts and depend upon those concepts that are common knowledge, they must depend more upon analytical skills to achieve statistical goals. With this dilemma in mind, it is not hard to understand why the results of achievement tests and IQ tests will often correlate highly. Both tend to emphasize general data widely accepted as "important."

Although achievement tests deal with more specific areas than do intelligence tests, their scores are *not* necessarily more precise. Both kinds of scores are best thought of as estimates, both can be affected by variables such as student illness, tension, and distraction, and both need to be interpreted in light of specific students and objectives. Some educators have found that achievement test scores can be made more useful if they are compared with norms constructed for a specific school rather than with national norms. There is an inherent danger in using scores from any standardized test as the sole criterion for establishing expectations of individual students or for making decisions about them.

Some of the commonly used achievement tests include the *California Achievement Tests,* the *Metropolitan Achievement Tests,* and the *Iowa Tests of Educational Development.*

Aptitude Tests. Whereas achievement tests focus on what students have already achieved, aptitude tests focus on their potential for future development. Aptitude tests function by grouping into occupationally oriented categories those items designed to measure specific abilities. For example, one of the most commonly used aptitude tests, the *Differential Aptitude Test Battery,* includes items involving verbal reasoning, numerical ability, abstract reasoning, space relationships, mechanical reasoning, clerical speed and accuracy, and language usage. Another commonly used aptitude test, the *General Aptitude Test Battery,* includes items involving vocabulary skills, numerical ability, spatial relations, form perception, clerical perception, motor coordination, manual dexterity, and finger dexterity. By evaluating the results of such tests, guidance personnel are able to suggest vocational fields in which students are most likely to experience success. Some fields, such as music and art, require unique abilities for success, and specific aptitude tests have been developed that focus very narrowly on those abilities.

It should be noted that few aptitude tests are known for their high predictive validity. It is not uncommon for a student who has shown a low aptitude in some area later to become interested in that area and go on to become highly successful in it. The importance of the student's own goals should never be minimized.

Interest Inventories.   Most interest inventories are similar to aptitude tests in that they are oriented vocationally. However, whereas most aptitude tests function by sampling specific kinds of skills, most interest inventories function by sampling student attitudes toward particular kinds of activities. Since students' likes and dislikes are subject to more rapid changes than are their abilities, interest inventories are generally regarded as less valid predictors than are either achievement tests or aptitude tests.

The most commonly used interest inventories include the *Kuder Preference Records*, the *Strong Vocational Interest Blanks*, and the *Thurstone Interest Schedule*.

General Utilization Factors

When using standardized tests, the teacher should keep two points in mind. First, all test administration directions must be followed explicitly. The generally high reliability of standardized tests stems partly from the fact that all students who take the test do so under conditions as nearly alike as possible. Every student is provided with the same materials and environment and is given the same amount of time in which to complete various sections of the test. As a general rule, students' scores will become less reliable to the degree that testing conditions are allowed to vary.

And, second, although a good deal of time, money, and expert help were probably used to construct, refine, and norm any given standardized test, the score a student earns on that test still reflects only a sample of ability. To avoid making wrong, unfortunate, and even tragic decisions concerning any individual, it is imperative to obtain as much and as varied data as possible. Standardized tests provide just one piece of information.

ALTERNATE EVALUATION PROCEDURES

Once the teacher begins to use specific objectives and focus on the ultimate skills students will be able to demonstrate, paper-and-pencil tests may receive less emphasis. There are few instances in which being able to pass a test is the ultimate reason for learning. Because the use of precise instructional objectives can increase the use of evaluation devices other than formal paper-and-pencil tests, and because these "alternative procedures" lend themselves so well to the evaluation of individual performance, the issue of how to make these alternative evaluation procedures valid and reliable needs examination. The following points can assist in building alternative evaluation procedures that will withstand critical scrutiny.

1. *Specify standards clearly.* Because spelling out standards clearly is so critical, it is reemphasized here. As an illustration, consider the following objectives.

Each involves a student construction, but in each case the product is less important than the cognitive skills necessary for its construction.

You will be able to:

A. Write a mailable one-page letter to a company or politician in which some problem is delineated, a desired course of action is outlined, and supporting rationales for that action are given. ("Mailable" is a business term used to denote a letter that is free from errors in spelling, grammar, punctuation, usage, etc., and ready for signature and mailing.)

B. Demonstrate your understanding of "power politics," in part, by assuming the role of leader of some small foreign government and describing, in less than three pages, (1) why some commodity under your control is critical, (2) why your current manipulation of that commodity (its price, availability, or use) is justified, and (3) how you plan to resist pressures to stop such manipulations.

C. Construct a 2′ × 3′ poster designed to sway people's opinion for or against some controversial issue and describe, in less than three pages, how each element (color, message, design, or figure placement) helps make the poster a powerful communicator.

The elements included as part of the minimum acceptable standards for these objectives partially spell out the criteria to be used in assessing achievement, and in each case the "product," by itself, is clearly insufficient. The objectives are designed to assess synthesis- and evaluation-level skills; unless students manifest these skills, they cannot meet all the criteria.

Suppose, however, the student wrote the following letter in response to the first objective.

Dear Sir:

I recently purchased a new Doohicky, and it does not work right. Neither the store I purchased it from nor your factory representative accepted responsibility for the Doohicky's malfunction, and now I'm tired of fooling with it and want a refund. Unless I get a refund within two weeks, I will turn the issue over to my attorney.

Sincerely yours,

This letter contains all the elements suggested in the objective, and the teacher may be pressed to give the student credit for achieving the objective. On the other hand, the letter leaves room for improvement. What can be done?

2. *Whenever possible, provide a model.* Models are helpful from a number of standpoints. Students will find them helpful because they will have an actual sample of the final product. Regardless of how explicitly written criteria are, actually seeing an acceptable product will help sharpen the student's mental picture of what is expected. The picture can be strengthened further if both good and bad models are provided and explanations of why they are good and bad are included.

Through the use of audio tapes, videotapes, and actual samples, as well as written models, you can provide models for virtually every kind of behavior or product students are to manifest. The possibilities are limited only by the teacher's imagination.

3. *Provide a checklist.* A checklist is really an elaboration of the stated minimum acceptable standards. It will be impossible, in most cases, to specify all important steps or criteria in every objective, but in the case of those objectives calling for the construction of some product, regardless of whether the product is a paper or a paperweight, a checklist can help students. In the case of the sample letter, for example, students could have been given a checklist for writing letters of complaint that included such items as, "Did you specify where and when you bought the product?" and "Did you explain exactly what your problem was?"

Checklists can function as both instructional and evaluative aids. As instructional aids, checklists provide students with a logical sequence of steps of points that, if followed or included, lead to the development of an acceptable product. As evaluative aids, checklists provide students (and evaluators) with a list of the specific points being sought in the final product, and since checklists can be much more detailed than the standards included in instructional objectives, they can be particularly helpful to students.

Checklists, like models, can be constructed to guide students toward the achievement of virtually every kind of expected behavior. If the checklists are clear enough, there is no reason why they, together with models, cannot be an aid in attaining a reliable grading system that enables teachers to differentiate between quality levels of students' work. The more teachers rely on measures of student achievement other than formal paper-and-pencil tests, the more students will see a practical value in what they are learning. What is learned is seldom important in and of itself; its importance stems from how it can be used.

ITEM ANALYSIS

Immediately after scoring a set of objective tests, the teacher should conduct an item analysis. To do this, the teacher should look at each item and mark down how many times each option was selected. This will result in a chart that looks something like the one that follows.

Item Number	Correct Answer	OPTIONS				
		A	B	C	D	E
1	A	20	–	–	–	–
2	C	–	20	–	–	–
3	E	10	1	5	2	2
.	.	.	.	.	.	.
.	.	.	.	.	.	.
.	.	.	.	.	.	.
24	D	4	3	4	6	3
25	B	2	15	1	1	1

The information is essential in interpreting the test results and in improving the test items. For example, the analysis above shows that everyone answered item 1 correctly. If the test was strictly criterion-referenced (pass or fail), this is no problem. If, however, a spread of scores was possible (0–100), then item 1 was not very useful; it failed to help identify those students who knew more than others. Perhaps that question should be replaced with one a bit more sophisticated.

The analysis shows that not only did everyone miss item 2, but that they all selected the same incorrect option. One likely explanation for this is a mistake on the answer key, but another is that students remembered one point when the teacher thought he or she was making a different point. The latter explanation is even more likely to explain the spread of choices in item 3. In both cases the choices that the students made are more likely to be due to a mistake on the teacher's part than to lack of knowledge on the students' part. This being the case, serious consideration should be given to deleting those items from the test and recalculating the grades.

Item 24 shows such an equal distribution of choices that the power of the item to discriminate is lost. The item should be reworded so that the distribution is closer to that shown in item 25. Item 25 shows that most of the students answered the question correctly, but some students chose each option.

The purpose of the item analysis is to enable teachers to examine each item and option in a test in order to polish those items. A test is most effective if it fairly assesses students' skills and knowledge and at the same time helps rank-order students on the basis of their skills and knowledge. As polished test items are accumulated, the length of time needed to construct tests will continually decline and that time can be used for other purposes.

CALCULATING GRADES

When teachers establish precise instructional objectives, they are establishing their instructional intent—the goals toward which students will work. As useful as those objectives are, they leave unanswered one very difficult but essential question. What is the very least that a student must do to earn the lowest passing grade? This question must be answered, because a teacher cannot justify giving a passing grade simply because a student attended class regularly or worked diligently. The attendance might suffice for a certificate of attendance and the effort for a letter of recognition, but neither equates with achieving the minimal competencies expected of students in the course.

If the lowest passing grade—D—is given, the teacher must be prepared to substantiate the fact that the student did complete at least the minimum course objectives that were approved for that course. The teacher would be providing false and misleading information if a grade of D was given and the student had not achieved those minimal objectives. Once this basic question is answered, the teacher can think about selecting a grading approach, but the basic question must be answered first and in writing (so that there is no question about the answer). What is the very least that a student must do to earn a grade of D?

Grade Contracts

To use a contract approach, a teacher develops sets of objectives that correspond to specific letter grades. The teacher begins by establishing the minimum objectives—those that must be achieved if a student is to get even a grade of D. The teacher must be sure that students are clear about those minimal competencies and must be prepared to explain those competencies to parents, administrators, and to anyone else who might question the basis for the grades.

It is likely, of course, that students will want grades higher than D. Therefore, the teacher should prepare sets of objectives that would enable students to earn successively higher grades. All the objectives would be cumulative in that students must complete the objectives for a D before working on those for a C and must complete those for a C before working on those for a B. The advantage of this approach is that students have some choice in deciding which objectives they work toward. The disadvantage is that the teacher will have more work to do in assessing students than if they all did the same thing.

Preset Levels

The most common grading approach is the preset level approach, in which standards are preset, such as A = 90–100, B = 80–89, C = 70–79, D = 60–69, and F = 0–59. The greatest advantage of this approach is that everyone understands it; it is the traditional approach to grading. Another advantage is that it is administratively convenient; a whole semester's work is summed up in one letter. A significant disadvantage is that the letter grades have no relationship to the complexity of the work required. For example, there is a significant difference between the level of work required for an A in a regular history class and that required for an A in an advanced placement class, yet the best students in both classes will get A's.

There are two common ways of using the preset level approach. One way is to say that a grade of 90 or above on a test or paper is an A, 80–89 is a B, and so forth. Sometimes teachers decide to vary the cutoff points, but as long as students know what the cutoffs are, they can easily calculate their current grade.

Another way of using the preset level approach is to calculate the total number of points that will be possible during the semester, and then decide what percentage of those points students will need to attain in order to earn an A, B, C, or D. The advantage of this approach is that the importance of any single score is minimized. For example, if the points available on all of the tests, papers, projects, and other assignments that will be used during the semester total 1000, students can see that a single low grade can be offset by higher grades. This point is usually true regardless of the grading approach used, but this particular approach makes it easy for students to understand why it is so.

The "Curve"

Another approach to calculating grades is to use a "curve." The curve refers to a mathematical construct known as the "normal curve." A normal curve results when a graph is plotted based upon the distribution of some characteristic such as height, weight, or IQ, among a very large population, such as the population of Chicago or New York. For example, in a large population, the average (mean) IQ might be 100. Since this would represent the average IQ, it would be at the center of the baseline (abscissa) under the highest point of the curve. To the left of the high point, and sloping down toward the baseline, would be successively lower scores, and to the right, again sloping down toward the baseline, would be successively higher scores. Neither side of the curve would touch the baseline, thus showing that some extreme scores, not shown, might exist.

Statisticians use procedures in which the resulting graph is divided into areas through the use of standard deviations (SDs). These SDs theoretically remain constant, with approximately 34 percent of the population falling between the mean (average) score and one SD above the mean, 34 percent falling between the mean and one SD below the mean, and most of the remaining scores divided between one SD and two SDs above and below the mean (see Figure 5).

Standard deviations and the normal curve are useful because they are based on the mean score rather than on some arbitrarily fixed point. Thus, if a particularly difficult test contains 100 items and the mean score happens to be 23, the teacher can still assign "A" to "F" letter grades by calculating how far above or below the mean each score is and then applying the standard deviation cutoff points. If the teacher had decided previously that an "A" was going to be any score one and one-half standard deviations above the mean, it would not matter whether the mean was 23 or 83. One and one-half standard deviations would be calculated from that point and the grade assigned.

There are a number of formulas by which approximations of the standard deviation can be calculated, but one often used because of its ease is that suggested by W. L. Jenkins.[5] The steps to this procedure are as follows.

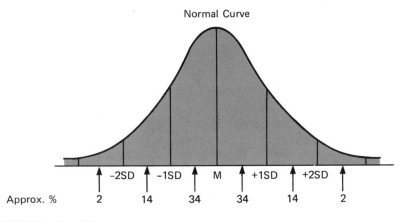

FIGURE 5   Normal Curve

(1) Arrange all the scores from high to low, (2) find the sums of the top one-sixth of the scores and the bottom one-sixth, (3) subtract the sum of the bottom one-sixth from the sum of the top one-sixth, and (4) divide the difference by one-half the total number of scores. In equation form the formula is:

$$\text{Approx. SD} = \frac{\text{sum of top sixth} - \text{sum of bottom sixth}}{\text{half the number of students}}$$

Suppose that a class of twelve students was given a twenty-item test worth 100 points. After 5 points were deducted for each incorrect response, the scores were calculated to be 95, 90, 85, 75, 75, 75, 70, 70, 65, 65, 60, and 40. Suppose further that the teacher had decided upon the following standard deviation cutoff points (where M = mean):

A $\geq$ M + 1.25 SDs
B = M + 0.25 to 1.249 SDs
C = M - 1.00 to + 0.249 SDs
D = M - 2.00 to - .999
F > M - 2.00 SDs

Grades for the class of twelve based on a curve could be estimated by the following procedure, using Jenkins' formula:

$$\text{Approx. SD} = \frac{\text{sum of top sixth} - \text{sum of bottom sixth}}{\text{half the number of students}}$$
$$= \frac{(95 + 90) - (60 + 40)}{6}$$
$$= \frac{185 - 100}{6}$$
$$= \frac{85}{6} = 14 \text{ (rounded to the nearest whole number)}$$

Next, calculate the point equivalents to the standard deviation cutoffs by adding the approximate SD to, and subtracting it from, the mean score.

$$\text{Mean} = \frac{\text{sum of scores}}{\text{number of scores}}$$
$$= \frac{95 + 90 + 85 + 75 + 75 + 75 + 70 + 70 + 65 + 65 + 60 + 40}{12}$$
$$= \frac{865}{12}$$
$$= 72$$

Since an A is any score 1.25 SDs or greater above the mean, the point equivalent can be found by multiplying 1.25 by 14 (the approximate SD) and adding the product (17.5) to the mean (72). The minimum A grade is therefore 17.50 + 72, or 89.5. Since the B range is 0.25 to 1.249 SDs above, its point equivalent can be found by multiplying 0.25 by 14 and adding the product (3.5) to the mean (72). The B range thus extends from 72 + 3.5, or 75.5, to 89.49. Similarly, the C range would be found by subtracting one SD (14) from the mean. The C range would extend from 72 − 14, or 58, to 75.49. The D range would extend from 72 − (2 × 14), or 44, to 57. The F range would be anything less than −2 SDs, or anything less than 44. The actual test scores might then be determined by using the following scale.

A = 90 or better
B = 76 to 89
C = 58 to 75
D = 44 to 57
F = 43 or lower

The grade distribution for the scores given at the beginning of this problem would then be

95 = A	75 = C	65 = C
90 = A	75 = C	65 = C
85 = B	70 = C	60 = C
75 = C	70 = C	40 = F

Practice Problems for Assigning Marks Using a Curve. Calculate the mean score and approximate standard deviation, to the nearest tenth, for the following 24 test scores using the Jenkins method and its equation as follows.

24, 22, 20, 19, 19, 18, 17, 17, 16, 16, 15, 15, 15, 14, 14, 13, 13, 13, 13, 12, 12, 12, 11, 11

First calculate the mean (average) of the scores (add all scores together and divide by the total number of scores). Compare the calculated mean to the work following:

13	15	17	24	
12	14	17	22	
12	14	16	20	71
12	13	16	19	82
11	13	15	19	96
11 +	13 +	15 +	18	+122
71	82	96	122 =	371

$$\begin{array}{r} 15.45 \\ 24\overline{)371.00} \\ \underline{24} \\ 131 \\ \underline{120} \\ 110 \\ \underline{96} \\ 140 \end{array}$$ Mean = 15.45

Now calculate the approximate standard deviation. Compare your work with that shown next. Check any discrepancies.

13	15	17	24
12	14	17	22
12	14	16	20
12	13	16	19
11	13	15	19
11	13	15	18

Sum of top sixth scores   = 24 + 22 + 20 + 19 = 85
Sum of bottom sixth scores   = 11 + 11 + 12 + 12 = 46

$$SD = \frac{85 - 46}{12}$$
$$= \frac{39}{12}$$
$$= 3.25$$

Assume that the school district wishes teachers to assign marks on the curve using the standard deviation scale given here:

MARK		SD ABOVE OR BELOW THE MEAN
A	$\geq$	+ 1.5 SD
B	=	+ 0.5 to + 1.49 SD
C	=	− 0.5 to + .49 SD
D	=	− 1.75 to −0.51 SD
F	>	− 1.76 SD

Assign the grades the students would receive using the scale given above to the scores provided. Compare your grade assignment with the answers given using mean = 15.45 and SD = 3.3.

Calculating A grades (scores 1.5 SD above mean and greater):

$$
\begin{array}{ll}
\begin{array}{r}
3.3 \ \text{(SD)} \\
\times 1.5 \\
\hline
165 \\
33 \\
\hline
4.95 \ \text{scores above mean}
\end{array}
&
\begin{array}{r}
15.45 \ \text{(mean)} \\
+4.95 \\
\hline
20.40
\end{array}
\end{array}
$$

Scores 20.4 and above get A's. There are two scores above 20.4.

Calculating B grades (scores between 0.5 and 1.49 SD above mean):

$$
\begin{array}{ll}
\begin{array}{r}
3.3 \ \text{(SD)} \\
\times 0.5 \\
\hline
1.65
\end{array}
&
\begin{array}{r}
15.45 \ \text{(mean)} \\
+1.65 \\
\hline
17.10
\end{array}
\end{array}
$$

Scores from 17.1 to 20.4 get B's. This means that the students with scores of 18, 19, and 20 would get B's. There are four scores in this range.

Calculating C grades (scores between 0.5 below the mean to 0.49 above the mean):

$$
\begin{array}{ll}
\begin{array}{r}
3.3 \ \text{(SD)} \\
\times -0.5 \\
\hline
-1.65
\end{array}
&
\begin{array}{r}
15.45 \ \text{(mean)} \\
-1.65 \\
\hline
13.80
\end{array}
\end{array}
$$

Scores from 13.8 to 17.1 get C's. This means that the students with scores of 14, 15, 16, and 17 would get C's. There are nine of these scores.

Calculating D grades (scores between 1.75 and 0.51 SD below the mean):

$$
\begin{array}{ll}
\begin{array}{r}
3.3 \ \text{(SD)} \\
\times -1.75 \\
\hline
165 \\
231 \\
33 \\
\hline
-5.775
\end{array}
&
\begin{array}{r}
15.45 \ \text{(mean)} \\
-5.78 \\
\hline
9.67
\end{array}
\end{array}
$$

Scores from 9.7 to 13.8 get D's. This means the students with scores of 11, 12, and 13 would get D's. There are nine of these scores.

Calculating F grades (scores more than 1.76 SD below the mean):

```
    3.3  (SD)                    15.45  (mean)
×-1.76                           -5.81
    198                           9.64
    231
     33
 -5.808
```

This means that students with scores below 9.6 get F's. There are no scores this low.

The assignment of grades would look like this:

```
A 24    C 17        14  13
    22      16      14  12
B 20        16    D 13  12
    19      15      13  12
    19      15      13  12
    18      15      13  11
```

Although estimating standard deviations and grading on a curve enables teachers to assign grades on the basis of statistical procedures, the procedure has rather serious disadvantages. Standard deviations originate from large samples in which the normal curve of percentages apply; that is, 50 percent of all cases will always fall below the mean, approximately another 34 percent will fall between the mean and one SD above the mean, and approximately another 14 percent will fall between one and two SDs above the mean. With small samples, such as those found in classrooms, these percentages are much less exact. Once you decide upon a set of cutoff points, you are virtually guaranteeing that there will be inequities because of the sample size. For instance, in the one example given, there are no D grades; in the other there are no F grades and only two A's.

Another closely related point concerns the fact that standard deviations are calculated with respect to mean scores. This means that in an advanced class a student might have to get a 95 to get an A, whereas in a slower class, a student might need only a 65. Since an A is an A in the final records, many educators have reservations about grading on a curve. The reservations are particularly great when grades are calculated on a curve in advanced classes in which students compete with each other for a handful of high grades, when such grades would have been assured had they been in a regular class.

Eyeballing

Another method of calculating grades consists simply of tallying the scores on a scale, looking for natural divisions in the distribution, and assigning letter grades to these divisions. Although this method seems haphazard, it is often used in practice, even though decisions are completely arbitrary.

It can be seen from looking at a tally of the scores in our first example that there are three natural divisions. A decision must be made as to the cutoff point for A's and B's and C's, and so on. There are no right or wrong answers here. Depending upon the teacher's assessment of how difficult the test was, how well the teaching had gone, or the like, the teacher may assign grades in a variety of patterns.

SCORES	FREQUENCY OF EACH SCORE
100	
95	1
90	1
85	
80	1
75	111
70	11
65	11
60	1
55	
50	
45	
40	1
35	
0	

Here are four possible eyeballing grading patterns for grade distribution:

100			100			100			100	A
95 1			95 1			95 1	A		95 1	
90 1	A		90 1	A		90 1			90 1	B
85			85			85	B		85	
80 1	B		80 1	B		80 1			80 1	
75 111			75 111			75 111			75 111	
70 11	C		70 11			70 11	C		70 11	C
65 11			65 11	C		65 11			65 11	
60 1	D		60 1			60 1			60 1	
55			55			55			55	
50			50	D		50	D		50	
45			45			45			45	D
40 1	F		40 1			40 1			40 1	
35			35	F		35	F		35	

Credit–No Credit

When working with precise instructional objectives, it soon becomes obvious that the key to success for students is to attain the minimum acceptable standard described in the objective or in supplemental checklists or descriptions. Many educators who are using such a model have gone to a "credit" system. It is, perhaps, the simplest of all methods available.

At the outset of instruction all the competencies are delineated. They may be modified by student input, but a final decision is reached. Each of them has a minimum acceptable standard or criterion level. As students demonstrate a competency, they are given credit and proceed to the next level. When all competencies are completed for the course, the student is finished. Under individualized instruction, the "normal curve" now reflects *time* rather than *scores*. Instead of the majority of students receiving an average grade, they will finish about the same time. Instead of receiving a high mark, a brighter student will achieve the competencies sooner.

Many schools have attempted to blend grading schemes with such programs. This is usually done by assigning an average grade for the basic competency and then encouraging "quest" or "enrichment" activities for high grades.

GRADING AND SUBJECTIVITY

All the grading methods examined have had one point in common. In each instance the method depended upon some subjective decision. The preset level method required a subjective judgment concerning the placement of the levels; the curve method required a subjective judgment concerning the standard deviation cutoff points; the eyeballing method depended entirely upon subjective decisions; and even the credit procedure required subjective judgments concerning the level of proficiency desired to receive credit.

Some educators argue that, since all grading methods ultimately depend upon subjective decisions, none is any better or worse than any other. The advantages and disadvantages balance out. Without intending to add to the argument, it can be said that any choice should be guided by at least two factors: (1) the circumstances (for instance, a particular school may have a set policy concerning grading) and (2) the importance attached to the material included in the test (very definite standards may be kept in mind for crucial material and more flexibility allowed with other material).

REPORTING GRADES

Assuming one or another of the many available methods to arrive at grades has been adopted, the question of how most effectively to communicate information regarding student progress still remains.

Many school systems have adopted a policy, at least with respect to standardized tests, of not reporting the student's exact score at all. To minimize the misinterpretations associated with "exact" scores, many school systems convert these scores to *stanines*. Stanine is a term that stands for "standard nine," a structured distribution that consists of nine equal intervals. The nine intervals account for 100 percent of any given population with the intervals representing 4 percent, 7 percent, 12 percent, 17 percent, 20 percent, 17 percent, 12 percent, 7 percent, and 4 percent of that population, respectively. Most standardized tests provide tables by which individual scores can be converted to stanines and thus placed in an appropriate interval. Because the intervals created by the stanine distribution are so large, teachers can be fairly certain that any given student's true score falls into the stanine interval indicated by the test score.

Stanines, like scores teachers calculate, are best reported to parents and students in a conference. The teacher can explain more fully the implications of particular grades as well as how the grades were calculated. Teachers find it important to be able to substantiate any grade given or comment made, and they can minimize parental uncertainty or anger by initiating explanations about grading procedures and providing reasons for using whatever grading scheme was selected. Having an understanding of the mathematics involved in a particular grading method means very little, however, if grades do not reflect achievement or nonachievement of specific instructional objectives. Parents are not normally interested in how sophisticated a grading system may be; they are interested in how well the grades reflect what their child has accomplished.

Teachers who are concerned with the need to report evaluations, rather than just grades, will find that parent-teacher (or parent-teacher-student) conferences or telephone conferences yield better results than do one-way communication methods such as the mailing of grades. Conferences enable the teacher to relate factors such as effort and dependability to the student's actual achievement. Conferences are even more valid if the student is present and can provide additional input, provided that the conference does not degenerate into an accusation/defense session.

Because conferences are sometimes difficult to arrange, educators rely heavily on some other reporting device—usually a report card. Unfortunately, grades on a report card do not really reflect a student's specific abilities, even though a great deal of importance is frequently attached to report card grades. If the school depends solely upon report cards, the teacher should explore the possibility of including with each report card a list of the instructional objectives for the class or course with indications of those that the student achieved. Such a list will provide parents with a much clearer picture of what their son or daughter has actually accomplished.

TEACHER EVALUATION

Any logical discussion of teacher evaluation must be based on the understanding that, when students, peers, administrators, and parents evaluate a teacher, each may use a different set of criteria and that, when the teacher engages in self-evaluation, still another set of criteria may be used. When students evaluate a teacher, for example (and they will, whether or not they are asked to), they may include among their criteria the ability to explain things clearly, fairness, and the ability to stimulate and maintain their interest. Peers might evaluate a teacher partially on the ability to come up with innovative instructional ideas and willingness to share those ideas. School administrators might include criteria concerning ability to get reports in on time, contributions to good community relations, and ability to maintain order in the classroom. Parents might have other criteria, and each teacher might have still others.

The point to keep in mind is that each individual who engages in teacher evaluation does so from a particular perspective, with particular expectations and with individual ideas of how the ideal teacher should look and operate. Evaluation(s) will be influenced by these factors, and teachers must take these factors into account as they attempt to make sense of the evaluations. It is suggested that teachers try to acquire as much feedback as they can concerning their performance and that they sift through this information looking for points (good or bad) that recur. It is likely that, if different people find the same aspect of performance worthy of comment, the teacher should look closely at that behavior with an eye toward capitalizing on it if it is a strength or remedying it if it is a weakness.

Regardless of how many other people evaluate teachers, teachers will likely be their own most persistent critics. Here are some specific techniques to acquire feedback concerning teaching performance.

Teacher Performance Tests

A teacher performance test (TPT) is simply a lesson planned specifically to evaluate a particular instructional procedure. The teacher should first specify one or two precise instructional objectives that students can achieve within a single class period. This is important to protect the evaluation from biasing factors such as student study after class and similar variables.

The second step in using a TPT is to preassess to ensure that students are not already able to demonstrate the objective(s) or, conversely, that they do not lack the necessary prerequisite skill. If some students fall into either category, the teacher should either find some other activities for them during this particular class or discount their evaluation results.

The third step is to specify the particular instructional procedure to be tested. Keep in mind that any given procedure may work well one time and not so well another time. Therefore, the teacher should try the same procedure again under conditions as nearly alike as possible, so the teacher will need an accurate description of what was planned and what was actually done.

The next step is to establish a minimum acceptable level of class performance. This standard is different from the minimum acceptable standard specified in the objective(s) in that here the teacher uses professional judgment to decide on a minimum percentage of students who must be able to demonstrate the objective(s) before the instructional procedure can be considered effective. There is no one "right" percentage.

The final step is to go ahead and teach the TPT. If the minimum number of students established as a cutoff point are able to demonstrate the objective, the teacher has empirical evidence that for those students, under the conditions that existed, the instructional procedure used was effective. Of course, the teacher should verify the findings by repeating the TPT a number of times. If the TPT results indicate that the instructional procedure is not effective with those students, under those conditions, it is advisable to look more closely at what actually took place during the lesson.

Audio and Video Recordings

So much takes place during a typical lesson that it is difficult to recall with accuracy afterwards all that went on during the lesson. Fortunately, technology can assist you. Most schools have audio tape recorders and many have videotape recorders as well. Arranging to tape the TPT (or any other lesson) can provide highly informative playback. A teacher may find, for example, that he or she tends to cut off students' responses or neglects to reinforce students for their contributions. Problems like these may be discerned by analyzing a taped lesson, and this kind of information is an excellent basis for self-improvement.

Interaction Analysis Techniques

In addition to simply listening to, or watching, a playback of the lesson, teachers can utilize any one of the various interaction analysis techniques. One of the most common of these, developed by Edmond J. Amidon and Ned A. Flanders, is known as *Flanders' Interaction Analysis*.[6] This technique is based on the delineation of nine categories of student and teacher verbal behaviors. The analyst uses the numbers assigned to each category of verbal behavior to encode, every three seconds, the kind of interaction (if any) that is taking place at that moment. The list of numbers can then be analyzed to determine if particular interaction patterns are used to the exclusion of other patterns and whether the interaction pattern recorded was what the teacher intended. The technique is useful for quantifying verbal interaction patterns and it is not intended as a technique for determining whether those patterns are good or bad. Judgments of that sort should depend more on the kind of interaction intended and the extent to which the interaction pattern facilitates students' achievement of the specified objectives.

Another interaction analysis system was developed by Morine, Spaulding, and Greenberg.[7] Either system can help ascertain what actually transpired during the lesson, and both help to quantify that information.

Student Evaluations

As helpful as the techniques cited are, teachers still want direct feedback from their students regarding their perceptions of teacher effectiveness. One way to acquire student feedback is periodically to ask for anonymous evaluations of what they like about the teacher's methods and what they believe needs to be improved. This technique will likely generate many comments concerning personality characteristics and interpersonal relations (as opposed to pedagogical skills), but the input is still useful in identifying strengths and weaknesses.

Another technique is to formulate a list of factors that students can evaluate fairly and ask them to respond to those points on a periodic and anonymous basis. As long as students are sure their evaluations will have no negative effect on their grades or on their relationship with the teacher, they will be truthful in most cases.

Peer Evaluations

The evaluations obtained from students will provide some information about teaching methods, but that information is likely to concern teaching style more than teaching effectiveness. Information about the latter point is best obtained from TPTs, pre- and posttest comparisons, and peer evaluations.

Peer evaluations are particularly useful if the subject selects the peer who does the evaluating. This is so because the subject tends to choose a teacher he or she respects and whose opinion is respected. That teacher can provide feedback concerning both process and product and, more important, can also suggest ways of improving.

Administrative Evaluations

Regardless of what other evaluation techniques may be used, the school administrators will also evaluate each teacher. The wise teacher asks the principal for a copy of the teacher evaluation form or list of criteria that will be used as the basis for evaluation. A perusal of this form or list will identify the particular points the administration considers important. One factor that will unquestionably be viewed favorably will be the measures taken with respect to self-evaluation and self-improvement. Administrators cannot help but think better of teachers who can document consistent efforts to assess their own effectiveness than if they make no efforts in this direction.

SUMMARY

Teachers use measurement and evaluation techniques in order to determine the extent to which students have achieved specific objectives. The information acquired also enables teachers to assess the effectiveness of instructional activities and materials, and it enables students to compare their abilities against specific criteria and against the abilities of peers.

Since tests only sample skills or knowledge, teachers can have greater confidence in the semester grades they record if those grades are based on the grades of at least ten tests and papers. The more grades that are averaged, the more likely the average will reflect the student's ability. Further, with ten or more grades, the lowest grade can be dropped, thus giving students an incentive to continue working even though they may have done poorly on one test or paper.

Variety is also important in measurement and evaluation because students have different abilities. Some may take objective tests well; others may do better on essay tests. Still others may demonstrate their abilities best by completing projects. Varying assessment methods increases opportunities for students to demonstrate their skills and knowledge.

Teachers should check the validity of their tests. Face or content validity reflects the extent to which the test assesses what was taught. Predictive validity reflects the extent to which performance on one test can be used to accurately predict performance on some other test or task. Construct validity concerns the extent to which a test measures psychological constructs such as honesty or tolerance.

Dealing with student effort is often difficult. One effective technique is to find ways in which students can demonstrate effort apart from sheer ability or willingness to do additional work. One way is to award extra points to papers that have no spelling, punctuation, or grammatical mistakes and to accumulate those extra credit points in a separate column in the grade book. At the end of the marking period, an examination of the extra credit column will help show how much effort the student demonstrated during that period.

Test reliability refers to the consistency with which the test measures whatever it measures. Reliability tends to increase with the number of items because as the number of items increases so do the areas of knowledge being sampled. The more adequate the sampling, the more likely it is that students will do equally as well upon testing with an equivalent form of the test. Reliability coefficients extend from 1.00 for perfect correlation, to .00 for no correlation, and to −1.00 for perfect negative correlation.

Criterion-referenced tests are those in which students either meet or fail to meet certain criteria. If the criteria are met, the student passes; if not, the student fails. Criterion referencing can be used to establish cutoff points for admission to programs or schools and for similar purposes, but most often teachers need norm-referenced tests.

Norm-referencing means that a student's performance is assessed in relation to the performance of students in some norming group. A norming group consists of members that have some relevant characteristic in common, such as age or grade level.

The most common type of evaluation instrument is the paper-and-pencil test. These tests present the same task, under the same conditions, to all students and result in a product that can be easily examined and analyzed. Objective tests are used to sample low-level abilities with respect to a fairly large topic. About 30 seconds should be allowed for each multiple-choice item, so about 50 items can be used per test. Essay tests are used to sample higher-level abilities, such as the abilities to analyze, synthesize, and evaluate. Since different thought processes are involved with each kind of test, students will do best if objective and essay items do not appear on the same test.

Assessments that require the integration of many sub-skills and pieces of information are most useful because they emphasize the application of what is learned. Before any test is administered, the teacher should have a formal review with the test in hand. The teacher should go over each part of the test explaining what topics are covered, what content is sampled, and how many items are in each part of the test. When reviewing for essay tests, the teacher should go over perhaps a half-dozen possible questions and the associated criteria. Students should be told that they will be asked to answer two or three specific questions.

Immediately after a test is administered, the teacher should conduct an item analysis to determine which questions and choices help differentiate among students of differing abilities and which do not. Then the teacher must assign grades using whatever system was decided upon. A preset cutoff system (such as A = 100–90, B = 89–80, etc.) has the advantage of being easy to understand, but it does not provide for tests that prove to be particularly easy or difficult for classes in which expectations differ. Grading on a curve, such as one based on standard-deviation cutoff points, provides for tests of differing difficulty levels since the scale moves up and down with the mean, but it too fails to provide for classes in which expectations differ. All grading systems have strengths and weaknesses. If the school does not mandate a specific system, each teacher must adopt or adapt one that he or she feels reasonably comfortable with and can defend.

Grades must eventually be reported to parents; the best way to do this is through a face-to-face meeting where questions can be answered and examples of the student's work shown. The use of report cards is least effective in communicating what a student has achieved, but it is the most common reporting method because it is most convenient. Standardized test grades are most often reported in terms of stanines or percentile ranks.

Teacher evaluation is just as important as student evaluation. A particularly useful approach is to videotape a lesson and then assess the extent to which it followed the lesson plan and the extent to which students could achieve the lesson's objective. Other techniques such as student, peer, and administrative evaluations may provide useful information, but no single piece of information should be considered conclusive. A good teacher is continually trying to improve and is continually seeking feedback. The single best feedback is the success of the students. A teacher's success is dependent upon the success of his or her students.

STUDY QUESTIONS

1. From an educator's standpoint, what is the most important reason for measurement and evaluation in education? What are two other reasons?

2. What are the five basic principles of effective measurement and evaluation discussed in this chapter?

3. Describe at least three characteristics of typical standardized tests, and cite examples of at least three kinds of standardized tests.
4. What purposes do tables of specifications and item analyses serve?
5. Compare the advantages and disadvantages of grading on a curve with the advantages and disadvantages of using an A = 90–100, B = 80–89, etc., scale?
6. Describe at least four techniques teachers can use to improve their own teaching.

NOTES

1. Robert L. Thorndike and Elizabeth Hagen, *Measurement and Evaluation in Psychology and Education,* 2nd ed. (New York: John Wiley, 1961), pp. 61–78.
2. Benjamin S. Bloom, ed., *Taxonomy of Educational Objectives, Handbook I: Cognitive Domain* (New York: David McKay, 1956), p. 104.
3. Thorndike and Hagen, *Measurement and Evaluation in Psychology and Education,* pp. 61–78.
4. Further data on the instruments included in this section may be obtained by referring to Oscar Buros, ed., *Mental Measurement Yearbook, Seventh Edition* (Highland Park., N.J.: Gryphon Press, 1972).
5. Paul B. Diederich, "Short-Cut Statistics for Teacher-Made Tests," *Evaluation and Advisory Series,* no. 5 (Princeton, N.J.: Educational Testing Service, 1960), p. 23.
6. Edmund J. Amidon and Ned A. Flanders, *The Role of the Teacher in the Classroom* (Minneapolis, Minn: Association for Productive Teaching, 1967).
7. Greta Morine, Robert Spaulding, and Selma Greenberg, *Discovering New Dimensions in the Teaching Process* (Scranton, Pa.: International Textbook, 1971), p. vi.

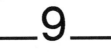

Classroom Management

INTRODUCTION

One of the greatest concerns felt by most beginning teachers is whether they will be able to establish and maintain a classroom atmosphere conducive to effective teaching and learning. In short, will they be able to control their classes? This chapter examines basic management principles, common causes of management problems, and effective ways to avoid or minimize these problems. It discusses some approaches to behavior modification and some of the legal factors that should be considered with respect to classroom management. The intent is to provide information and techniques that teachers can use to prevent most common classroom management problems and to deal humanely and effectively with any that do arise.

SAMPLE OBJECTIVES

When you complete this chapter, you will be able to:

1. Orally explain at least two basic management principles and their supporting rationales.
2. Select any two levels of needs described by A. H. Maslow and orally explain at least two things that can be done to help students satisfy those needs in a classroom.
3. Orally explain the meaning of *in loco parentis*.
4. Orally explain the general steps that should be followed when dealing with a continually disruptive student.
5. Describe, in writing, the major difference between an operant-conditioning approach to behavior modification and a reality-therapy approach.

THREE BASIC MANAGEMENT PRINCIPLES

There are many classroom management rules and principles, but the following three have been shown to help secondary students mature while enabling teachers to provide a reasonable teaching-learning environment. The first principle is that the goal of classroom management efforts is to help students develop self-control. The second principle is that, when given a choice, most people prefer to be successful rather than unsuccessful. The third principle is that people tend to follow a leader who sets goals that they see as appropriate and who has a reasonable plan by which the goals can be achieved.

The Goal Is Self-Control

One of the primary missions of all teachers is to assist students to act as responsible citizens. In order to do this, students must learn to control their own actions and take responsibility for those actions. Young children lack the foresight to anticipate the consequences of many of their acts, so parents and primary-grade teachers assume portions of that responsibility and protect youngsters from impetuous actions that might be harmful. As children get older and more experienced, they become more able to anticipate consequences and thus more aware of the need for self-control, but many parents and teachers find it difficult to give up control of their students' lives. In considering this problem, consider the steps of learning to ride a bicycle. It is helpful to have someone hold the bicycle when a child is first learning to balance, but if the helper does not let go, the child will never master the skill or be able to use the bicycle to its fullest advantage. Teachers need to "let go of the bicycle" as soon as possible. They need to let students practice the skill of self-control so they can master it.

One way to do this is to minimize the number of rules imposed. Teachers are required to enforce all rules set forth by the school board and the school administration. These are usually written in a handbook that is given to each student at the beginning of the school year. All teachers, but particularly beginning teachers, should read the school rules carefully because they are contractually obligated to enforce them. This point should be made clear to students. Beyond those rules, however, teachers have a great deal of flexibility. Some teachers, for example, find that they need just one rule: You may do whatever you like as long as you do not disturb anyone else.

Such a rule may sound like an invitation to chaos, but it is not. One reason for this is that the rule is so reasonable that students are reluctant to violate it. Teachers who take such an approach must do so with care. Those who want to use such an approach might find the following steps useful:

1. Before the semester begins, teachers should construct knowledge structures and unit plans that focus on the acquisition of useful information. They must make sure that they can show students the personal and social significance of the material to

be learned. One step toward this is building rationales that answer the question, "Why should I learn this stuff?"

2. On the very first day of class, teachers should distribute and then discuss the course syllabus. The discussion of the objectives and week-by-week schedule will communicate to students that the teachers have done their homework, that they have thought seriously about the course and its relevance to the students, and that the students can, in fact, achieve worthwhile goals.

3. Teachers should explain that they will help students learn the skills and information described in the syllabus, but that the teachers can control only their own actions, not the actions of each student. Therefore, though the teachers intend to do their best to conduct interesting and informative lessons that will help students achieve useful objectives, each student must decide whether he or she wants to learn. That choice is available to each student. The choice to disturb others is not. If a student does not want to learn, he or she can doodle, daydream, or do other work, as long as students who wish to learn are not disturbed or distracted. Because students have the option of simply sitting quietly and doing nothing, if they choose to cause a problem, their choice pits them against the rest of the class. Few students want to appear unreasonable to their peers, so the reasonableness of the rule acts as a deterrent against disruptions.

Another reason the do-not-disturb-others rule works is the idea of natural consequences. Teachers who use this approach take great care to point out to students that there are natural consequences to their choices. For example, if a student chooses to daydream during class, the natural consequence is that he or she will miss some information and will not be able to use that information on tests or outside the classroom. The teachers explain that if people wish to be successful, they must choose to do those things that make success possible. Teachers can help, but students must make the choices and they will reap the resulting benefits or problems.

This approach to classroom management shifts responsibility for proper student behavior from the teacher to each student, where it belongs, and it gives students the opportunity to develop self-control. That opportunity is denied them if teachers closely supervise and control their every move.

Help Students Be Successful

People would rather be successful than unsuccessful, and to the extent that teachers can help students achieve success, the students will tend to be cooperative. Success means the achievement of some goal or the satisfaction of some need or desire, so the first thing teachers must do in order to help students be successful is to identify some of the basic needs and desires that motivate their behavior. As it happens, the groundwork has already been done.

MASLOW'S HIERARCHY OF NEEDS

In 1943, Abraham H. Maslow described a hierarchy of human needs beginning with basic physiological needs and extending through needs for safety, love, esteem, and self-actualization. He theorized that people would devote their attention to at least partially satisfying their most basic needs before they diverted their efforts to satisfying less basic needs.[1] For example, the reader might at one time or another have had to miss part of a play or movie in order to use a restroom. The physiological need was more powerful than the desire to watch the entertainment. Teachers can make use of Maslow's work because the needs he described are the motivating forces behind many student actions. Understanding the hierarchy of human needs may help teachers understand how they can help students meet those needs in the classroom. This will help minimize or eliminate many classroom management problems.

One word of caution. In thinking about why particular students may be causing problems, teachers need to keep their own qualifications in mind. Unless the teacher is a certified psychologist or a licensed physician, he or she should not try to diagnose or treat any suspected psychological or physical problem. Teachers are employed to teach the content they are certified to teach, not to play amateur psychologist, physician, or minister. Any attempts to do so may do more harm than good (regardless of good intentions), and they may delay or prevent the proper thing from being done.

Physiological Needs

Maslow identified physiological needs as the most basic and powerful of all human needs. For example, the first concern of a person who is drowning, starving, or dying of thirst is to satisfy that crucial need for air, food, or water. Teachers do not often encounter situations involving actual survival; nevertheless, physiological needs can prompt behavior problems.

Air.   People work best when they are reasonably comfortable. If a room is too cold or too warm, smells bad, or simply lacks adequate air circulation, students will soon begin paying more attention to the discomfort than to the lesson. Teachers who ignore such problems will appear to be unreasonable or unaware of the world around them. Neither image is helpful. A better course of action is to acknowledge the problem and try to solve it. Sometimes it helps to simply open a window, but in rare cases it might be necessary to arrange to move to a different place. In any case, the acknowledgment of the problem and the effort to solve it are important. These steps show students that the teacher cares about them. This alone will help minimize potential behavior problems.

Food.   One could argue that it is the responsibility of parents to feed their children, but since the passage of the National School Lunch Act in 1946, schools have taken on part of that responsibility. Most students come to school adequately fed, but they are in a period of rapid growth and are frequently hungry. Do not be surprised, therefore, if students are somewhat less attentive toward the end of the period immediately preceding lunch. Hunger is a powerful force, and hungry students would rather contemplate a hamburger than an algebraic equation. This does not mean that teachers should allow students to snack during class (it is likely to disturb the teacher and the rest of the class) or that a teacher should end instruction early, but understanding the need should help teachers be more tolerant of student inattention.

If a teacher suspects that a student is getting too little to eat or is suffering from malnutrition (perhaps from dieting too rigidly), the proper course of action is first to discuss the issue privately with the student and then, if necessary, to alert the appropriate school administrator. A teacher's primary function is to provide food for thought. Others are employed to deal with the question of food for the body.

Water.   The need for water is not usually a great problem, but callous teachers can make it into one. If a student asks for permission to get a drink of water and is refused for no good reason, the teacher will appear to be unreasonable. If students believe that a teacher is unreasonable, the teacher will find it difficult to elicit student cooperation and can expect continual challenges to his or her authority.

On the other hand, some students use requests for drinks as a way of avoiding work or disrupting the class. One effective way to handle this problem is to meet with such students privately and express concern for their health. Students should be told that their requests will be carefully monitored and, if the problem persists, that they will be referred to the school nurse. If the requests were just excuses, the idea of having to talk with the school nurse will quickly end the problem. If the requests continue, there might be a real problem and a visit to the nurse would be appropriate.

Elimination.   The need to eliminate bodily wastes is a very real and basic need. A request to go to the bathroom should be granted immediately. If a teacher suspects that students are making the requests in order to avoid work or to disrupt class, the strategy for dealing with problem water-drinkers should be used. The teacher should meet with the students privately, express concern for their health, and explain that if they cannot attend to their needs before or after class, that an appointment will be made for them to see the school nurse. Students are even less likely to want to discuss their toilet habits with a nurse than to discuss their requests for drinks, so the problem will quickly end. If the need is real, a referral might result in finding and treating a disease or malfunction at an early stage.

Sleep.   Today's teenagers have full schedules. In addition to attending school and doing homework, many students engage in extracurricular activities and some hold part-time jobs. As a result of trying to attend to so many things, some students do not get the sleep they require and may therefore doze during class. Certainly such students are less likely to sleep if a class is interesting and informative, but even when it is, some students may still fall asleep.

The first time a student falls asleep it would be appropriate to indicate, via nonverbal cues, that a nearby student should awaken him or her. It is important to avoid embarrassing the sleeper. Once awake, the student can be brought into the class activities by being asked a not-too-specific question or by being asked for an opinion. At some other time the teacher might also announce to the class that anyone who feels sleepy should feel free to get up and stand in the back of the room for awhile. If the problem persists, the teacher should meet with the student privately and explain that the sleeping distracts others.

The student is likely to express a desire to stay awake and to offer some explanation for sleeping. If the problem seems to be beyond the student's control (he must work to help support his family, or it is impossible to get to sleep at a reasonable time because of noise, for example), it should be referred to an appropriate administrator. A teacher's primary responsibility is to teach. Others are employed to deal with out-of-school problems.

Sexual Interest.   Interest in the opposite sex is normal, and it begins to manifest itself during the early teen years. Educators are well aware of the hormonal changes affecting students, and they try to help students adjust to their new needs by providing instruction about reproductive systems, social expectations, and how to avoid sexually transmitted diseases. This instruction provides students with useful information, but in some cases the hormones appear to override the thinking process.

Teachers should be aware that teenagers are sometimes preoccupied with sex; they have just undergone pubescence, and they are naturally curious about their bodies and their attractiveness to the opposite sex. Some concern about physical development and some flirtatious behavior are to be expected. If the concern interferes with academic performance, then the teacher needs to intervene. The intervention should take the form of a private conference to discuss with the student the need to separate physical concerns from academic concerns. Since the issue is a sensitive one for most students, one conference is usually enough. If the preoccupation continues or if the student brings out a concern that may reflect a physical problem, referrals to appropriate school staff may be in order.

Safety Needs

Once physiological needs are at least partially met, people will turn their attention to the next most powerful need, physical safety. As was the case with physiological needs, safety needs refer to survival—not being killed by wild animals or by other people. In today's schools, most students and teachers have relatively little concern about actual survival, but the need for safety is still real. Consider the following facts.

In Boston schools during the 1987 school year, "55 students were expelled for carrying guns and 2,500 must report to police probation officers for past offenses."[2] In 1985, California, one of the few states that collects data on school crimes, reported "three on-campus, school-related homicides, two with student victims."[3] Nationally, it is estimated that at least 38,000 secondary students were assaulted at school during 1985,[4] and not only students have cause for concern. Teachers, too, are assaulted. According to a National Education Association (NEA) Member Opinion Poll, attacks per 100,000 teachers stood at 4,000 in 1984, 3,000 in 1985, and 8,000 in 1986.[5] The concern for safety on the part of students and teachers is real.

For students, there are three main sources of physical harm: other students, the curriculum, and teachers. There is little that teachers can do to protect students against violence by other students, because most of that violence takes place when teachers are not present, as in restrooms, before or after school, or in congested, hectic situations, such as crowded hallways or lunch rooms. If such violence is a serious problem, the school administration may decide to have police patrol the school grounds and hallways. Having to take this step is unfortunate: it is an admission that education alone is not sufficient to induce social order, and it is expensive. It reduces the number of dollars available to meet other educational needs. In some cases, however, there is no choice. Without that protection, education in some schools is not practical.

While teachers may not be able to do much about violence outside their classrooms, they can take steps to eliminate it in their classrooms. One such step is to establish and follow a routine. If a teacher begins each class on time, greets students, takes attendance, makes announcements, and then moves into the lesson, students will understand what to expect in that class and what is expected of them. This understanding will help generate among students a sense that the classroom is a special place, a place to learn, not a place to continue out-of-class discussions or fights. The classroom becomes more of a safe and secure haven.

A second source of safety concerns for students is the curriculum itself. Handling a welding torch in a shop class, putting a cake into a hot oven in a home economics class, or jumping off a diving board in a physical education class are activities that may, depending upon the previous experiences of individual students, cause them great concern. It does not matter that the activity is one that can easily be performed safely; what is important is the student's perception of danger. The teacher must deal with the student's perception, because that is what is real for the student.

It is best to avoid problems, so teachers are wise to examine their planned activities and to identify any that have caused concern for students in the past or that might cause concern for students. The teacher should make a special effort to show students how those activities should be done and how to avoid common mistakes. Even more important, the teacher should offer to work privately with any student who is afraid of having difficulty with the activity. The point is to let students know that having concerns about some things is not wrong or "dumb" and that the teacher is willing to work with them.

It may happen that a student does not come for extra help but shows great reluctance to engage in the activity during class. The student should not be pressured, either physically or by fear of ridicule, to engage in the activity. The teacher should move on to another student and discreetly arrange to talk with the fearful student after class or after school. Under no circumstances should a teacher point out a student's fear to others or ridicule the student. The way the problem is handled will not be lost on the other students and will do much to strengthen or weaken a teacher's rapport with the class.

When meeting with the student privately, the teacher should discuss the problem and offer additional time and help. It should be made clear, however, that credit for achieving the objective can only be given if the objective is, in fact, achieved. The student's fear may be so great that he or she chooses to lose credit for the objective rather than attempt the activity. Make it clear that this is an acceptable choice. It is counterproductive to take the position that unless that particular objective is achieved, the student's academic career is ruined. There are other objectives that can be achieved and other things the student can learn. Further, an understanding attitude may, over a little time, prompt the student to return to the problem activity and overcome his or her fear. A teacher's job is to help students succeed. Helping them overcome fears helps them succeed.

A third source of student concern for safety is physical punishment. Although hundreds of years ago teachers such as Hillel and Comenius argued that physical punishment has no place in the instructional process, the practice is still with us. In fact, as recently as 1988, 50 percent of 2,118 adults surveyed approved of the use of physical punishment.[6]

The legality of corporal punishment is in the hands of each state, because there is nothing in the U.S. Constitution about education. In 1977, the Supreme Court, in *Ingraham vs. Wright,* ruled that the provision against cruel and unusual punishment does not apply to school children.[7] Nonetheless, many state boards of education have banned the use of corporal punishment. Within those states that have not formally banned corporal punishment, many local school boards have done so. Even in districts that have not banned it, many principals have done so. Once a rule or law is passed at one level, no one at a lower level has the right to unilaterally change that rule.

The arguments against physical punishments are strong. First and most important, using force rather than reason contradicts the intent of the educational process. Educators are trying to help students learn to solve problems by using brains rather than brawn. If educators themselves use force, the brains versus brawn argument is seriously weakened.

Second, though physical punishment may be expedient and may provide some immediate satisfaction to the punisher, it teaches the student very little other than not to get caught. If a teacher is unable to explain the rationale for or against a particular act with sufficient clarity to convince a student, it is unlikely that a session with the paddle will do the job.

Still further, while educators might be able to use physical punishment in the lower grades because they are so much bigger than the students, older students are unlikely to submit meekly to such treatment. In the interest of self-preservation, teachers should abstain from physical punishment.

If a student is subjected to physical punishment, the teacher should not administer it. The teacher's role as concerned helper is too important to jeopardize by assuming the role of bully. Further, if physical punishment is administered, it should be done in the presence of at least two adults. Lawsuits are likely to arise out of charges of physical abuse, so a witness may be needed in court. Avoid the problems. With the exception of occasional congratulatory pats on the back, teachers should keep their hands off students.

Love Needs

Maslow's description of love needs centers on the love that usually exists between husband and wife, between parents and children, and among siblings. The need for this kind of nurturing love and sense of belonging is only indirectly related to classroom management because a teacher's sincerest concern for a student cannot replace the love and concern of a mother, father, brother, or sister.

Teachers should be aware, however, that students who are deprived of love at home suffer a deficiency as debilitating as that resulting from the deprivation of food or sleep. Students who suffer from a lack of parental concern, nurturing, and love are likely to be less stable emotionally and more easily depressed than their more typical peers. A teacher who learns of such a problem can make special efforts not to amplify the problem at school.

One thing that a teacher *can* do with respect to love needs is to establish a sense of unity among the students in each class. This sense of unity is fostered by working toward common goals, by mutual respect between students and the teacher and among students, and by maintaining high but achievable standards. These practices may generate among students a feeling of belonging to a group—something that might be lacking in some students' lives.

Esteem Needs

The need for esteem is the need for a sense of worthiness in one's own eyes and in the eyes of others. Although this need is less basic than the preceding needs, it is more directly related to classroom management and more amenable to teacher manipulation.

One aspect of esteem is a person's sense of him- or herself as a person—the need to be accepted as one is. Teachers should make it clear by words and actions that their first and greatest concern is for each student as a fellow human being. Human beings are not perfect, and it is reassuring for students to know that when they make a mistake, they will not be regarded as inherently bad. When they make a mistake, it is the act, not the person, that rates the disapproval. This stance enables teachers to continue working with students who sometimes cause problems. It becomes a matter of "John, I do not like what you did, but I believe that you have done better and will do better," rather than, "John, I do not like what you did and therefore I want as little to do with you as possible." The first stance allows for cooperation in the future, whereas the second tends to end the relationship.

Internal Recognition.   The need for esteem is met in two basic ways. The first and most important way is for the individual to perceive that he or she is being successful (that he or she is developing new abilities, new knowledge, or new control over his or her life, or is acquiring some other desired thing or state). Think back to the time you learned to ride your bicycle or to swim. The chances are good that one of the first things you did after learning the new skill was to show off your new ability to Mom or Dad. You were proud and you felt good about yourself. That is what self-esteem is all about—earning a sense of accomplishment.

Earning the sense of accomplishment is crucial. Students are unlikely to feel good about themselves if they get high grades for relatively simple work. The symbol (whether it is a gold star, a high grade, money, or some other reinforcer) is not sufficient in itself to produce the feeling of pride and accomplishment that builds self-esteem. To exist at all, the feeling must be earned: it must be based on having made a real gain.

One way teachers can help students achieve is by helping them help themselves. For example, if a student is having difficulty learning a skill, it might be useful for the teacher to break the skill into separate components and encourage the student to work on each component independently with minimal teacher assistance. This "systems analysis" approach should help the student eventually overcome the larger problem. The procedure requires careful monitoring of each student's progress, but it helps students more accurately perceive their abilities, and it builds their self-esteem as they see their abilities increase through personal effort.

Sometimes students are so caught up with their failures that they lose sight of the fact that they have made some progress. When a student is not doing well in a class, the teacher should examine the student's overall performance and isolate the things that the student does well. If the teacher then takes the student aside and points out that progress is being made and that more can be made, the student is helped to develop a feeling of accomplishment. Such a student may not feel great about his work, but he won't feel hopeless either. Teachers cannot give students a sense of accomplishment as they would give a five-dollar bill, but they can help students realize their actual achievements, and that is important.

External Recognition.   A second way self-esteem can be developed is by outside recognition of accomplishments. Remember running to show Mom or Dad that new ability? You did not do that until you were confident that you had acquired the skill—that had to come first. Immediately thereafter, however, you wanted everyone to know. Much the same is true of your students. Having worked and practiced to develop new skills that they perceive to be important, they will want others to know of their accomplishments when the skills have been developed. Acknowledging students' achievements boosts their self-esteem. Posting students' good work on bulletin boards is a common way elementary school teachers share students' achievements, and grades on report cards are common at all levels. However, if a teacher is serious about helping students feel good about themselves, a phone call to their parents once in a while to tell them about a piece of good work or some good class participation will go a long way. The parent will certainly tell the student about the call, and the student will feel good. Most people feel awkward about blowing their own horns, but few object if someone else does it for them. The teacher should take the time to point out the accomplishments of students to parents, other teachers, and administrators, making sure that the accomplishments represent real gains in skills and abilities. The better students feel about themselves, the better work they are likely to do. The more successful they are, the more successful you will be.

The need for peer acceptance is great among teenagers. If they cannot satisfy that need by doing well in some socially accepted arena (such as school, music, or sports) they may try to satisfy the need by demonstrating to peers that they can challenge an authority figure—a teacher—and win. From the student's standpoint, winning may be measured by the degree to which they can get away with some rule infraction, by publicly proving that some rule is outdated or logically inconsistent, by causing a teacher to lose patience, or by using up class time. Regardless of the outcome, such students accomplish part of their goal simply by focusing attention on themselves.

Challenges and confrontations can be minimized if teachers follow a routine of beginning class promptly, explaining the objective, and moving directly into the lesson. This routine focuses the attention of the class on a specific objective. Once the lesson is underway, any issue raised that is not relevant to the work at hand should be deferred. Students raising such issues should be told that the work at hand must continue but that the issue can be discussed immediately after class. By refusing to engage in give-and-take during class, the teacher minimizes the peer reinforcement that the student can get and, equally important, provides a cooling-off period that increases the likelihood that the issue can be discussed objectively.

Teachers need to be careful not to use sarcasm, ridicule, or humiliation as control devices. For example, grades should be treated confidentially. If grades are posted they should be keyed to an identification number, not to students' names. If you were getting the lowest grade in a class, would you want everyone to know it?

It is particularly important to guard against sarcasm. Teachers have many opportunities to make remarks that seem clever and perhaps even funny but that may offend some students. Think twice before speaking. A sharp tongue can inflict deep and lasting wounds, and it can surely destroy any rapport that might be developing. Perhaps the best advice here is the oldest. "Do not do unto others what you would not have them do unto you." In this case, teachers must temper the golden rule with the realization that they are adults and that their students are in the process of becoming adults.

Self-Actualization Needs

The last need described by Maslow is the need for self-actualization, or the need to develop as fully as possible.[8] This need is directly related to classroom management; students who believe that their time and efforts will help them make useful and relevant gains in abilities or will open up new areas of personal development are more willing to cooperate in the instructional process.

One of the most crucial steps teachers can take to help students meet their need for self-actualization is to ensure that the course objectives include some at the higher levels of the cognitive or psychomotor domains. Such objectives require the integration of skills and knowledge and usually reflect important abilities. The teacher should discuss these abilities with students, and, further, show how the content clearly relates to current events in business, industry, research, the arts, or some other human endeavor. These steps will help students see that they will be learning interesting and valuable information and that they are, in fact, enhancing their own abilities.

It is also important for students to use their newly acquired abilities. Individual or group projects can provide opportunities for students to utilize new skills and to see how their study has paid off. Further, to the extent that the projects have some out-of-school components, the students will be demonstrating their abilities to different adults, thus helping build their self-esteem.

In review, many classroom management problems can be avoided if teachers recognize that many student actions are motivated by basic human needs. By consciously helping students satisfy those needs, teachers will eliminate many of the causes of classroom management problems.

GUIDELINES FOR PRECLUDING DISCIPLINE PROBLEMS

Using the background information on human needs, along with other psychological principles and common sense, the following set of ten guidelines can be helpful in organizing to preclude discipline problems.

Eliminate Physical Distractions. As has been pointed out, students who are concerned about their physical well-being are likely to pay less attention to classwork at hand. Simple steps, such as assuring a continual flow of fresh air through the room, maintaining a comfortable temperature, eliminating glare on the chalkboard, and establishing a reasonable policy concerning leaving the room for drinks or trips to the restroom, can help eliminate the causes of many "discipline problems."

Treat Students with Respect. Remember that students are fellow human beings and deserve to be treated with the same degree of respect and courtesy that adults extend to any of their peers. Students are likely to treat you the same way you treat them.

Elicit Student Help in Planning. A frequently cited cause of student discontent is the feeling that the material they are asked to learn or the activities in which they are asked to engage are irrelevant. If teachers take the time to think about the rationales for the objectives and take the time to discuss those rationales with students, the problem of irrelevancy will decrease.

Maintain Reasonable Expectations. It usually does not take long for teachers to discover that mild student frustrations can be used to increase learning. The mildly uncomfortable feeling on the part of students, which continues until they achieve a goal, assists in speeding up the learning process. If teachers expect too little from students, this sense of frustration will be lacking, the work will be viewed as busy-work, and the final sense of achievement students could otherwise have experienced will be minimized. At the same time, unattainable goals or artificial barriers to goal achievement must be eliminated or students will become overly frustrated, and this frustration can be manifested in the form of discipline problems.

Use a Variety of Instructional Experiences.   An admitted cause of discipline problems is student boredom. Teachers can combat this by building into their lessons a variety of different learning experiences. Not every student will be equally inter-ested in each experience, but by having a number of different experiences in each lesson, teachers increase the probability of gaining and holding the interest of stu-dents more of the time. Interested students are less likely to cause discipline prob-lems.

Provide Prompt Feedback.   Students are generally extremely interested in finding out "how they did" on any given task. If a report is not forthcoming soon after the task is completed, students are apt to think that the teacher did not regard the task as very important and therefore feel they wasted their efforts. This feeling will continue to grow as such instances multiply, with the eventual result that students will feel that whatever they do in that particular class is of little value. Such an environ-ment is open to the generation of discipline problems. As a general rule, a second assignment should not be given until the first is corrected and handed back.

Provide Positive Reinforcement.   When evaluating students' work, many teachers concentrate upon the identification and correction of errors. If teachers continually emphasize what students do incorrectly without recognizing those things they have done well, students will become discouraged and resentful. Their needs for esteem and self-actualization will go unsatisfied and they may seek other, undesirable sources of satisfaction. Teachers should point out sections of students' work that are well done and should encourage students to use those sections as models for the less well-done portions. Sincere, positive reinforcement can go a long way toward mak-ing corrections more palatable and toward satisfying student needs.

Be Consistent.   If students perceive inconsistencies in a teacher's reactions to problems, or if they believe a teacher is being unfair, their respect for that teacher will decrease. Once a teacher loses the respect of his or her students, discipline problems will begin to increase.

Foster Peer Approval.   As was pointed out earlier, peer approval or disap-proval is an important element in the life of most adolescents. At times this force may motivate students more than any other single element. Teachers who gain the respect and approval of the majority of their students can tap this force and use it to help maintain an environment conducive to learning. Students who are "with" a teacher can assist, in many subtle ways, in controlling their peers.

It must be pointed out that, although teachers can accept most forms of student support and can allow most forms of peer pressure to bear on students causing discipline problems, the tool cannot be used indiscriminately. Manifestations of peer pressure such as physical reprisals, ridicule, sarcasm, and humiliation cannot be tolerated. If teachers condone the use of such measures, the very student respect that generated the support in the first place will be lost.

Avoid Punitive Action. This principle is one of the most difficult for beginning teachers to follow. Many people have become accustomed to an eye-for-an-eye philosophy, and when teachers are inconvenienced by a student, their first inclination is often to inconvenience that student at least as much. There is little evidence, however, to support the idea that punitive action will have any lasting effect on deviant student behavior.

The selection of appropriate punitive action is not easy, nor is the prediction of consequent student reaction certain. An examination of common punitive actions follows:

1. *Detention.* This option punishes teachers as much as students, since someone must supervise the detention. Often the student is bused to and from school or has an after-school job, and the hardship caused makes the punishment excessive. In other cases, students may be involved in sports or some after-school club and the detention may therefore deprive them of one of the few school experiences that is keeping them from dropping out.

2. *Extra schoolwork.* There seems to be no evidence to support the idea that assigning extra schoolwork is helpful in eliminating discipline problems. In fact, it is likely that the assignment of such work will cause students to associate all schoolwork with unpleasant experiences and thus cause more harm than good.

3. *Repetitive sentences and the like.* The use of repetitive sentences and similar busywork assignments has been widespread among teachers for years. There must be teachers somewhere who have found this device effective in maintaining good discipline, but locating such a teacher proves to be difficult. Such tasks are likely to cause students to equate schoolwork with busywork and to dislike both.

4. *Special seating assignments.* Special seating assignments usually take one of two forms. In the first form a seat is isolated from the rest of the class and students are assigned to it essentially as objects of ridicule. Ridicule is not effective as a discipline device.

Another form of special seating is to attempt to separate friends or arrange seats in a way that will minimize student interaction. This procedure is less satisfactory than using friendships in a positive way to foster intrinsic motivation. Further, separated students will still find ways to communicate despite the teacher's efforts.

5. *Physical labor or exercise.* The use of physical work or exercise is fraught with danger. A student who is asked by a teacher to do as little as move a desk and

who is hurt in the process is in a position to bring suit against the teacher. In some states physical labor assigned to students is specifically forbidden.

Exercises, such as running the track, push-ups, and so on, are often used in physical education classes as punitive action. The same reservations apply here that applied in the assignment of schoolwork as punishment. How are students going to build an intrinsic desire for more exercise if the teacher considers it distasteful enough to use as punishment?

Occasionally a teacher in a classroom will use push-ups or some other physical action as punishment. Unlike the physical education teacher, who at least knows whether the student is physically able to do the assigned exercise, the classroom teacher may make an unjustified assumption about a student's physical abilities. It is possible that a student would rather injure himself or herself attempting the assigned exercise than lose face with peers, and it is unlikely that parents would lose the legal battle that could follow.

6. *Lowering of grades.* In some school districts there are policies that condone the lowering of an academic grade for disciplinary reasons. This practice is analogous to withholding a diploma as punitive action when all necessary requirements have been met. In this case the courts have ruled that the diploma must be awarded.[9] In the case of grades, however, teachers can cloud the criteria for grading to the point where a grade could be lowered consciously or unconsciously because of discipline problems. This cannot be defended logically, since once a student has achieved an objective and demonstrated a competence it is senseless to deny the accomplishment. Teachers who engage in this practice will be deemed unfair by their students and will quickly lose a large measure of student respect.

7. *Banishment from the classroom.* Along with lowering grades are the procedures that can cause students to earn lower grades, for instance, actions that deny the student access to ongoing instruction. Insisting that the student stand outside the classroom may solve a problem for the moment, but the teacher will eventually need to spend extra time teaching the material to the student if academic achievement is considered important. Further, teachers are legally responsible for their students while class is in session. By banishing a student from the room, the teacher removes that student from direct supervision and may therefore be held liable if the student is injured or gets into additional trouble.

BEHAVIOR MODIFICATION: OPERANT CONDITIONING

Operant conditioning is the formal name given to the process of encouraging people to behave in particular ways by systematically rewarding desired behaviors. This process is also known as contingency management because the rewards are provided only after the desired behavior is demonstrated. Put in more technical terms, the reinforcement is contingent upon demonstration of the desired behavior. Obvious examples of operant conditioning techniques include the use of praise to encourage the completion of homework and the use of prizes to entice students to do well in school.

In order to better explain operant conditioning, we will find it useful to define some terms. *Positive reinforcement* occurs when the presentation of a stimulus results in an increase in a desired behavior. For example, if Diane is given a candy bar every time her homework is done well, and she begins to do her homework well more often, then the candy bars are functioning as positive reinforcement.

Negative reinforcement occurs when the withdrawal of a stimulus results in the increase in a desired behavior. If Adam's parents, who usually nag him to do his homework, stop the nagging, and he starts doing the homework, then stopping the nagging acted as a negative reinforcement.

Punishment occurs when the presentation of a stimulus results in a decrease in the undesired behavior. If Gary is required to stay after school if he forgets to do his homework and he does his homework in order to avoid staying after school, then staying after school is a punishment.

If the above seems too complex, consider what the situation would be if Diane were very weight conscious. Then the candy bar might not function as the expected positive reinforcement. In fact, it might even be perceived as punishment. What would happen in Adam's case, if the only attention he got from his parents was the nagging? He might well feel that the nagging was better than no attention at all. For him, the negative reinforcement (the stopping of the nagging) might function as punishment. In Gary's case, suppose that if he did not stay after school he had to go to work—which he disliked even more than school. In that case the "punishment" might be positive reinforcement. The point here is that the only way to determine whether a stimulus is a positive reinforcer, a negative reinforcer, or a punishment is to see its effect on the target behavior.

Proper utilization of operant conditioning requires a careful and systematic series of steps intended to isolate and modify the undesirable behavior of a particular student. Let us suppose that Tom periodically disturbs the class, and his teacher has decided to try to modify his behavior via operant conditioning. Steps that would be appropriate follow.

Determine What Generally Triggers the Student's Misbehavior. Does Tom begin whispering when a particular stimulus is presented (e.g., when discussion of assigned homework is initiated) or when a stimulus is withdrawn (e.g., when you shift attention away from him)? Although it may seem as though the student in question is always misbehaving, a careful analysis (after observation) will usually reveal the triggering stimulus. In this case the teacher determines that Tom begins whispering when the class starts to discuss the previous night's homework assignment.

Determine What Generally Happens Each Time the Student Misbehaves. When Tom begins whispering, what is the teacher's reaction? What is the reaction of the other students? This analysis of what happens immediately after the student misbehaves is important, and it can be highly revealing. In this circumstance, the analysis shows that, as soon as Tom begins whispering, the teacher interrupts the class and forcefully tells him to stop. Further, immediately following the chastisement, other students giggle and snicker, and Tom usually responds with some wisecrack.

Devise and Try Countermeasures. At this point, the analysis has begun to point the way toward the solution of the problem. The teacher knows, for example, that Tom's disruption of the class usually begins with whispering to neighbors, which, in turn, is triggered by the announcement that the class will begin discussing the homework assignment. Further, the disruption intensifies after a chastisement for whispering. The teacher's outbursts may be functioning as positive reinforcement.

A number of countermeasures are available. One option is to ignore Tom's whispering, thus depriving him of reinforcement from the attention focused on him. While this option may work, it may be undesirable because other students may misinterpret the lack of action, particularly if Tom is a leader. A second option would be to move Tom to a different seat where neighbors would be unlikely to whisper back. This option might work, but it may be less desirable than other possibilities because it is unlikely to bring about a lasting modification in Tom's behavior. A third option could emerge. For example, it may be that there is a cause-effect relationship between Tom's whispering and impending discussions of homework. It might be determined that Tom rarely does his homework and that his whispering is an attempt to acquire survival data prior to the discussion.

Operant conditioning could be initiated by waiting for a time when Tom is able to participate in a discussion of homework and then praising him for his good work and valuable contributions. If the praise or other positive reinforcement were forthcoming each time he contributed to the discussion without whispering beforehand, the whispering might soon cease, because he would recognize that it was no longer necessary. This procedure, while effective, depends upon waiting until Tom does his homework and could turn out to be a long-term approach.

A fourth option to speed up the reinforcement process could be initiated. Keeping in mind that the class disruption is caused in part by Tom's whispering and in part by the teacher's reaction to that whispering, the teacher might find the following steps effective:

1. Make specific homework assignments for each student.
2. Privately encourage Tom to do the assignment.
3. Call on some students to discuss their homework, but call on Tom the first day only if he has done his homework and ignore whispering if it occurs.
4. Again make specific assignments and privately encourage Tom to do his.
5. As soon as Tom has made an effort to do the assignment, even if it came only as the result of heavy prompting, call on him during the discussion and praise his contribution. Again ignore his whispering if it occurs.
6. Repeat steps 4 and 5 each day, praising Tom's contributions and ignoring his whispering. The whispering should decrease and disappear within a few days. If it does not, the analysis must be reexamined for alternative explanations for the behavior.

The point of the operant conditioning process is to focus attention on desired behavior and to provide an incentive for the student to engage in that behavior. The incentive may be praise, points, or any other reward valued by the student, and the expectation is that the desired behavior will soon become self-reinforcing and will replace the undesirable behavior, which is never reinforced.

Keep in mind that sometimes the removal or withholding of a stimulus (for example, the denying of an opportunity to receive attention and reinforcement from peers) is as effective as the presentation of a stimulus (for example, the giving of praise or rewards). Once the right stimulus is found for any individual, a procedure can be established to help bring about lasting behavioral changes via operant conditioning.

As a process, operant conditioning is not concerned with root causes of undesired behaviors. Instead, attention is focused on discovering and capitalizing on particular rewards that will help individuals to modify their behavior. This emphasis on rewards rather than causes seems superficial to many educators and has caused many to express reservations about using operant conditioning techniques.

Among the arguments used by opponents of operant conditioning techniques is the opinion that they may cause as many problems as they solve. When teachers use operant conditioning techniques, the basic process is to identify the specific behaviors they wish to increase and reward the student when the desired behavior is demonstrated. Some educators maintain that it is not long until other students observe that one way to get extra attention or rewards from the teacher is to misbehave and then behave properly on cue. These educators also insist that operant conditioning techniques can be unfair to those students who behave properly.

Still another concern of many educators is that operant conditioning techniques imply that appropriate behavior should be demonstrated only because such behavior will generate an extrinsic reward such as praise, candy, money, or free time. They maintain that the use of rewards for appropriate behavior obscures the fact that such behavior has its own intrinsic rewards and will not, in fact, bring extrinsic rewards in the "real" world. They claim, therefore, that operant conditioning techniques mislead students by giving them a false impression of reality.

A further criticism leveled at operant conditioning practitioners questions the right of the behavior manipulator to make judgments as to what other people's behaviors should be. Operant conditioning practitioners must decide which behaviors are "good" and which are "bad" and use rewards to cause students to modify their behavior without necessarily making the students aware of the process. Such decisions, however, must be made daily by teachers to maintain an atmosphere conducive to the educational process. It is interesting to note that, in one survey concerning behavior modification, of the 406 educators questioned, 85 percent agreed that it was ethical to "manage behavior regardless of the techniques employed."[10] If nothing else, the finding speaks eloquently of the importance educators attach to "good" behavior on the part of students.

Many of the attacks on operant conditioning have been prompted by aversion to its abuses by individual teachers who use it indiscriminately and without regard for its ramifications. When used properly, the rewards often pertain to student fulfillment of basic needs, such as the needs for esteem and self-actualization. Further, when teachers fully understand the ramifications of the technique, they are quick to point out to students the intrinsic rewards of the desired behavior and thus lead students away from continued extrinsic rewards.

BEHAVIOR MODIFICATION: REALITY THERAPY

Reality therapy is a behavior modification tool made popular by Dr. William Glasser.[11] It utilizes student needs, but its philosophical orientation is significantly different from that of operant conditioning. In operant conditioning, individuals undergoing the conditioning are often unaware that their behavior is being manipulated. No attempt is made to treat individuals as responsible people, to make them partners in a joint effort to modify behavior, or to help them see the cause-effect relationships between their behavior and its long-term consequences.

Reality therapy, on the other hand, makes individuals the prime movers in the modification of their own behavior. Reality therapy is predicated on the idea that people engage in those behaviors they believe will bring them relatedness and respect (i.e., which will satisfy one or more perceived or unperceived needs) but that some individuals have either a distorted idea of what their goals are or a distorted idea of how to achieve them. Reality therapists see their role as a "perception sharpener"—one who attempts to help the individual perceive the reality of the situation. The assumption is made that the students know right from wrong.

Reality therapy begins with the current situation. Although reality therapists are well aware that many problems have roots in past events, they are not willing to allow those past events to become excuses for future actions. The individual's attention is focused on the behavior to be modified, not on the root causes of that behavior, and the individual is helped to see the consequences of continuing the undesirable behavior as well as the consequences of modified behavior. The following step-by-step procedure is illustrative of how a teacher might use reality therapy to deal with Tom's whispering.

Help the Student Identify the Undesirable Behavior.   In this case, the teacher would arrange to see Tom privately. In the process of discussing the "problem," the teacher elicits the identification of the problem from Tom. It is important that Tom identify it, because then he is taking the first step toward its solution. If the teacher makes the identification, Tom is likely to look to the teacher for the solution to the problem rather than to seek that solution for himself.

Care is exercised not to ask Tom *why* he is engaging in the undesired behavior (whispering). To do so would provide him with an opportunity to offer an excuse for his actions and to focus attention on the excuse rather than the action. Again, the reality therapist does not deny that there may be legitimate reasons for inappropriate behavior—he or she simply insists on beginning with the inappropriate behavior rather than with a series of antecedent events. Nothing can be done about the past, but something can be done about the future. After discussion Tom should identify whispering as an inappropriate behavior.

Help the Student Identify the Consequences of Undesirable Behavior. It is important that the consequences identified be real and logical. If the environment is manipulated so the consequences of a particular action are unreasonably harsh or virtually meaningless, the situation becomes contrived and unreal. In such a situation reality therapy is less effective. In this case, for example, telling Tom that he will be suspended from school if whispering continues is unreasonable. Similarly, it would be unreasonable to tell him that inappropriate behavior will have no consequences. It is appropriate, however, to point out that consequences are often cumulative and tend to get more and more severe.

Through discussion it is determined that Tom's whispering disturbs other students and that part of the teacher's responsibility is to maintain an atmosphere that is quiet and conducive to concentration. In keeping with that responsibility, Tom should conclude that continued whispering will logically result in some form of exclusion from the group, which, in turn, will adversely affect progress.

Help the Student Make a Value Judgment about the Inappropriate Behavior and Its Consequences. The purpose of this step is to help the student see that the inappropriate behavior is contributing more to eventual unhappiness than to immediate or long-range happiness. The student is likely to have inaccurate perceptions about the effects of the behavior and may need help in making a value judgment about its desirability or undesirability. If the student does have difficulty making a value judgment about the behavior itself, then the focus is directed at making a judgment about the consequences of that behavior. In any event, the student is helped to conclude that the inappropriate behavior is undesirable or that it will bring more unhappiness than happiness. In the example, Tom admits that whispering can bother other students and that one student should not interfere with the right of other students to learn.

Have the Student Formulate a Plan for Changing the Behavior. Once Tom has concluded that the behavior is not, in fact, in his own best interests, the next step is for him to suggest alternatives to that behavior. If possible, he should be encouraged to propose an alternative behavior, for example, he will:

1. Simply stop whispering.
2. Admit to not knowing an answer or not doing his homework rather than try to acquire last-minute information via whispering.
3. Tell the teacher before class when he is not prepared and then will not be called upon to answer questions.

Of these three alternatives, the last is the least acceptable, and the teacher should reject it if Tom does not see its inappropriateness, because it forces the teacher to share responsibility for his action when, in fact, that responsibility belongs to him. It is important that Tom recognize that (1) the current situation is a result of his own behavior and (2) he can be extracted from the situation by engaging in behaviors that are both socially acceptable and conducive to achievement of his own and other people's success and happiness.

Have the Student Select and Implement a Specific Alternative. After Tom (perhaps with the teacher's help) has generated alternatives, he should decide which alternative to utilize. At this point, the teacher's role is to monitor carefully to determine how well Tom is following the plan and to offer supportive praise.

As was pointed out earlier, the differences between the operant conditioning approach to behavior modification and the reality therapy approach are many and significant. It is unlikely that both approaches will appeal to all teachers or that all teachers will be able to use both with equal effectiveness. It is suggested, therefore, that before either approach is decided upon, teachers assess their own philosophical position concerning classroom control and behavior modification. Haphazard or indiscriminate use of either or both of these procedures can not only be frustrating and futile, but it can also harm a teacher's rapport with students. Used properly, however, these procedures can enable teachers to bring about lasting behavioral changes.

THE THIRD PRINCIPLE—HAVE A REASONABLE PLAN
FOR DEALING WITH PROBLEMS

Earlier in the chapter we spoke of three principles. The first was that the goal of classroom management procedures should be the development of self-control among students. The second was that, given a choice, most people prefer to be successful rather than unsuccessful. The third principle is that the teacher should have a reasonable plan for dealing with problems. Regardless of how carefully teachers plan and how skillfully they conduct their lessons, there will still be minor disruptions of the ongoing classwork that can develop into major discipline problems. In the mind of every teacher is a conceptual model of an "ideal" instructional environment. Each teacher's model varies from those of other teachers, and some teachers are willing to tolerate a much broader range of deviant student behaviors than are others. Remember that it is the teacher who decides what a deviant behavior is. All teachers will find, however, that their typical classes will deviate, in one degree or another, from the ideal model and that there will be some points at which the degree of deviation approaches unacceptable levels.

When the teacher feels that some overt action is necessary to maintain a reasonable instructional environment, he or she must decide whether that action will cause a greater disruption than will the continuation of the deviant behavior. Jacob S. Kounin reports that teacher-initiated disciplinary acts (which he and his associates labeled "desists") can have significant effects on the other students in the class who are not the target of discipline. These effects have been called "ripple effects." In one study it was found that teachers who use angry or punitive desists often cause other students in the room to refocus their attention from the work at hand to the disturbance and the teacher's reaction to it. Simple reprimands, on the other hand, tend to have a lesser negative ripple effect.[12] Kounin also reported that interviews with high school students indicate that, if a teacher is viewed as fair and is generally liked by the students, his or her desist actions are less likely to cause ripple effects destructive to the teaching-learning environment.[13] One could conclude, therefore, that to deal successfully with most discipline problems, teachers should establish good rapport with their students and should use simple reprimands to deal with occasional deviant behavior. Mild desists can include actions such as moving toward disruptive students, standing by them, glancing at them, and directing questions at them, as well as direct reprimands. Further, reprimands should be in the form of direct statements rather than questions. "Would you please stop talking?" is less desirable than "Please stop talking," because it does not invite a verbal student response.

If the mild desists used are not effective, and the previously discussed preventive measures are being used, or if reality therapy or operant conditioning techniques have failed, the teacher needs a plan of action. In some schools, teachers are told exactly what disciplinary procedure to use. If such a policy exists, it should be followed precisely. If no complete policy exists, the teacher should develop one based on whatever policies do exist. The following procedure is predicated on the possibility that the student may need to be referred to the school disciplinarian, and it capitalizes on the fact that people tend to follow a leader who communicates a clear plan and a reasonable way to accomplish the plan.

1. *Each time a student engages in behavior that interferes with the teaching-learning process, he or she should be told to desist.* As was pointed out, if the teacher is respected and utilizes a mild reprimand, the danger of ripple effects will be minimal.

2. *If the deviant behavior persists, tell the student to remain in the room after the class is dismissed.* If the class precedes a lunch break or the end of the school day, the subsequent conference can be more leisurely. If the student is scheduled for another class immediately, the teacher should keep the conference as brief as possible and should write a note to the teacher of the student's next class explaining the tardiness. In either case the purpose of the conference should be to explain to the student that violations of proper classroom behavior have occurred and to attempt to obtain a commitment from the student that such misbehavior will not reoccur. (Note the difference between this tactic and its counterpart in reality therapy.) The conference should be brief, businesslike, and to the point. It should be recorded on an anecdotal record card with a specific explanation of the offense and date. The student should sign the card and the teacher should retain it. This will help convince the student that the teacher is serious and intends to follow through. The point is to convince the student that cooperation will be far less troublesome than noncooperation.

3. *If the offending student continues the disruptive behavior, schedule a mutually convenient time for a longer conference with the student.* The reason for assuring

that the time for the meeting is mutually agreeable is that students will find reasons why they cannot meet at teacher-decided times. The teacher should be willing to meet before, after, or at an appropriate time during the school day. Make sure that the student understands the commitment to meet. If there is any doubt about the student's showing up, make two copies of the time and place and mutually initial each copy.

It should be made clear to the student that such a conference is not synonymous with detention. The purpose of this conference is to review the student's offenses and to outline the consequences of future offenses. The teacher should explain why the offenses cannot be tolerated (because they disrupt the teaching-learning process and keep other students from learning). The focus of the conference should be on identifying and eliminating the misbehavior, not on the student personally. A record of the conference, offense, date, and so forth should be added to the anecdotal record card and the student should again sign the card.

At this point the student should begin to feel that the procedure and conferences are a bother (or even a little painful) and will also realize that the teacher means business. Notice that no punitive action has been taken. The emphasis is on changing the behavior of the student, not on punishing him or her. The student should be told at this point that further misbehavior will result in his or her parents' being contacted.

4. If the misbehavior persists, enlist the aid of the student's parents. Since the student was apprised, as part of step 3, of the consequences of continued misbehavior, he or she should not be surprised at the initiation of this step if the misbehavior persists. At the next offense, remind the student as he or she leaves the room that the parents will be contacted and their support enlisted. Once this step is announced it is important that the contact with parents be made as soon as possible, preferably before the end of the school day. If this is not done, the student may arrive home before the teacher's call and set a stage that is difficult or impossible to cope with. Once the contact is made, the teacher should go through the anecdotal record explaining the actions taken and enlisting support. A record of the home contact should be made on the anecdotal record card.

5. If the problem persists, the student is referred to the school disciplinarian. Before making this referral, contact the disciplinarian and discuss with him or her the anecdotal record with the list of offenses and corrective efforts. This is important because the disciplinarian must understand that the teacher has had a minimum of two conferences with the student and has contacted the parents. Once the disciplinarian understands that the problem is not superficial, he or she can try working with the student. If the disciplinarian decides upon some punitive action, the choice will be his or hers, not the teacher's.

6. Steps 3, 4, and 5 are repeated. Before referring the student to the office again, another conference should be held and another contact with parents made. This cycle should continue until (a) the student's behavior changes as home, class, and office pressures mount, (b) the disciplinarian removes the student from the class, (c) the school term ends, or (d) the student removes himself or herself from the class.

Obviously the teacher will be most satisfied if the student modifies the behavior voluntarily, but his or her primary responsibility is the education of the entire class, and if one student is thwarting that education and refuses to modify his or her behavior, the teacher is obligated to take all reasonable measures to fulfill the educational commitment to the rest of the class.

POTENTIALLY DANGEROUS PROBLEMS

It is probable that most teachers will eventually encounter what can be labeled a "potentially dangerous problem," for instance, fighting, verbal or physical abuse of staff members, drinking, drugs, overt defiance, sexual assault, or malicious destruction of property. In such a situation it is almost always too late to attempt remedial action. Because of the legal ramifications, such problems are handled best by experienced administrators. Unfortunately, it is not easy to decide the best course of action in these volatile situations. In some cases the student will be rational enough to proceed directly to the office alone. In other cases the teacher may need to accompany the student to the office. If escorting a student to the office entails leaving a class, the teacher should ask a nearby teacher to monitor the class. In many schools, classroom-office communication is possible and the teacher is able to summon help without leaving the room. The immediate goal is to keep the students from causing harm to themselves or to others.

HYPERACTIVITY AND CHEMOTHERAPY

Sometimes when teachers see a student who is continually restless, given to sudden outbursts, or unable to concentrate on the work at hand, they attribute it to hyperactivity. Hyperactivity is generally thought to be caused by the inability of an individual to assign priorities to the many sensory inputs constantly bombarding the brain. Most teachers are simply not qualified to diagnose such problems, but many try to do so anyway. What occasionally happens is that a teacher mistakes lapses of attention, restlessness, or even the normal exuberance of youth for hyperactivity. Having "diagnosed" the problem, the uninformed teacher may call the student's parents (or have the school nurse call them) and suggest that they take the student to a physician and "have the doctor give him something to control hyperactivity."

Unfortunately, some physicians will, after only a cursory examination, accept the teacher's "diagnosis" and prescribe a treatment on that basis. The typical treatment for hyperactivity is the prescription of amphetamines such as Ritalin and Dexedrine. Although these drugs act as stimulants for adults, they act as depressants for children. It is difficult to predict accurately the exact effect of any specific drug on any specific child, and many children are being adversely affected by such chemotherapy. Even worse, because of the increasing instances in which drugs are prescribed for students on the basis of inadequate diagnoses, many students are exposed to drugs who do not need to be.

If a teacher suspects that a student may be hyperactive, the initial step should be to double-check the basis for the suspicion. The procedures include keeping a written record of the frequency of each "hyperactive" act, checking with teachers to see if the student is demonstrating similar behavior in other classes, and engaging in discussions with the school nurse and guidance personnel to see if they have been told of any specific problems the student may be having.

If the suspected behaviors are persistent and not just isolated examples, the collected data should be discussed with the guidance department and nurse. If the results of this conference indicate that an examination by a physician is in order, then the parents should be involved in a separate conference in which such an examination is recommended. At this conference the parents are provided the list of incidents without suggestions that the student is hyperactive or that he or she needs drugs. The *doctor alone* should diagnose the problem and prescribe any treatment.

Assuming that the teacher is informed of treatment, it is then his or her responsibility to continue to monitor the student's behavior. In this way the effectiveness of the treatment can be determined and its eventual elimination hastened. The ultimate goal, of course, is to help the student to control his or her own behavior without the use of chemicals.

LEGAL TERMS AND ISSUES

In most cases, teachers are able to resolve classroom management problems quickly and easily. Few problems require the involvement of parents and even fewer require the involvement of school administrators. Nonetheless, situations that have legal ramifications may arise, so it is useful to know some of the legal terms that might be encountered.

"In loco parentis" is Latin for "in place of the parent." Courts of law generally recognize that a teacher acts in place of a parent during school activities. If a question is raised about the propriety of a given action, such as breaking up a fight or detaining a student to prevent him or her from engaging in a harmful act, the question that is most likely to be asked is whether the teacher acted as a *reasonable and prudent* parent would have acted. A judge or jury would answer that question on a case by case basis (case law) because each situation is likely to be unique.

In loco parentis offers some protection to teachers as they go about the task of helping students, but it does not offer immunity to bad judgment. For example, if a student confides in a teacher that he or she is taking drugs, the teacher is placed in an uncomfortable position. A reasonable and prudent person might be expected to try to get help for the student, perhaps by notifying his parents, a counselor, or a school administrator. If the teacher does not do this, and the student dies of a drug overdose, how would the teacher feel? His or her intervention might have saved a life. If it is school policy to report such situations and the teacher does not do so, he or she might be charged with negligence: "the omission to do something which a reasonable man, guided by those ordinary considerations which ordinarily regulate human affairs, would do, or the doing of something which a reasonable and prudent man would not do."[14] On the other hand, if the teacher does notify someone, students might perceive that action as a betrayal of trust, and that perception would seriously weaken the teacher's rapport with all students. The choices are not always easy.

Sometimes teachers witness illegal acts. For example, if a student is forced or frightened into giving his lunch money to another student, that action is not just "a shame," it is extortion: "the obtaining of property from another induced by wrongful use of actual or threatened force, violence, or fear, or under color of official right."[15] A student might also menace someone by showing "a disposition to inflict an evil or injury upon another."[16] A more serious threat is an assault: "any willful attempt or threat to inflict injury upon another, when coupled with an apparent present ability to do so (or) any intentional display of force such as would give the victim reason to fear or expect immediate bodily harm."[17] If the student actually carries out the threat and makes bodily contact, the offense of battery has been committed.

While teachers are rarely the victims of assault or battery, they are often the victims of slander. Slander is "the speaking of base and defamatory words tending to prejudice another in his reputation, office, trade, business, or means of livelihood."[18] Students sometimes say things about teachers that are not true. To the extent that such comments do not go beyond one or two students, they may be no cause for concern. If such comments or rumors become widespread, however, they may result in a formal or informal inquiry about the teacher. Depending upon how much trouble the comments or rumors cause, the teacher might consider filing charges of slander against the perpetrators. Libel is essentially slander in writing.

Sometimes, despite the best efforts of a teacher, it is necessary to remove a student from the classroom. A teacher usually has the right to remove a student for part or all of a class period by having the student go to some other supervised place in the school—a detention room or the main office. Such a removal is referred to as an in-school suspension. Because a teacher is legally responsible for a student while that student is assigned to his or her class unless some other appropriate adult assumes that responsibility, sending a student from the room as a disciplinary measure is unwise. Be sure that all students are appropriately supervised at all times.

A principal usually has the right to suspend a student from all activities for up to a week. The suspension may be an in-school suspension (the student comes to school but spends the time in a detention area usually away from other students) or an out-of-school suspension (the student is not allowed into the school during the suspension period). In-school suspensions are most often used when there is doubt as to who would be supervising the student if he or she were out of school.

Students who commit serious breaches of school rules are sometimes expelled. Expulsion is such a serious matter that most school boards take it upon themselves to impose that penalty. When a school board expels a student, it generally bans the student from attending school or school functions for a specified period of time and establishes the conditions upon which the student may return to school after the expulsion period.

SUMMARY

The goal of classroom management procedures should be to help students develop self-control. This development is facilitated by freeing students from as many restraints as possible. This freedom requires students to think about and control their own behavior rather than mindlessly following rules. Some teachers find that they can extend student freedom to the point of needing only one classroom rule: You may do whatever you like as long as you do not disturb anyone else.

The key to helping students develop self-control is to help them be successful. The first step in this process is to recognize basic human needs and plan the instructional program so that students can satisfy as many of those basic needs as possible. Abraham Maslow identified the following basic human needs: physiological, safety, love, self-esteem, and self-actualization. Physiological needs refer to the maintenance of life and may be reflected in a classroom by a student's need for a drink, for sleep, or to visit a restroom. Physiological needs are powerful enough to override other needs and often must be met immediately. Students sometimes use these same needs as excuses to avoid work or to disrupt class. In these cases, the teacher may speak privately to the student, expressing concern over the student's repeated need for water or the bathroom, and offer to refer the student to the school nurse (or a similar staff member) for a checkup.

Safety needs refer to physical safety. Concern over physical safety may surface in a class where a student refuses to participate in a particular activity, or it may relate to a fear of physical abuse from peers. It is important to remember that regardless of whether a student's fear is real or imaginary, it is real to the student. Students are often embarrassed about being afraid; the teacher should minimize the potential for embarrassment by working privately with the student to help him or her overcome the fear step by step. If fear keeps a student from completing a required objective, however, the student cannot be given credit for achieving that objective. With respect to safety, students should know, by the words and actions of the teacher, that they are safe both physically and psychologically in the classroom. Teachers can help students meet safety needs by establishing a routine and treating students as people with feelings.

Love needs refer to the kind of love shared by parents and children and as such has little relevance to the classroom. There is, however, at least one point of relevance. With the increasing number of divorces in the nation and the high mobility of the population, the classroom may be the only social unit with which a student can identify. Teachers should strive to make that environment as pleasant and nurturing as possible.

The need for self-esteem refers to the development of a positive self-concept, and it is the need that teachers can best help students meet. Self-esteem is founded on a sense of satisfaction about oneself. Teachers can help students achieve this sense of satisfaction by conveying to students that the work they are doing is serious and worthwhile. This can be done by developing a course syllabus that contains relevant objectives; setting up a calendar showing what will be covered when, due dates of papers, and test dates; and choosing appropriate grading criteria. On the first day of class this syllabus should be distributed to students and discussed. This approach lets students know that the teacher has given serious thought to the course and has outlined a reasonable plan for helping them achieve the objectives.

A student's sense of achievement is fostered by internal and external recognition of achievement, premised upon the student's attainment of some significant goal. The teacher, therefore, must be sure that the objectives of the course are set at a reasonably high level. If students feel they are improving their skills, abilities, or knowledge in ways that seem valuable to them, they win the internal recognition of achievement necessary for meeting self-esteem needs. External recognition refers to having others (such as parents, peers, or authority figures) acknowledge a student's achievement. Favorable grades, phone calls to parents (giving good news), and the sharing of students' work are ways of attending to the need for external recognition.

The highest need, self-actualization, refers to lifelong continual growth and improvement. Once again, the course objectives play a central role. If those objectives were formulated with long-term utility in mind, they will be seen as contributing to the satisfaction of the need for self-actualization.

Regardless of how diligently a teacher tries to help students meet their needs, classroom disruptions may still occur. One way to deal with them focuses on convincing students that such disruptions will not be tolerated and explaining the procedure that will be used to handle them. That procedure consists of first telling a student to stop the undesired behavior. If the behavior continues, the teacher begins an anecdotal record, which will document the student's name, the date, the problem, and what was done. The student may be asked to initial the entry to show that he or she is aware of it. If the problem persists after two or three private meetings with the teacher (each with its own entry in the anecdotal record), the student's parents will be contacted. If the problem persists after that, the school administration will be brought in. This course of action demonstrates to the students that the teacher means business, enables the teacher to follow a consistent, nonpunitive procedure, and documents the history of the problem and the attempts made to solve it. The teacher may try more specific procedures, such as operant conditioning and reality therapy.

With respect to legal issues, teachers will find that if they fulfill the responsibilities assigned to them and act as reasonable and prudent parents would act, they have little to fear from the courts. For example, the usual test applied in negligence suits is whether the teacher had a clear responsibility to the student, whether the teacher willfully failed to fulfill that responsibility, and whether the student suffered actual harm as a consequence of the teacher's failure to fulfill the responsibility. Teachers should not utilize corporal punishment because it is educationally unsound even if it is legal in their school district.

If teachers are humane and recognize that students have basic human needs that must be at least partly fulfilled, and if they establish and maintain a classroom management program aimed at helping students learn to control their own behavior so they can function as effective citizens in a democratic society, they will have few, if any, classroom management problems.

STUDY QUESTIONS

1. What should be the main goal of a classroom management program?
2. What are the arguments for and against having only a do-not-disturb-others rule?
3. Explain each of the levels of Maslow's hierarchy of needs and cite an example of how each level might apply to the classroom.
4. What is the relationship among teachers, administrators, school boards, state government, and the federal government with respect to establishing school rules?
5. What legal rights and obligations are conferred by "*in loco parentis*"?
6. What are the reasons for maintaining anecdotal records of behavior problems?

NOTES

1. A. H. Maslow, "A Theory of Human Motivation," *Psychological Review* 50 (1943): 370–396.
2. "Getting Tough," *Time* 131, no. 5 (Feb. 1, 1988): 54.
3. "Kids Who Kill and Are Killed," *NEA Today* 6, no. 7 (February 1988): 11.
4. Ibid.
5. Ibid.
6. "20th Annual Gallup Poll of the Public's Attitudes Toward the Public Schools," *Phi Delta Kappan* 70, no. 1 (September 1988): 32–46.
7. *Ingraham et al. v. Wright et al., United States Reports,* Cases Adjudged in The Supreme Court at October Term, 1976, Vol. 430 (Washington, D.C.: U.S. Government Printing Office, 1979), p. 651.
8. Maslow, "A Theory of Human Motivation," p. 382.
9. Anne Flowers and Edward C. Bolmeier, *Law and Pupil Control* (Cincinnati, Ohio: W. H. Anderson, 1964).
10. Sherman H. Frey, "Teachers and Behavior Modification," *Phi Delta Kappan* 55, no. 9 (May 1974): 635.
11. William Glasser, *Reality Therapy—A New Approach to Psychiatry* (New York: Harper & Row, 1965).
12. Jacob S. Kounin, *Discipline and Group Management in Classrooms* (New York: Holt, Rinehart and Winston, 1970), p. 49.
13. Ibid., p. 142.
14. Henry Campbell Black, *Black's Law Dictionary,* 5th ed. (St. Paul, Minn.: West, 1979), p. 930.
15. Ibid., p. 525.
16. Ibid., p. 1137.
17. Ibid., p. 105.
18. Ibid., p. 1244.

—10—

Individualizing Instruction

INTRODUCTION

Among the ideals continually advocated by educational theorists has been individualized instruction. Educational psychologists point out that, because every student is unique and has different readiness levels, teaching should ideally be individualized. The term "individualization of instruction" has, however, come to stand for a variety of ideas: (1) special individual lesson plans, (2) self-paced instruction, (3) self-selected curriculum, and (4) large-group instruction with individual help. This chapter explores possibilities for self-pacing via the use of self-instructional materials. It also presents, in the form of a self-instructional package, the fundamental steps necessary for building self-selected curriculum (one in which virtually all courses are selfselected).

SAMPLE OBJECTIVES

When you complete this chapter, you will be able, in writing, to:

1. Explain, in a paper of two pages or less, at least two advantages and two disadvantages of the use of self-instructional materials in your own teaching field (analysis).
2. Construct a self-instructional package that meets the criteria set forth in this chapter and is suitable for use in your teaching field (synthesis).

THE SYSTEMS APPROACH TO INDIVIDUALIZING

A self-instructional package approach can achieve self-pacing in a variety of ways. One is to operate separate classrooms as self-contained units wherein each teacher decides how to achieve the objectives. Another is to combine several classrooms, departments, or the entire school under one larger system for instruction. Whatever the administrative procedure adopted, systems approaches are based on the construction of sets of self-paced instructional packages that have objectives encompassing a variety of domains and levels. Following is a description of a typical middle school system's concept for self-instruction. It is not a description of any particular school but has elements of many that are in operation. Included are some of the processes necessary to engage in a changeover from a traditional school, although a more complete analysis is the province of texts on supervision or curricular development.

After achieving staff agreement (no easy chore in itself) that a thrust toward a self-paced systems program is desirable, the hypothetical school can initiate a first phase toward a gradual changeover. The recommended first step is an agreement among staff members of each department on the objectives of that department. These objectives will undergo the critical examination described in Chapters 2 and 3, including an analysis of terminal and en-route objectives, and identification of the necessary prerequisite skills for each objective identified.

After the identification of objectives, a procedure for building self-paced instructional packages and pilot testing is organized, using small numbers of students. No attempt is made at this point to convert classrooms to a systems approach. The packages are offered as supplements to or temporary replacements for the regular instructional program. The students' packages include built-in evaluation procedures for each constituent part (for example, questions such as "What learning activity was helpful?" and "Did you understand the objective?"). In this way, the packages are polished and improved.

As a department increases its stock of proven self-instructional packages to the point at which all objectives of a particular course are covered, that course may be put on a systems basis. Assume that there are three teachers of eighth-grade English during the third period each day. When self-instructional packages have been built for the entire course, the decision can be made to try the packages as a system that includes all three classes.

At this point the role of the teacher changes dramatically. The teacher's new responsibilities will focus on four basic activities. First, a teacher will have a responsibility to the system that replaces responsibility to a single class. For instance, instead of keeping track of grades for each student in the one class, a teacher may keep track of the packages completed by students in all three classes. In return, another teacher who previously kept track of materials for his or her own class may now keep track of materials for all three classes.

Second, the teacher will be expected to write new packages and to review old and new materials. Continual additions and improvements are necessary to keep a system viable. If there is a problem with a particular package, immediate alteration is required. The teacher most concerned with that particular package must be willing to modify it quickly to ensure success of the system. This package building implies a growing need for proficiency in the production and selection of media. Most packages need a variety of learning modes to be successful. As new information and ideas appear in the content areas, the teachers should be alert to the possibilities of including good new ideas in the packages. Microcomputers are ideally suited to use on a self-instructional basis.

Third, the teacher should expect to serve on content-area committees that will continue to examine the selection and evaluation of objectives in terms of overall school goals and community changes. A perfectly good set of terminal objectives for last year's student population may become obsolete because of the influx of a new type of student population during the course of the year. The committees may also consider many other issues connected with the operation of the system, such as new package adoption or revision of old packages.

Finally, the teacher becomes an advisor and counselor in addition to a content-area specialist. The student-teacher contacts become more one-to-one as the teacher assists each student with particular concepts or procedural details.

The role of the students also changes as they work through a course using self-paced materials. Assuming that the required objectives of the course have become the objectives of learning packages, the student may consult the teacher about which package should be worked on next. A plan and appropriate materials may already have been prepared individually for the student, and he or she may only need to consult that plan, or the student may consult a routing sheet that all students are following. After determining which is the next learning package, the student may select that package from his or her personal set of materials or may go to a central location and check out an individual package. Once the package is in the student's hands, work can begin.

Packages take a wide variety of forms, but most contain a preliminary statement of the skills that will be demonstrated upon completion of the package. If the student does not fully understand the precise instructional objective as stated, he or she will need the assistance of one of the teachers. At this point (depending upon the sophistication of the package), the student may take a preassessment test that will enable him or her to determine (1) which learning activities to complete, (2) which learning activities may be omitted because of prior knowledge, or (3) whether he or she already has the competency and can go immediately to the final evaluation instrument. In some cases a preassessment may be set up under test conditions, and the student may demonstrate the competency directly after or during preassessment.

After determining the specific learning activities designed to build the skill needed to demonstrate the competency, the student begins to work at these activities. It is at this point that many programs succeed or fail. The learning activities must be interesting. They need to include a variety of learning modes and should be based on sound learning principles. Films, filmstrips, guest speakers, records, multimedia kits, lab work, and field trips are just some of the learning modes that students can use to acquire skills and information. Reading is not the only option available in the self-instruction packages.

After completion of the learning activities, the student is ready for evaluation. Evaluation can take many forms. If it is to be a test, the student may acquire a copy of the examination from the teacher and go to a special area to take it, or the student may be tested at a central location in the school that has its own support staff. Results from this test should include feedback if the necessary minimum competency is not attained so that the student can determine which learning activities should be reemphasized or whether an alternative learning activity is more appropriate to specific needs.

The system for informing students of their progress and for keeping accurate records can range from individual record-keeping by teachers to a computer-oriented surveillance of an entire school. The information is vital for continuous process adjustment.

By blending a combination of required packages with a variety of self-choice packages, students can begin to have some control over curriculum content. Though it is obvious that eighth-grade students need to continue to write to improve competency in written communication skills, the choice of content—between science fiction and sports short stories for instance—can be left to the students if both types of literature will help them to attain the same skill competency.

THE EFFECT OF SELF-INSTRUCTIONAL PACKAGES ON THE CURRICULUM

The Purpose of Package Programs

The most persuasive reason for the increased popularity of self-instruction package programs is their potential for individualizing instruction. Although educators' implementation of this long-advocated position on individualization is far from complete, self-instructional packages provide an effective beginning.

A second reason for the implementation of self-instructional package programs is the opportunity they afford for rigorous curricular examination. When the question is asked, "What is the student going to be able to do after completing the self-instructional package?" the reply necessitates examination of a behavioral objective, and the result may be a clean-up of outdated curricular inclusions.

A third reason for self-instructional package programs is that they eliminate duplication of material and ensure inclusion of important material. It is well known that, when course guides are displayed for classes in the secondary school, they often do not reflect the actual teaching. Teachers may neglect certain content areas and overemphasize or reteach other areas. Self-instructional package programs eliminate this problem, since, once a student can demonstrate a competency, he or she need not rehash the old material again.

A fourth reason for considering the use of self-instructional materials is they can be of great use in meeting the needs of mainstreamed students. Since these students may need an individualized instructional program in some parts of the course, the use of self-instructional materials might help the teacher meet the needs of those students in an educationally sound and expeditious manner.

The Teacher as Advisor

When a self-instructional package program is underway, the teacher assumes a new set of responsibilities. Without describing in detail the extent of this change, it is worthwhile here to point out a new phenomenon in the relationship between student and teacher generated by a self-instructional package systems approach.

Under a traditional education system, the student's perception of the teacher-student role often approaches that of an adversary. The instructor assigns the work, teaches the class, administers tests, and hands out grades. The student competes with other students for attention and grades and learns that the teacher is the most powerful element in the process. Often, learning is inhibited by the threat of competition with peers, the possibility of alienation of the teacher, fear of the subject content, or previous unsuccessful experiences.

In a self-instructional package program, the student is not competing with peers but is striving to achieve a predetermined competency level. The teacher in this situation has the opportunity to work *with* the student to reach this mutual goal. The student's success becomes the teacher's success, and together they can take mutual pride as competency in each area is proven.

Teachers taking full advantage of this role possibility will find a more relaxed interchange building up between themselves and the students.

Packages as Enrichment Activities

One problem faced by all teachers handling large classrooms is how to accommodate the bright student who has conquered the current material. One common technique utilized by textbooks and teachers is to provide a set of topics and encourage the students to generate a project of their own. There are several disadvantages to this approach if a complete independent study program is not in effect. The first is that independent study projects can be a time-consuming enterprise for the teacher. Four or five active "independent scholars" in addition to a room filled with other students can increase the work load beyond feasibility. A second disadvantage is that, without structure, the topic limits and approach of the projects can easily get out of hand. A third problem is that at just about the time the bright student gets rolling on the project, the class has caught up and is starting work in a new area. The bright student must stop the project (generated from an interest in the last topic) and shift gears into the new area. Students may have lost interest by the time they are able to return to the old project.

Having a series of supplemental self-instructional packages for each topic can offer relief for several of these problems. The student may pick among them according to interest and, because of their calculated length, complete as many as time permits before the next unit.

Things do not always go in practice exactly as in theory, so there will be occasions when there will not be enough packages and more will have to be built and other occasions when the student will assert that none of the possible packages is interesting. But a self-instructional package program can certainly assist in providing enrichment for many bright youngsters.

Remedial Use of Packages

When there is no point in having a student continue in a classroom topic because he or she has fallen too far behind, the student can be shifted to a self-instructional package program on an individual basis. This technique is applicable in those instances where the course is broken down into discrete topics. In these instances, the student need not continue in frustration in that unit but can move to a series of slightly less difficult objectives in a self-instructional package program where he or she can experience success. When a new topic is started, the student can be shifted back to the classroom with a fresh start in that topic.

When the class content builds throughout the year and each new piece of information depends upon mastery of the previous information, the student may be shifted to a self-instructional package program at the point at which learning from class presentations is no longer profitable. That is, enough new terminology and concepts are being used in the course of instruction that the student does not benefit from the presentations. The student may or may not be on a package program for the rest of the course. In some instances, the self-instructional package program may allow him or her to catch up with the class. Even then, however, the student often prefers to stay in the package program because of the success experienced.

Extended Absence

In some instances when self-instructional package programs are available as a counterpart to the traditional classroom situation, the student who is absent because of illness or other circumstances can keep pace with the class by undertaking self-instructional package programs at home. One drawback, of course, is that packages are often not self-contained and refer the student to other material, which must be obtained from the school, the public library, or other sources. In addition, when the packages have several possible learning modes, students may be faced with the problem that the best learning modes for them are available only at school. In spite of these obstacles, many students while physically away from school have been able to keep up with their schoolwork through the use of self-instructional packages.

Partial Package Programs

In some classrooms teachers are blending packages with regular classroom instruction. In one popular approach to partial programs, the students are involved in topics related to the content of the regular class during time opened specifically for self-instructional packages. Students might be doing traditional classwork on Monday, Wednesday, and Friday; on Tuesday and Thursday, however, they work on any of the several available self-instructional packages. During this time they operate independently and are given credit for competencies gained.

A second approach has the self-instructional packages built more closely into the curricular content of the traditional class. There may be less of a variety of selfinstructional packages, sometimes as few as three or four, and they are reproduced in enough quantity so that the class may be broken into groups by interest areas or ability.

Each group area works on the related self-instructional packages for a portion of the time. In some cases, students can start the self-instructional packages with some group work and then branch out to individual work. In other instances, a subgroup of students with the same self-instructional package can be brought together during the work period for a particular learning activity and then returned to individual work.

Modified Systems Programs

Some programs combine aspects of a traditional classroom with a total systems approach. Various procedures are used but only one is examined here.

Students are broken into three groups, and each individual starts to work on the self-instructional package assigned to that group. The time allotted for completion of the package is enough so that about two-thirds of each group will have demonstrated the competency by a specified date. During these work periods, occasional compulsory traditional classes may be held as part of the learning activities described in the package. At the end of the allocated time, the two-thirds of the students who demonstrated the competencies move on to the next set of self-instructional packages. The one-third who did not yet complete the package join with those students just beginning it and move through the activities again with the new group. In this fashion a student will have three "cycles" to complete a self-instructional package in which some of the learning activity is based on traditional classroom-type instruction. After a particular package is repeated three times, other forms of instruction are substituted for the classroom part of the learning activities.

MODEL OF A SELF-INSTRUCTIONAL PACKAGE

Part 1: Objective for Model Package 1

Following a model and a set of instructions, you will be able to construct a self-instructional package in your content area suitable for use by pupils and containing a minimum of five prescribed elements listed in this package. These elements must exhibit the minimum qualitative criteria described in the evaluation section of this package (synthesis).

Part 2: Self-Preassessment

If you have already built one or more self-instructional packages, you may compare them with the criteria in the evaluation sections to see if they meet the criteria. If so, they may be submitted to your instructor for evaluation. Since you were not working with the instructor on the project, be prepared to answer technical questions about it to demonstrate clearly that it is your own work. Even if you have already built an instructional package, you may wish to build another to satisfy this competence, because (1) the more times you work at this skill the better you will become, and (2) no teacher ever has enough self-instructional packages to satisfy all the needs of students.

Part 3: Learning Activities

You will:

1. Study the section "Constructing Self-Instructional Packages" found in this package.
2. After this preparation, you are ready to begin construction of your package. Follow the steps described in the section "Constructing Self-Instructional Packages" and in the evaluation section of this package.
3. Use the "Checklist for Constructing Self-Instructional Packages" to check each component of your package.
4. Schedule a help session with your instructor if you feel it is necessary.

LEARNING ACTIVITY 1:
CONSTRUCTING SELF-INSTRUCTIONAL
PACKAGES

This self-instructional package on self-instructional packages will serve as our model to guide you step by step in the construction of your own self-instructional package. You will want to prepare your own with care so you can use it in your work.

We shall build each of the four basic divisions in the self-instructional package separately, always being careful that each step focuses exactly on the objective. Before we are done, your self-instructional package should at least include

1. A clear, precise instructional *objective.*
2. A procedure for students to *preassess* their ability in the subject area and guide themselves to appropriate activities.
3. An interesting set of *learning activities* that will build the student's ability as described in the behavioral objective.
4. An *evaluation process* that will assess whether or not the student has acquired the competency described in the behavioral objective.

In addition to these four basic sections, your self-instructional package may include other elements, such as

1. A list of materials that the student will need to complete the package.
2. An enrichment section to guide the student to additional activities in the same content area.

3. A discussion of the approximate time needed to complete the entire package or parts of the package.
4. A rationale explaining why it is important for the student to acquire the skills or information described in the objective.
5. Optional learning activities to help students attain the objective, not necessary if the student engages adequately in the required learning activities.
6. Self-evaluation prior to the final evaluation to provide feedback of competency before actual attempts are made at final evaluation.
7. A section early in the package alerting the student to schedule certain items in advance, for instance, when any learning experiences involve scheduling a room, special material, or group sessions.
8. Any other sections that may seem appropriate because of the unique nature of the content of a particular package.

CREATING THE PACKAGE

In theory, a package could evolve from mutual student and staff recognition of curricular need. For instance, it could become apparent in a home economics class that students lacked ability in personal money management. If enough students felt frustrated because of personal money mismanagement, a self-instructional package on that topic would evolve.

Since you may not yet have had enough practical experience to be able to identify areas of student frustration in your own teaching field, simply select some topic in which you are interested (or which may have caused you some difficulty) and use that topic as the basis for your self-instructional package.

Step 1. From a school library, obtain a typical text in your content area that might be used in a high school. Locate in that text a topic you find interesting. If you choose, you may utilize sources of content material other than a textbook.

Step 2. Translate this content into precise instructional objectives. At this point you may need to review Chapters 2 and 3 to write good instructional objectives. You should include more than just lower-level cognitive objectives. In the objectives for this model package, there are both knowledge-comprehension objectives and higher-level objectives. You may particularly wish to review the part of Chapter 3 dealing with the taxonomic levels in the cognitive domain before proceeding.

Suppose you are an industrial arts teacher and you have chosen to develop your self-instructional package somewhere in the area of metalwork. In looking through the chapter on "Layout Tools," you decide that a self-instructional package could be built on the use of inside calipers. There seems logically to be two levels to a self-instructional package on this topic: first, we wish the student to comprehend information *about* calipers; and second, we wish him or her to be able to *use* calipers. After some thought, objectives such as the following are generated:

1. After studying specific material on the care and use of inside calipers, the student will be able to demonstrate comprehension of that material by answering correctly nine out of ten written completion-type questions.

2. When presented with a set of inside calipers, a steel rule, and a piece of iron with five holes drilled in it, the student will be able to use the calipers to measure the inside diameter of four of the five holes to within one-sixty-fourth of an inch.

The first objective is at a skill level lower in the cognitive domain than that required in the second objective. The second objective is a combination of the cognitive skill *application* (level 3) and psychomotor skills.

This procedure of delineating what you wish your student to be able to do after the instruction should cause you some real thought and introspection. Do not be satisfied with an objective because it was easy to build. Try to analyze what it is that you really wish the student to be able to do and translate that into words that communicate powerfully. The student should be able to understand immediately from the objective what competency will have to be demonstrated. If some of the words used in the objective are complicated and are only later defined in the material in the learning activities, it is absurd to assume the objective will perform its intended function.

Step 3. Although the order of the self-instructional package as used by the student has the preassessment section next, you are generally better off arranging the rest of your self-instructional package first and then returning to build the preassessment. This enables you to set the link-ups to the corresponding learning activities from each part of the preassessment activity.

Let us return to our example. We ask ourselves, "How can I transmit the necessary background information about the use and care of inside calipers most easily to the student?" and "What alternative learning procedures for this objective can be made?" Some of the possible ways to transmit this information are by having the student

1. Read material from a text.
2. Read articles on the subject from trade magazines.
3. Read specially produced material prepared by the teacher (usually the material most precisely tuned to your objectives).
4. Listen to commercially produced audio tapes on the subject.
5. Listen to audio tapes produced by the teacher.
6. Modify items 4 and 5 of this list by listening to the tape(s) while viewing accompanying handouts.
7. View a filmstrip made either commercially or locally.
8. View and listen to a tape-slide presentation—either commercially or teacher-produced.
9. Refer the learner to a student who already has the competency. The "tutor" uses a special guide to make sure all the points required are covered and receives some credit for successful demonstration of the competency by the "pupil."
10. Arrange short help sessions during lulls in the class for the students who have signed up on a special sheet.

11. View and listen to a filmstrip on the subject while filling out an accompanying worksheet that emphasizes the important points in the filmstrip.
12. Engage in a single linear programmed learning sequence covering the material.
13. Engage in a more complex, branched program using a microcomputer.
14. Engage in any other learning activity deemed appropriate.

After you decide upon instructional modes for the learning activity, the material that will make the learning activities come alive must be built. For the first objective, in which the student is learning about the care and use of calipers, let us assume that the learning activity chosen is a teacher-prepared sound filmstrip. All the content material is gathered and arranged into a script. The script is then recorded on a tape cassette. It is found that the entire taped content runs twelve minutes. Simple photographs are then taken of the main points emphasized in the script, and the student is told in the script when to move to the next slide. A good way to focus on the important points would be to have an accompanying worksheet, which students could fill out as the tape-slide sequence is viewed and from which they could later study.

Some teachers are concerned about their work being of professional quality. It certainly does not hurt for the slides to look as though they came out of a magazine and for the voice on the script to sound like Richard Burton, but it is not necessary to have perfection in order to have a high degree of learning take place. In fact, students identify with everyday photos of other students used in the slides and respond to the taped voice of someone they know. Using a tape cassette, a set of slides clearly numbered from 1 to 30, and a simple hand-held slide viewer can be as effective as a slick professional treatment. If alternate learning activities are desired, the script may become reading material generously illustrated with the prints and made available as checkouts from the materials center.

For purposes of learning to *use* the inside calipers, it is obvious that the student should engage in the equivalent practice necessary to gain the proficiency. For this, the second objective points clearly to the self-instructional learning activity required. A series of various-sized holes are drilled into pieces of metal and identified with a key. Students simply engage in the necessary amount of practice until they are measuring the inside diameter of the holes correctly. (Our example objective's criterion level is probably too low, since after one gets the "feel" and some practice with inside calipers and micrometers, measurements accurate to within 0.005 inch should be possible.)

This objective happens to align itself well with the equivalent practice, providing immediate feedback to students. Other learning activities, such as this self-instructional package on building self-instructional packages, may not be so easy to design. For instance, if a student uses this book independently, the only way to check the objectives designed for the package is to compare them with the objectives in this package, the objectives at the beginning of many of the other chapters, and the samples in Chapters 2 and 3. If a student uses this book in conjunction with a class, the instructor should also be able to give advice as to the appropriateness of objectives and the rest of the self-instructional package.

You should now try your hand at building your instructional learning activities. It may be that your objective leads you to a particular activity. You may want to ask yourself the following questions to guide your choice and work:

1. Are the materials necessary for building the activity available?
2. Is the importance of the objective large enough to warrant multimodal activities?
3. Is the target population of students who will use the package confined to a particular level, thereby restricting the range of the possible learning activities?
4. What restrictions does the content of the objective place upon learning activity development?
5. What do I know about learning activities that have been used for this content area in the classroom that will be effective for a self-instructional package?

After building the learning activities, it may be possible, even though the entire package is not complete, to explain the objectives to a small sample population and obtain suggestions improving the learning activities. A trial run can often save a lot of headaches. It can be especially helpful to ensure the alignment of the objective with the learning activities. You may also be able to get ideas from your peers or your instructor at this point to help polish the activities.

Step 4. Without forgetting that we will return to build our preassessment section, the next step is to design the evaluation for our self-instructional packages.

Whatever skills we described in our objective will be checked to ensure that the student can now demonstrate the described competency at the minimum criterion level. The first objective in our example leaves little doubt about our check. We wanted the student to show comprehension of facts about the care and use of inside calipers, and we were willing to accept as a demonstration of that competency "correctly answering nine out of ten written completion-type questions." We have left out of the objective other conditions surrounding the demonstration of the competency, so the first thing our evaluation section should do is communicate any and all conditions. Let us assume that there is a test center in this school, so the instruction may be something like, "When you have completed the learning activities, filled out your worksheet, and feel that you understand the material, report to the test center for the short completion exam on this material. If it is the first time that you have taken the exam, ask for Test #0034 on *Calipers*—Form I. If you have taken the test before, ask for Form II. You will be expected to complete nine out of ten completion questions correctly on this test."

If we had decided to include a trial test, then the preceding instruction would be modified to encourage the student to take this self-administered trial test and check his or her work against provided model answers. In this circumstance the trial-test answers would direct the student to the approximate part of the worksheet for review in case of missed answers.

A sample item of the form described in the objective might be, "An inside caliper is a two-legged, steel instrument with its _____ bent outward." (See Learning Activity 2, slide 4, or Learning Activity 3, page 5 for review.) Answer: Legs.

The second objective also leads us to an obvious evaluation. It implies the use of inside calipers, a rule, and a piece of metal with holes drilled in it. The operation of the typical test center may or may not preclude the student from using these materials there. Let us assume that we cannot use the test center. Then our instructions might read: "When you have completed the learning activities in this self-instructional package and you feel that you can successfully use inside calipers to measure the inside diameter of holes drilled in metal, ask your instructor for the steel bar for testing and the test answer sheet for this objective. Bring a 6-inch steel rule and an inside caliper with you at this time. You will need to measure four out of five holes to within one-sixty-fourth of an inch to demonstrate this competency."

If you know that you will be involved in a self-instructional package program with certain restrictions, build them into your instructions. For instance, if you know that you will be evaluating only on Tuesdays and Fridays, then say so in your evaluation section.

A much less satisfactory procedure for this objective would be to describe and illustrate a series of inside caliper measures on a straight written test administered in the test center. In this instance the student would answer questions about the descriptions and pictures. We could assume that, if the student could honestly answer such questions, he or she could find the inside diameter of drilled holes. Such assumptions are risky and should be avoided, although analogous situations can be found throughout school systems.

You should now build your evaluations for your self-instructional package. The trial test is a sound procedure and should be used if possible. Make sure test items are straightforward and clear. At this point you may wish to refer to the section in Chapter 9 on evaluation for guidance in the construction of criterion-referenced test items.

It is often hard to determine initially how well the student must perform on a new test instrument on untried learning activities. Fortunately, as your skill as a package writer increases, your intuitive notions about the proper criterion level will increase rapidly. A flat 80 percent proficiency level for all tests in a system is unrealistic. It is obvious that for this purpose alone, conducting trial runs is worth the effort.

Step 5. We are now ready to return to the preassessment section. We have postponed it until now because, even though the behavioral objectives in your package tell you exactly what the students are going to be able to do at the end of instruction that they could not do before, they do not consider the instructional approach to be used. Building the learning activities and the evaluation section has structured an approach to help the student achieve the objectives, and this approach can now provide a basis for sequencing and referencing preassessment questions.

There are many facets to the problem of preassessment. Chapter 4 covers several approaches to rapid assessment for the readiness of individuals for learning. For our purpose we are interested in giving students a procedure to judge their own knowledge and skills in relation to the knowledge and skills presented in the package. Two procedures are often used. One is to ask a series of questions about the content. Students go through the questions carefully and attempt to answer them. Whenever they encounter a question they cannot answer, they can refer to a designated section in the accompanying articles. If students find that they cannot answer very many questions, then it is definitely best simply to start with the learning activities and go through them. If students know that they learn best from an alternative mode to reading, the slide filmstrips and audio tapes that accompany those learning activities can be used. If students know most of the answers and choose to use the preassessment to figure out which portions of the material they need to cover, the slide filmstrip and the audio tapes are more difficult to survey to find various parts. Therefore, it probably would be best to begin at the beginning, review all the material, and *empha-size* the parts that the questions have referred them to.

A second type of preassessment is described for this self-instructional package. In this case, the evaluation will be of a product—a self-instructional package. The student either has or has not completed a self-instructional package in the past. If he or she has and if it meets the qualitative criteria listed in the evaluation section, the student may immediately submit it to the instructor for demonstration of the competency.

Various procedures are acceptable for preassessment purposes. In some packages concerned primarily with a very specific set of facts, the preassessment, trial test, and final test may be virtually the same instrument. For instance, in the case of a set of precise safety rules for the chemistry lab, when the rules are specific enough and 100 percent competency is mandated, the three test instruments may be changed only enough to ensure comprehension and to avoid the rote memorization of a list of correct answers.

Going back to our example of the inside calipers, let us describe a third alternative. For purposes of illustration, assume that the shop teacher has a senior student who has majored in metalwork and is now a student assistant. For our preassessment we ask the students who believe they can use inside calipers to see the student assistant to demonstrate their ability. The assistant has a short checklist, and the pupils who feel that they already have the proficiency simply demonstrate each skill on the list. If they reach a certain level on the checklist, they need not engage in the package.

If this package is one of many covering the use of hand tool skills, the preassessment process could be the same for all of the packages. If that is clearly understood by all students, then there need not be any mention of preassessment in each of the separate packages. Instead, the condition can be announced generally and posted. On the other hand, it is always a good idea to repeat any uniform instruction in each package, so that nothing is left to chance and the instructor is protected.

At this point you should build your preassessment procedure and any instruments for the procedure. You will then have the four basic parts to your package completed; again, a trial run to check the complete flow is encouraged.

Step 6. From the trial runs and self-analysis you may now have the feeling that other embellishments are needed to make the package complete. You may want to go back to the introduction of this article on "Constructing a Self-Instructional Package" and review some of the additions that are often helpful. For instance, this model package has a checklist to use when constructing your own package.

In our running example of the inside calipers, students may be alerted in a separate early section of the self-instructional package to schedule their final evaluation (proving they can use the inside calipers accurately) the day before the demonstration is to take place. This will enable the evaluator to schedule a mutually convenient time and to be sure all needed materials are on hand.

Step 7. Before turning in your self-instructional package for final evaluation, use the Learning Activity 2 checklist to make sure you have included all the minimum requirements for a successful package.

*LEARNING ACTIVITY 2: CHECKLIST FOR BUILDING
A SELF-INSTRUCTIONAL PACKAGE*

1. Does your self-instructional package contain the minimum requirements of (a) precise instructional objective(s), (b) preassessment, (c) learning activities, and (d) evaluation?
2. Do the objectives contain
   a. An observable terminal behavior that tells students what they should be able to do after completing the package?
   b. A minimum acceptable standard that explains how well they must be able to accomplish the objective?
   c. The conditions that describe the circumstances under which they will demonstrate the competence described in the objective?
3. Is the objective a valid one for the field?
4. Can the objective be evaluated in precise terms?
5. Does the preassessment section describe a procedure that will give the student the necessary information to determine their background in relation to the anticipated outcomes?
6. Is the procedure described in the preassessment section workable and not cumbersome?
7. Are there a variety of learning activities available in the learning activities section?
8. Can the student locate the cited material easily?
9. Do the learning activities concentrate on preparing the student to be able to accomplish the objective with a minimum of digression?
10. Are the learning activities designed at a level the student can understand?
11. Are the learning activities lively and interesting?
12. Does the evaluation truly check the competency described in the objective?
13. Will the evaluation tell the student and the teacher where the breakdown in learning occurred if the competency described in the objective is not demonstrated?
14. Are the instructions for the evaluation stated clearly so that there is no question in the mind of the student as to how to proceed?
15. Are all the additional sections you have included necessary?
16. Would additional sections be helpful?

Part 4: Evaluation

The evaluation of this objective is a judgment as to whether or not a package constructed by you meets the following minimum qualitative criteria:

1. One or more objectives that contain an observable behavior, conditions under which the behavior will be exhibited, and the criteria upon which it will be judged.

2. A preassessment of the competence already possessed by the student in the area described in the objectives. The preassessment should guide the student to the appropriate learning activities.

3. Precise learning activities (at least two), explained so that students clearly know what they are to do to acquire the competency. These learning activities will preferably have more than one instructional mode so that the students may select instructional procedures they enjoy or learn from best.

4. An evaluation description with precise directions as to exactly how the student will be evaluated, including where to go, whom to see, and to whom to submit products.

5. Evaluation instruments. If the evaluation is to be a test, then that test must be prepared. If the evaluation is to be the assessment of a skill, then a checklist to guide assessment should be prepared. If the evaluation is to be the construction of a product, then a model and qualitative criteria should be provided.

6. Internal consistency. The objectives, preassessment, learning activities, and evaluation should all zero in on the same competency. Material extraneous to that goal and subtle differences in the thrust from one section to another must be eliminated.

7. Any or all of the supplemental parts of packages that are mentioned in the article "Constructing Self-Instructional Packages," such as worksheets, checklists, and self-tests, may be included.

8. Compliance with the "Checklist for Building a Self-Instructional Package" found in this package.

When you are done with your package, make sure that you have covered items 1 through 8 of this list of qualitative criteria and see that you have complied with all of them. If appropriate, turn in your completed package to your instructor for final evaluation.

SUMMARY

The phrase *individualizing instruction* refers to a variety of educational procedures generally aimed at providing instruction geared to the needs of individual students. In this chapter we have applied the term to the idea of self-pacing through the use of self-instructional packages.

Self-instructional packages are useful for presenting new information, but they are used more frequently to provide remedial or enrichment material. The basic parts of a self-instructional package are (1) precise instructional objective(s), (2) a preassessment section, (3) a learning activities section, and (4) an evaluation section.

It is important to keep in mind that, though self-instructional packages can be highly effective instructional and motivational tools, students still profit from the teacher's attention. In the final analysis, people learn best from people.

STUDY QUESTIONS

1. Some educators have advocated the idea that, in spite of the enormous cost, one-on-one instruction should be provided for every child. Is such an idea feasible? What are its pros and cons?

2. The systems approach is another name for a form of competency-based education. What are the fundamental differences between competency-based education and traditional education? Which is superior? Why?

3. Many educators believe that some content areas cannot be taught effectively using a systems approach. What could be some of these areas? How could they be taught in a more individualized way other than the systems approach?

4. A school is changing over to a systems approach for all its classes. Please discuss some of the potential problems of the change and ways they could be solved. Include considerations of cost and the reactions of teachers, students, and administrators.

5. Systems approaches have been criticized because of the problems of monitoring the students' progress. If the competency to be demonstrated is not evaluated by a paper-and-pencil test, then some special procedure must be organized. What are some of the competencies that would be difficult to evaluate? How could the problems be solved?

6. Assume that a package program has been initiated. The minimum competencies have been identified and packages for each designed and constructed. Now students are working at their own pace. The able and ambitious students are finishing the complete series with three and four weeks left in the semester. What are some ways to handle these students?

__11__

The Management
of Co-Curricular
Activities

INTRODUCTION

A secondary school principal once asked the staff of his school to rank each subject-matter area and various student co-curricular activities according to how well they helped students reach the goals described in the seven cardinal principles: health, command of the fundamental processes, worthy home membership, vocation, citizenship, proper use of leisure time, and ethical character.

After their responses, it became obvious that the co-curricular activities program was a crucial factor in the school's attempts to meet those goals. Even the teachers most adamant about the sanctity of the classroom and the importance of their subject admitted that, overall, the co-curricular activities program was meeting more needs than any one subject area.

SAMPLE OBJECTIVES

When you complete this chapter you will be able, in writing, to:

1. Describe in your own words at least three common arrangements for student government structure in a typical secondary school (knowledge, comprehension).
2. Given an application for student council cash boxes for a club sale, fill out the application and describe procedures for obtaining the cash box (comprehension, application).
3. Given a hypothetical assembly theme, organize a program that will be entertaining to a group of high-school students and involve all members of the hypothetical club you are sponsoring (synthesis).

4.   Given a hypothetical club situation in which a club is deciding upon which of several objectives to pursue, judge which of several suggested objectives would be of most benefit to the students to adopt and defend that choice by submitting at least four logical rationales (evaluation).

5.   After selecting a hypothetical sponsorship role, write a series of at least six precise instructional objectives appropriate to the club or activity being sponsored (synthesis).

EXTRA PAY

One of the problems that must be faced in regard to teacher participation in co-curricular activities is the continuing controversy over extra pay. For many years, it was assumed that all teachers should participate in a minimum amount of co-curricular activities sponsorships and that this responsibility would be divided approximately equally among the staff. As certain activities took more and more time, the notion of extra pay evolved. Usually the athletic staff was the first to receive extra money. Then the band director was awarded a few extra dollars. This was soon followed by the drama teacher (three plays a year), the sponsor of the yearbook, and so on.

There is no easy solution to the problem of extra pay because it is so difficult to make extra pay equitable. As an example, about the time an extra-pay schedule is closely reflective of the actual work put in by staff members, one of the staff may retire. Perhaps he is the choir director and received $250 extra pay for directing the choir at two PTA meetings, one music concert in conjunction with the school band, and the Winter assembly. He is replaced by a young, energetic teacher who attracts many students into the choir, adds an a capella choir after school, raises funds from the community, and organizes a series of assembly presentations at neighboring schools. Everyone is happy with the new publicity the school is receiving. The parents are pleased at the attention given their children, and the new teacher organizes an "awards banquet" at the end of the year, giving small trophies to the "most outstanding choir member," "most inspirational," and so on.

The next year the board of education wants to raise the extra pay for choir directors to reward this teacher for all his hard work, but in the other high school in the district, the choir director is continuing with just the usual two PTA meetings, one musical concert in conjunction with the school band, and the Winter assembly.

An exaggerated case? Not at all. Besides, even if the board could raise the salary of the choir director at one school and not the other, at about that time the teacher may very well have been recognized as outstanding and have been offered a job at the local community college as choir director at an increased salary.

What happens when extra pay is in the salary schedule? The school district usually has a specific amount of money for paying salaries. In some instances, without realizing it, teachers who want extra pay are taking dollars from all teachers and redistributing those dollars to a few. On the other hand, if everyone is given extra pay, schools may as well be back on a salary schedule without extra-pay considerations included.

In some schools no extra pay is given, but teachers who involve themselves heavily in co-curricular activities are given fewer classes to teach. That is, if the normal daily load is six forty-five minute classes, the varsity football coach may only teach three physical education classes and then start coaching at the beginning of the last period of the day. Often, the band and choir are scheduled classes. With modular scheduling, more of this type of time compensation for teachers is possible.

TYPES OF SPONSORSHIP

A teacher in a secondary school usually becomes involved in various kinds of co-curricular activities programs. Some patterns of co-curricular organization key all activities around the school to clubs, which sponsor all the dances, sales, and the like. In other schools, the student government seems to be the driving force behind activities. In large schools, often a teacher has emerged in a subtle or recognized administrative capacity as activity director, and all activities seem to emerge from his or her office. Regardless of the organization, however, the following descriptions are typical of the possible involvement a teacher can choose.

Clubs

The quality and quantity of clubs on a high school campus vary tremendously. Few campuses have no clubs. Some seem to have many clubs, but they function in name only, holding few meetings and conducting few or no activities. Others have a number of very active clubs. Clubs function best and will involve sponsors and students most when they are an outgrowth of a subject-matter field. It is probably difficult not to find at least a remote link between any special-interest club and some aspect of the curriculum, but the more remote the link, the more tenuous the position of the club. In addition, the strength of the club and its members is almost always related to the sponsor: weak sponsor, weak club. In some instances, it is the special interest of a sponsor that makes a club successful, and when the sponsor leaves the school, the club disbands.

A comprehensive list of clubs is impossible, but a few here deserve comment.

CLUB	COMMENT
Foreign language clubs	In larger schools there is often a French club, a Spanish club, etc. In small schools one club seems to work. Events held might include the Roman banquet and assisting in the foreign exchange-student program.
Science clubs	Sometimes broken into more specific areas (e.g., physics club), these are usually active in getting students involved in science fairs and field trips.

CLUB	COMMENT
Girls' athletic associations	Most girls' physical education departments organize an active club that not only sponsors on-campus activities but also engages in intra- and/or intermural sports. With current reemphasis on girls' participation in sports, blending of girls' and boys' athletic clubs is taking place.
Lettermen clubs	The athletic program in a school may sponsor several clubs. Sometimes a big football school will have a separate club for football players only. This fragmentation is unnecessary, with the athletic club logically being involved in the annual sports awards banquets.
Pep club	On some campuses pep club membership is a prerequisite to being a drill team member or yell or song leader. This group often arranges for buses to away games and involves itself in rallies.
Forensics	Many schools have debate as a part of their regular curriculum and as co-curricular activities. Involvement of members (as with athletics) can become intense.
Thespians	A drama club usually emerges if the drama classes result in well-received productions. As with the forensics, national affiliations are possible.
Industrial arts	Often broken down into subclubs such as "car clubs," these clubs provide more opportunity for students to use shop equipment on their own time with school supervision.
Creative writing club; library club	Except for forensics, the English department of most schools generally has trouble generating a real special-interest group. Membership is usually small. When successful with such a club, the publicity can be a positive force for the club and school.
Math club	The math clubs on some campuses have become very active. Interschool competitions have emerged in some areas.
Glee club; pep band	Sometimes much of the music program on a campus is in the form of co-curricular activities. Members of clubs of this nature can receive important reinforcement from their public appearances.
Foreign exchange-student clubs, world friendship club, field services	Clubs with a singular purpose in mind, to bring a foreign exchange student to the school and to send students to other lands, often are very successful. Their objectives are defined.

CLUB	COMMENT

Other clubs
  Ski club
  Chess club
  Scuba diving club
  Sailing club
  Riding club
  Surfing club, etc.
	These clubs have more trouble linking themselves directly to a specific content area of most school curriculum. They live and die in terms of their sponsors. Many of these needs can be filled through sponsorship by an outside organization or agency other than the school.

Student Government

Teachers may also sponsor student government. The structure of student government varies considerably from school to school, but the most common organization is one that roughly approximates that of the U.S. government. That is, an "executive" branch is composed of the student body president, vice president, secretary, treasurer, and so on. The "legislative" branch is made up of a representative from each homeroom, a particular academic area such as social science class, or a representative from each class operating at a specified time of day. Often a "judiciary" branch is supposed to interpret the associated student body constitution, make parliamentary rulings, and run elections. In a very few schools there is a student court system, but success with peers' standing in judgment of peers sometimes is fraught with problems. As a counterpart to the state governments, each grade level usually has a set of elected officers that meet and generally hold one or two functions each year. For instance, a junior class may conduct the junior-senior prom as its big annual event.

There is usually a "student council" or "cabinet" composed of various representatives that meets regularly. A typical structure might be composed of the student body officers, representatives from the pep squads, and the presidents of the classes. Sponsors may be assigned to any of these subsections of student government. Generally, one or the other of them emerges with the real control over student affairs, often the student council or cabinet. Sometimes this group meets daily as a class in "leadership" or "government" and because of this consistency can play and execute a wide variety of events more thoroughly than can other government segments limited to after-class meeting times.

Pep Groups

Teachers also sponsor the band, pep band, drill team, song leaders, yell leaders, flag twirlers, baton units, and the like. Sometimes all these meet during a period of the day under the direction of the band leader. In other schools, the band and drill team may meet regularly after school, and teachers are advisors to subsections. A teacher is unlikely to inherit the sponsorship of one of these groups unless he or she was involved in one of these activities as a student, but sometimes circumstances will make a teacher without any experience a sponsor of such groups. When this happens, the teacher will need to burn the midnight oil to learn new skills in a hurry.

Service Organizations

A teacher may also serve as advisor to a service organization. These groups—the Key Club, "societies," or whatever—usher at evening assemblies, acquire support for needy students, serve at banquets, and so on. Almost every school has one or more of these groups, and, when sponsored well, students will want to be a part of them and will gain in self-concept, poise, and confidence.

Classroom-Associated Organizations

The final type of sponsorship mentioned here is usually handled partly in a teaching period. These are organizations formed to handle such things as the annual, school newspapers, glee clubs and other singing groups, drama, debate, and coaching assignments. All these are usually stipulated at the time of employment, and the teacher has had a specific background that qualifies him or her for that job. In all cases, however, a large part of the activity is taken care of outside of regular school hours and is considered co-curricular.

Events

Various types of events are usually a part of any co-curricular program. Any or all of these may be the big event of the year for a particular group. The sponsor should be prepared to support, encourage, and guide the students as they work to make such an event a success.

Trips

For some schools a trip of some kind is a tradition for one of the classes or for a group. For instance, the honor society may go annually to the nearest large city for a play. Some districts have strict regulations about such trips, and it is wise for the sponsor to know these regulations precisely before making any commitments to a group. Some clubs seem to be organized with a trip in mind: for instance, the ski club's annual trip to a ski resort over Christmas vacation or the geology club's field trip to collect mineral specimens.

On occasion, a group such as the debate club may have a championship team that qualifies for a national championship tournament. The financing for such trips has often not been planned, and special fund raising has to be set up. In this event, the sponsor may have to spend a lot more time on the activity than expected.

Even when there is not a trip per se, clubs may have to hold an event either on- or off-campus. Again, specific school regulations usually govern this, and sponsors need to be aware early as to what these rules are. By and large, no purpose is served by holding events off-campus when they can be held on-campus, but the sponsor can become involved in disputes with students who for some reason feel that an off-campus location somehow enhances the event. One of the main reasons for keeping events on-campus is the issue of legal liabilities. The law is well established that teachers are not liable for student injuries incurred on the way to and from school. But students while on their way to and from other locations for school-sponsored events (involved in accidents) have a different legal ground on which to sue. There are, of course, some things that simply should not be done, for instance, loaning a senior student the sponsor's car to pick up some decorations for an event. If the student is involved in an accident, the teacher may be held liable. When events are held off-campus, it is more likely that supplies will not be there, and there is a greater chance that students will have to be sent on more errands.

Dances

Another commonly sponsored event is the dance. Dances take a variety of forms. There are, for example, after-the-game dances, informal record hops, dances with small guitar groups, and formal dances with big bands. Each of these involves more planning than the students (and often the sponsor) realize.

SALES AND MONEY MANAGEMENT

Every club seems to get involved at some point in the task of raising money. The obvious way to raise money is to buy something at wholesale in large lots, divide it up among the members, and sell it at a profit. Simple? It seems to be, but without good organization, sales can emerge as a major problem.

There are several types of sales. First, there are food sales. Some schools and states have regulations against certain types of open food sales. For instance, for years—and still today in some locations—students have held bake sales. The club has no outlay and all cash collected is profit. The problem, of course, is the question of cleanliness and cookie ingredients. Let a group of students turn up with food poisoning, and the sponsor is confronted with a lawsuit.

Students sometimes behave in unlikely ways. On one campus, for example, on each Tuesday for a month students purchased and ate enough dill pickles to fill a barrel, thus making a tidy profit for a club attempting to sponsor a Korean orphan. When the idea of a pickle sale was introduced, the sponsor had visions of a club stuck with a barrel of dill pickles and no student purchasers. But in fact, pickles sold like hot cakes. Other open food sales, such as pancake breakfasts or selling snow cones and popcorn, can also be used if school regulations permit.

The other type of food sale is the closed container sale, mostly of candy. In many large schools, a class or group is able to raise several thousand dollars within a week by selling candy to the community. Many candy selling programs exist, and the club's sponsor should insist that students talk with several salesmen before embarking on a project. There are programs with various prices at various volumes, prizes for students who sell the most, 40:60 dollar splits, 50:50 dollar splits, poor-quality candy and good-quality candy with special school labels. It pays to deal with a firm that has been established for some time.

Other sales involve nonfood items. Key chains, good-luck charms, school emblems, pep stickers, football programs, and sports cushions are all offered for sale at various times by schools. Again, sometimes unusual things go over well. A well-organized campaign once sold over 2,000 toothbrushes in four days. It should be noted that food is generally easier to sell than are unusual items. Sponsors should engage dealers who will accept the return of unused merchandise.

When involved in any sale, the club must follow certain procedures. No matter how honest the students are, tight controls on checking out goods must be established, if for no other reason than to serve as an example of sound money management practices. A checklist must be kept of each student in the organization, showing how much merchandise was checked out and when. Deadlines for returning the money and unsold goods must be set up and kept. If there is a sale of tickets, each should be numbered and the numbers recorded. Without such procedures, money and goods will inevitably be lost.

Most schools have an organized procedure for the collection of cash. A common practice is for the treasurer of the club to fill out a requisition for an appropriate number of cash boxes and change. Usually a secretary in the school has the responsibility for handling routine matters concerned with student body funds in the school, and the request reaches her desk. A typical cash box requisition is shown in Figure 6.

After the sale has been completed, the student treasurer and sponsor will deposit the money with the secretary or staff member in charge of student body funds. Usually each organization has its own "trust" account that makes up a portion of the larger total student body funds. A typical deposit slip for funds is shown in Figure 7.

When events are held at night, depositing funds with the secretary or school official will not be possible until the next day. In the case of a large event, many schools have provisions for night deposit at the bank that is used by the student body. In the case of a championship football game, gate receipts can total several thousand dollars. In this case, not only are night deposits necessary, but a paid police escort is needed.

Unfortunately, in a few schools the entire organization for handling student body funds is slipshod. Some organizations and clubs prefer to operate independently of regular school channels. Such things as candy sales will be organized by a club, candy sold, and profits made and spent without reporting to the central student body

Cash Box Requisition
(Fill out in duplicate)

Organization   *Pep Club*

Event   *Button Sale*

Number of cash boxes requested   *2*

$34   Cash   Composition:

10	$1 bills	*$10.00*
4	$5 bills	*20.00*
0	pennies	*.00*
20	nickels	*1.00*
10	dimes	*1.00*
10	quarters	*2.50*
		$34.00

Date and time of pickup   *11/25/83   3 p.m.*
Date and time of return   *11/26/83   8 a.m.*

Organization's Treasurer   _____
                                         Signature

Organization's Sponsor   _____
                                         Signature

FIGURE 6

accounting procedure. Sponsors must guard against being involved in this practice. Many teachers have found that coins collected in coffee cans and hidden in the bottom drawers of locked desks have a way of disappearing. A basic principle of any co-curricular activity program is to function as an example of good business practices.

If a club or group decides to sell a particular product, these products must be purchased. Usually the school requires the club to requisition such items through

---

School Organization Slip
(Fill out in Duplicate)

Organization's name _____ *Girl's League* _____

Account number _____ *22* _____

Sponsor's signature _____

Treasurer's signature _____

Date _____ *3/24/84* _____

Composition of deposit:

25	pennies	$	*.25*
32	nickels		*1.60*
44	dimes		*4.40*
14	quarters		*3.50*
2	halves		*1.00*
22	$1 bills		*22.00*
12	$5 bills		*60.00*
14	$10 bills		*140.00*
1	$20 bill		*20.00*
14.05	Total in checks		*14.05*
		Total deposit	*266.80*
		Less cashbox change	*34.50*
		Net deposit	*232.30*

FIGURE 7

proper channels. A typical requisition form is shown in Figure 8. What the sponsor and club treasurer may get in return is a completed purchase order, ready to send, or the office may send the purchase order directly. On occasion, the sponsor and club committee may hand carry the purchase order to a local vendor and pick up the product themselves. In a third alternative, the sponsor may request a check and pay for the item at the time of pickup instead of giving the vendor a purchase order.

In some schools, all checks are requested from a central office. In others, the principal signs all checks. In still others, an activities director may sign the checks and the student body treasurer may countersign. Whatever the procedure, the club sponsor will need to request checks before a particular event takes place and antici-pate who needs to receive checks. In a very few schools each club has its own

Purchase Order
Requisition

For Office Use Only

Organization _____   Purchase order no. _____

Account no. _____ Date _____   Appropriation _____

Date needed _____   Date _____

Sponsor _____

Treasurer _____

Approved _____
                    Administrator

Complete Description of Articles or Services	Quantity	Unit	Unit Price	Amount
			TOTAL	

Complete Name & Address of Suggested Vendors:

FIGURE 8

checking account at the bank. This practice is less efficient and makes central reporting of student body funds difficult. In addition, certain states have sales tax reporting on items sold, and widely dispersed accounts make collection of data difficult.

ELECTIONS AND APPOINTMENTS

One area of sponsorship that is fraught with potential problems is that of elections and appointments. By appointments is meant the choosing of students to perform any student body role by a process other than election. The following is a list of roles that may be filled by a variety of procedures:

1. Student body government officers
2. Drill team membership
3. Varsity band
4. Pep band
5. Dance band
6. Cheerleaders
7. Baton twirlers
8. Flag twirlers
9. Song leaders
10. Class officers
11. Senate, homeroom representatives
12. Student court
13. Queens, princesses (homecoming, junior and senior prom, etc.)
14. Club officers
15. Special committees
16. Membership in honorary groups
17. Participants in talent shows
18. The casts of plays
19. Sports squads

Election for student body officers may take place in the spring or fall or both. Some schools elect for a semester, some for a school year. Some school elections are high powered, with voter registration, intense campaigning, primaries, and inaugural addresses. Other schools have little fuss. It is important that the sponsor get to know election procedures early and well. For instance, if there is a regulation on the quantity and size of publicity posters, a sponsor may be called upon to make judgments of possible rule violations.

The big warning here is that, as a faculty member involved in student elections, the sponsor must make sure that election procedures are delineated and are carried out to the letter. This is not just to make the election an example of the larger public elections but to ensure that there are no repercussions throwing the election in a bad light because of a procedural question. Rumors spread like fire across a high school campus. If there is a technical slip, the school can be thrown into a temporary turmoil.

Probably the most important aspect of the election procedure is the counting of ballots and the subsequent announcement of victories. This counting must be organized and overseen by sponsors. Scrupulous attention to detail is mandated.

An even more ticklish area is that of appointments. If an election can be questioned, what of the appointment of the drill team or other pep squads? If an area has the potential for controversy, heartache, and ill will, this is it. Yet there seems to be no alternative. What *must* happen is that whatever procedures are to be used must be as fair as possible—and followed to the letter.

An often-used system for selecting pep squads is to have a preliminary tryout, during which a committee will cut the number of candidates to a reasonable size, perhaps twice the final group. As an example, suppose thirty-three girls are trying out for six song leader positions. A committee composed of the pep group sponsor, one academic faculty member, a visiting pep sponsor from another school, a visiting song leader from another school, and two senior song leaders use a rating sheet to assess each girl. Using these ratings, the group can be cut from thirty-three to twelve. These twelve are then placed on the student body election ballot and the six song leaders are elected from them.

It sounds like a fair process, yet, sooner or later, an irate parent and daughter will be crying "favoritism," and the subsequent agony of procedural review will have to be made. When this happens, the sponsor must have smooth procedures and straight records.

CONTRACTS

The school may or may not use many contracts. It is a good idea for the teacher to make up written contracts, even if informal, with each merchant dealt with outside the school. The need for a contract with any bands or orchestras has already been mentioned. Any hiring of halls or other outside facilities should be negotiated formally. All sports events with other schools, along with the split of income from ticket sales, should be contracted. Ring sales, pictures, and the like are all contract negotiations.

The reasons for the contract is to make clear *before* the actual sale or event exactly who will be responsible for what and who pays for what. Without this arrangement, the sponsor may well be left holding the bag. Even with a contract, it is hard to foresee unexpected events. For instance, donkey basketball and donkey baseball games have been big money-makers in various parts of the country. Many promoters of these types of programs will ask for a flat fee, but upon negotiation, a contract may be signed that puts much less risk on the school and sponsor through a procedure using a percentage of the gate as the basic fee. Arrangements such as these are often available for a variety of shows and entertainers.

WORKING WITH OFF-CAMPUS ORGANIZATIONS

In addition to the multitude of possible merchants who offer services and goods, the teacher may also become involved with various off-campus organizations. Sometimes service clubs, business leaders involved in junior achievement, Little League coaches, and the like get ideas that can mean the involvement of a particular sponsor and club. For instance, suppose that a local club decides that because of a rash of car accidents they want to make a batch of posters about safe driving to post in local shop windows. They may run a poster contest, or they may come to the sponsor of the art club and offer to throw a poster party for all the club members at which all students in the club can get free goodies (cookies and punch), listen to records, and make lots of posters.

This type of project seems innocent enough, but the sponsor must make sure of several things. Where will the poster party be held? Perhaps in the artroom? If so, how will the teacher make sure that the supplies used are not furnished by the school?

The sponsor of a club may be expected to furnish the place, materials, food, and records in exchange for a check from the service club that covers materials. Even this is not bad if the art club is enthusiastic about the project and is willing to set up the committees and do the necessary work to make it go. If, on the other hand, the club members feel that this is just a job that has been forced upon them, then the sponsor will end up doing most of the work. The sponsor should find a way to let the service club know that the objectives and goals of the club do not mesh with the poster party idea without alienating the service club. At times this can be difficult.

When working with a community organization, a sponsor must maintain congenial relations by explaining the purposes of the club being sponsored so members of the community organization can see what activities of the club are appropriate for mutual benefit. Keep the school administration informed of what is taking place. Certainly organizing all club members to sell a product for the profit of a community organization that does not help to sponsor the high school club directly is not an acceptable activity.

ASSEMBLIES

Many schools have a regular procedure for scheduling assemblies. Some hold only assemblies that involve students from their own and adjacent high schools. In others, outside speakers are used. In a few, no assemblies are scheduled, often because of a lack of a facility to gather the students together. Often assemblies are held on a shift basis, where part of the students will attend one period and part of the next period. The problem of organizing an assembly-day schedule is up to the administration, so it will not be dealt with here. But faculty sponsors may well be in charge of a particular assembly.

Some of the common student assemblies are the Winter assembly, talent assembly, awards assembly, and assemblies sponsored by various clubs. For instance, it may be traditional that every other year the science club sponsors an assembly. For the sponsor, this means gathering together ideas, organizing them into a sequence of displays, skits, and so on, and going through various procedures until convinced that things will go smoothly.

If the science club so decides, it could raise money and pay a science speaker for the assembly, or it may be able to line up one of the many speakers that work for the electric, telephone, or other companies who speak at such assemblies without charge. Whatever the ideas and result, the sponsor must guide the students as they make all the necessary arrangements and have the answers when questions arise.

DISRUPTION OF CLASSES

One problem that haunts the sponsors of clubs is that of class disruption. There seems to be certain unavoidable times when classes are disrupted by students involved in activities. For instance, all candidates for student government offices need to report a few minutes before an assembly to take their places and get set. As long as this assembly can be scheduled immediately after a longer break, there is no problem. But if that is not possible, then the candidates must leave their rooms early, which can disrupt the teaching flow. When schools operate under a modular schedule, disruption problems of this sort seem to be minimized.

Sponsors should do everything in their power to arrange club activity schedules so as not to disrupt classes or keep students out of classes. When this is not possible, sponsors need to make sure they work through the procedures set up by the school and keep the administration informed of what is happening. Sponsors of clubs may be doing a bang-up job with their club participants but inadvertently be alienating some of the staff by seemingly instigating a series of classroom disruptions.

OBJECTIVES AND CO-CURRICULAR ACTIVITIES

Existing clubs should have procedures set up by the school for the recognition of their existence. Usually these procedures involve the prerequisites of a minimum number of students interested in the club, a staff sponsor, and a constitution that has been approved by the administration, student council, and sometimes the board of education.

The constitutions of most clubs have a section delineating the purposes and goals of the organization. These sections suffer from the same problems of ambiguity with which their objectives traditionally have been guilty. A sponsor may have the opportunity to help club members add bylaws and amendments to their constitution that will spell out the objectives of their club more precisely.

A second use of the principles of precise objectives comes as the sponsor works with the students. Students and sponsors must realize that clubs function and stay healthy by committing themselves to a series of worthwhile projects. Often clubs will get involved in fund-raising projects or hold an annual fund-raising project without a purpose for the disbursement of those funds. Fund raising is a means to an end, not an end in itself. The more worthwhile the end, the easier it is to rationalize the enterprise. As a resident of an area, would a homeowner be more willing to buy a box of candy to raise money to help bring a foreign exchange student to the local high school or to help the freshman class throw a party? Both are common fund-raising objectives, but one obviously has a more worthy goal.

The sponsor should see that as many objectives as possible are verbalized in behavioral terms. Many times these may be in the affective domain. Of these, many will not be shared with the students as a cognitive objective would in the classroom, although there may be instances where the learning is cognitive and direct. For instance, if club meetings are disorganized and disorderly, the club sponsor may teach and involve the students in the use of Roberts' *Rules of Order*.

More often, however, the sponsor will notice a club member who could be helped to develop a social skill or attitude change and, by arranging his or her committee assignments and relations with the group, be able to assist the student in self-improvement. Again, the objective may be verbalized only in the mind of the teacher, but it helps guide decisions.

Objectives will initially have a less formal place in the operation of co-curricular activities than in the operation of classrooms because the goals of the club or organization are usually stated less precisely. As activities and purposes evolve during the course of the school year, meaningful objectives are formulated by the club members and sponsor that can be used to defend any activity in which they engage.

As an illustration, consider the sponsor of a girls' service organization. One of the goals in the constitution of the club is to help students with special problems. During the year a student is burned badly in a fire and is undergoing skin transplant operations. The students in the club find out that the family needs $5,000 to complete the operation and they vote to try to raise the money.

The goal of helping others has now been translated into the precise objective of raising $5,000 for a worthy cause. During the implementation of the raising of the money, the sponsor can identify various roles that can be handled by club members that will assist them in various forms of growth. At the conclusion of a successful project, the sponsor can point out in meetings how each girl fulfilled her commitments and reinforce the growth that has taken place. On occasion, individual talks and encouragement for specific girls may be necessary during the course of the project. If the goal is not reached, then a real learning experience can result as the problems are analyzed and possible alternatives discussed that would have resulted in success.

A main problem to avoid as a sponsor is a general fragmentation of activities without a commitment to some clear goal. In such circumstances, students spin wheels and jump from project to project without completing anything.

THE SCHOOL CALENDAR

Almost all schools have an activities calendar that contains the entries of all club meetings, events, and use of facilities. In some cases this calendar is developed a year in advance to keep conflict of events to a minimum. Sponsors must ensure that all club events have been cleared with the administrator in charge of the school calendar, so that it is not discovered too late that one event is competing with another.

In some cases, avoiding conflict is impossible. For instance, the fall play may be scheduled right after football season. However, if the school has a championship team, the team may enter some sort of playoff. If so, conflict with the play is inevitable.

If a calendar is available, judicious planning on the part of a club may allow them to find a time slot during a lull period that can help to ensure an event's success.

SUMMARY

Club sponsors may find that involvement in activities encompasses unfamiliar areas. School rules and regulations governing clubs and organizations must be kept in mind as the teachers deal with students in settings other than the classroom.

Elections, money handling, and appointment procedures can be painful unless organized and documented carefully. Scrupulous attention to detail is essential, lest a student or parent level accusations of unfairness.

The use of contracts will help protect the sponsor and the school and expedite the accomplishment of a club's objectives. Other areas of concern are (1) maintaining good relations with off-campus organizations that involve themselves in student activities and (2) minimizing classroom disruptions because of activities.

Sponsors need to keep the organization's objectives in mind. It is easy to become involved in activities that lead the students away from the goals set up in the organization's constitution. Fund raising is a means to a worthwhile end, not an end in itself.

STUDY QUESTIONS

1. Describe at least three conditions that might prompt or require a teacher to participate in out-of-class activities.
2. Describe at least three school concerns over which student councils might be given a large degree of autonomy.
3. What basic human needs (as described by Maslow) might students meet more easily in out-of-class activities than in regular classroom activities?
4. Describe steps that teachers can take to help students become aware of the relevance and importance of participating in some out-of-class activities.
5. What legal or ethical problems might an out-of-class activity sponsor face as a result of confidences shared by students or as a result of acts of questionable legality perpetrated by students?
6. Describe at least three ways in which the school calendar should affect out-of-school events.

Appendix

Lovett, Kenneth
C&I 216 (01)
Nov. 30, 1988
Unit Plan

THE FORMING OF THE EARTH'S SURFACE

I. Introduction
   A. Course: Earth Science
   B. Target Population: 9th Grade
   C. Title: The Forming of the Earth's Surface
   D. Overview: This unit deals with the natural and human-made forces that have shaped and are continuing to shape the earth's surface, including plate tectonics, mountain building, erosional processes, and urbanization.
   E. Length of time: Approximately four weeks

II. Unit objectives
   Upon successful completion of this unit, the student will demonstrate each of the following objectives, in writing
   A. Define and exemplify terms such as: continental drift, Pangaea, mid-ocean ridge, deep-sea trench, sea-floor spreading, geothermal energy, hot spots, asthenosphere, lithosphere, faults, Richter scale, volcanoes, mountain types, erosion, glaciation, and acid rain.
   B. Name the seven major plates that make up the earth's crust.
   C. Describe the process by which continental plates move, citing at least one modern-day example as evidence.
   D. Describe what geothermal energy is and how humanity exploits it, citing at least three examples to defend or rebut its usefulness to humankind.
   E. Describe the process by which an earthquake occurs, then list two positive and two negative effects an earthquake has on the earth's surface today.

F. List the two types of volcanic eruptions and the resulting landform of each, citing at least three distinguishing characteristics of each volcanic type.

G. List and describe at least three types of mountains and give at least one modern example of each.

H. List the three types of erosion and describe the process by which each transports materials of different size and shape.

I. Given examples of different landforms, describe the process by which each was formed and list at least two examples of the landform's effect on humanity.

J. Given a particular erosional process, such as wind, describe at least two examples of humankind's successful and unsuccessful attempts to control the process.

K. List at least two examples of humanity's continuing influence on the surface of the earth and logically defend the positive or negative effects this influence has had on the earth.

L. Describe at least two ways in which modern technology has changed the effect humanity has on the earth's surface.

III. Content

    A. Earth's internal structure

        1. Three layers of the earth

            a. Crust—the outermost layer of the earth

                (1) Composed of silicate (SiO_2, sand) minerals

                (2) Thickness: 16 km (ocean floor) to 40 km (continental mountain ranges), (10–25 mi)

            b. Mantle—the rock layer beneath the crust

                (1) Surrounds the core

                (2) Composed of olivine (mixture of magnesium and iron

                (3) Thickness: 2895 km (1800 mi)

            c. Core—the center of the earth

                (1) Composed largely of iron and nickel

                (2) Consists of a liquid outer layer and a solid center

                (3) Temperatures lie between 4000° and 5000° F

                (4) Diameter: 6950 km (4320 mi)

        2. Lithosphere—the part of the earth's crust made up of solid rock. Litho = rock.

        3. Asthenosphere—soft, weak layer of rock material, which separates the lower crust and the upper mantle. Astheno = weak.

            a. The rock material present is close to the melting point (2000° to 3000° F)

            b. "Plastic" characteristic

        4. Convection cell—areas within the asthenosphere in which the "plastic" rock material circulates as a result of constant heating and cooling

            a. The hotter material is always rising to the top

            b. The cooler material is falling to the bottom

            (This is the basis for sea floor spreading and plate tectonics.)

(To illustrate the layers of the earth, make a transparency of a cross-sectional view of the earth depicting the planet's interior. Identify the relative boundaries of each layer and describe how the convection cells work. These terms will be a good introduction to continental drift and plate tectonics.)

    B. Plate tectonics

        1. Continental drift theory

            a. Proposed by Alfred Wegener in 1912

   b. The breakup of a parent continent, Pangaea, starting about 230 million years ago, resulted in the present arrangement of the continents and intervening ocean basins

(A transparency showing historical configurations of the continents and how they have drifted since the formation of Pangaea will give the students an idea of the present movement of the continents.)

   2. Sea-floor spreading—the pulling apart of the oceanic crust along the mid-ocean ridges
      a. Convection cells circulate molten rock close to the surface
      b. Molten rock propagates through the cracks along the mid-ocean ridges
      c. Molten rock reaches the surface and cools rapidly, creating new sea floor
      d. Newly formed sea floor causes the plates, which make up the crust, to move
      e. Average rate of sea floor spreading is 6 to 12 cm per year (2.3 to 4.6 in)
      f. Mid-ocean ridges—a great undersea mountain range
         (1) Stretch nearly 70,000 km (43,500 mi) around the earth
         (2) Rise steeply to heights of up to 3 km (almost 2 mi)
         (3) In some places this ridge reaches the surface of the ocean and forms volcanic islands, such as Iceland
         (4) Largest is the Mid-Atlantic Ridge, which is currently moving the Eurasian and African plates away from the American plates

(A transparency showing the ocean floor and mid-ocean ridge system and another showing the seven major plates will help illustrate this topic.)

   3. Major plates of the earth's crust
      a. Pacific—largest plate, covering one-fifth of the earth
      b. Eurasian—one-sixth of the earth
      c. Antarctic—almost one-sixth of the earth
      d. North American—one-eighth of the earth
      e. African—almost one-eighth of the earth
      f. South American—almost one-tenth of the earth
      g. Austral/Indian—almost one-tenth of the earth

(These are the seven major plates, but there are several minor plates, which play an important role in shaping the earth's surface.)

   4. Plate boundaries
      a. Continental rock, due to composition, is less dense than sea-floor rock
      b. As a result of sea-floor spreading, there must also be plate destruction (otherwise the earth would not remain round)
      c. When two plates collide, one of three results may occur
         (1) Continent–ocean plate collision
            (a) The continental plate is lighter than the ocean plate
            (b) The continental plate rides over the ocean plate
            (c) This creates a deep ocean trench
               1. The ocean plate is pushed down, back into the asthenosphere
               2. The rock material is then melted

        3. The molten rock is then recirculated in the convection cells

        4. The deepest of these ocean trenches is the Marianas trench east of the Philippines at the depth of 11 km (almost 7 mi)

    (d) The most common result of a continent–ocean plate collision is a chain of volcanic mountains along the edge on the continental plate

        1. The most notable example is the east coast of South America, the Andes Mountains

  (2) Continent–continent plate collision

    (a) The plates are of relative equal density; therefore each is attempting to override the other

    (b) Results in a huge mountain range made up of the rock that at one time was the edge of the continental plate

    (c) Mountains grow very rapidly (as compared to the other types of mountains)

    (d) Associated with the highest mountains on earth—Himalaya Mountains in south Asia

  (3) Ocean–ocean plate collision

    (a) The plates are of relatively equal density; therefore both are attempting to push the other plate down

    (b) Deep ocean trench is created

    (c) Undersea volcanic mountain range is created

(When these volcanoes reach the surface of the ocean, a volcanic island chain is formed, such as the islands of New Zealand.)

  5. Evidence of plate tectonics—three facts supporting the theory of continental drift and plate tectonics

    a. Similar continental boundaries—"puzzle-piece" match-up can be seen on a globe of the world, looking at the eastern side of Africa and the western side of South America

    b. Similar fossil types—fossil types of particular regions can be found on both Africa and South America

    c. Regions that are presently different climatically and geographically show evidence in similarities of climate and geography (plant types and soil profiles). Therefore the continents would have had to be connected in the past. Similar examples can be found on the continents of North America and Eurasia.

    d. Similar rock types—rock layers have been found to be the same in composition and post-depositional deformation in areas of South America and Africa. Similar examples can be found in North America and Eurasia.

C. Other tectonic features

  1. Hot spots

    a. Regions around the earth where convections cells are located just below the surface of the crust

    b. Not a part of the process of continental drift

    c. Volcanoes or volcanic activity prevalent

    d. Spots appear to drift as a result of their location under a moving plate

e. Two notable examples of this activity are the Hawaiian Islands and Yellowstone National Park

(A discussion on the phenomena of Hawaiian Islands and Yellowstone Park can be based on their formation and their "control center," which is molten rock very close to the surface of these regions that forces its way to the surface. In the Hawaiian region, a volcano is created. If continental drift were not present, Hawaii would be one huge island, like Iceland. In Yellowstone, the hot spot is deeper beneath the earth's surface than in Hawaii. About 500,000 years ago, this hot spot was much shallower than it is presently, and the molten rock worked its way to the surface, making a ring-shaped cut in the crust. The result was a hole about 500 feet deep, about 50 miles across, and about 100 miles long. Today in Yellowstone, groundwater percolates down through the rock, is super-heated into steam, and is explosively shot out of cracks in the ground—geysers.)

2. Volcanoes
   a. Volcanoes can be created two ways
      (1) Collision of plates
      (2) From hot spots
   b. The shape of the volcano is determined by the type of eruption, and the type of eruption is dependent upon the composition of the molten rock.
      (1) Explosive eruptions
         (a) Lighter, continental type of rock
         (b) Gaseous and volatile lava
         (c) The pressure of the gas forces the molten rock to the surface, causing the lava to explode out of the volcano
         (d) Pyroclastic (fire-broken) material, solidified lava, in the form of ash (dust size, under .10 in), cinder (pebble size, .10–.50 in), and bombs (.50–24.0 in), is thrown from the volcano
            (The typical lava flow associated with volcanic eruptions is not present.)
         (e) An explosive eruption that does not include lava is a *nuée ardente*
            1. A super-heated gas cloud containing steam and ash is expelled from the volcano
            2. Temperature often in excess of 3000° F
            3. Moves at very rapid speeds regardless of slope
            (In 1902 an eruption on the island of Martinique in the Caribbean was of this type. All but two of the 30,000 inhabitants were killed instantly.)
      (2) Nonexplosive eruptions
         (a) Rock material is from the ocean floor
         (b) Does not contain the gases and volatile material present in continental rock material
         (c) Pressure exerted on the lava is released once the vent of the volcano has been cleared
         (d) The lava oozes out of the volcano in large flows
         (e) Lava can be classified by viscosity (fluidity)
            1. *Aa*
               a. Thin

        b.   Fluid in molten state

        c.   Forms a jagged layer of broken pieces of lava as it cools

        d.   Sounds like pieces of glass clinking together as the flow moves

    2. *Pahoehoe*

        a.   Thick

        b.   Less fluid than Aa in molten state

        c.   Outer layer appears smooth and billowy (rolling mass, like smoke) as it cools

  c. Three types of volcanic cones

    (1) Cinder cone

      (a) Small

      (b) Steep sided

      (c) Composed largely of loose volcanic cinder or ash

      (d) Associated with explosive volcanoes

      (e) Paricutín in Mexico

    (2) Shield cone

      (a) Nonexplosive

      (b) Broad

      (c) Gently sloping

      (d) Composed almost entirely of layers of lava

      (e) The Hawaiian Islands

    (3) Composite cone

      (a) Explosive and nonexplosive eruption

      (b) Large

      (c) Built of alternating layers of lava and cinders

      (d) Volcano first erupts violently, sending ash and cinder into the air

      (e) Second eruption produces a quiet lava flow covering the ash and cinder layer

      (f) Mount Vesuvius in Italy and Mount St. Helens into Washington state

3. Faults and earthquakes

  a. Often associated with volcanoes

  b. Earthquakes can sometimes indicate a future volcanic eruption

  c. Earthquakes are associated with faults

    (1) Fault—a fracture in the ground along which slippage occurs

    (2) Cause: Progression of the following

      (a) Crustal movement due to plate tectonics

      (b) Tension created at a fracture in the crust due to the movement

      (c) Slippage along the fracture occurs as stress factors overcome shear factors

      (d) Slippage creates shock waves, which are interpreted as earthquakes

(Clay models are available to illustrate how tension building up as a result of tectonic activity can actually cause solid rock to move and bend.)

    (3) Types of faults

      (a) Normal fault—the hanging wall (side above the fault)

has moved down in relation to the foot wall (side below the fault)

(b) Reverse fault—the hanging wall has moved up in relation to the foot wall

(c) Thrust fault—a very low angle reverse fault

    1. Rock has been heavily folded as a result of slow, continuous pressure

    2. Shear factors of the rock have not been overcome due to the gradual application of pressure, therefore the rock folds instead of breaks

    3. Pressure becomes forceful and the stress overcomes the shear factors of the rock, causing the rock to break and thrusting the hanging wall over the foot wall

(d) Strike slip or transform fault—the fault is relatively perpendicular to the surface. Two sides of the fault slide laterally past each other rather than vertically

(A popular example of this type of faulting is the San Andreas Fault in California.)

(Sketches of the different fault types with a rock bed highlighted will help to show how movement is different in each fault.)

(4) Shock waves

(a) Measured as seismic (earthquake) waves

(b) Categorized by the direction in which they travel through the earth away from the fracture

(c) Three types

    1. L—long waves or surface waves

        a. Slowest of the three waves

        b. Travels no deeper into the earth than the crustal layer

        c. Resembles the waves on the ocean surface

        d. Causes the major damage during an earthquake

    2. P—primary waves

        a. Fastest of the three waves

        b. Can pass through solids, liquids, and gases

        c. Considered push-pull waves because they push the rock ahead of them and compress the rock. When the wave passes, the rock pulls back to its original position

    3. S—secondary waves

        a. Not quite as fast as P waves

        b. Can pass through solid material, but not liquid or gases

        c. Moves the rock from side to side

(5) Magnitude of an earthquake

(a) The magnitude of an earthquake is measured by recording the L-waves using a *seismograph*

(b) Plotted on a logarithmic scale

(c) *Richter Scale*

    1. Ranks the magnitude of the earthquake from 1 to 10 while it is occurring

2. Each increment of one increases the magnitude of the earthquake by 30 times
3. Visual criteria used to estimate the magnitude of an earthquake
   1—Not felt at all or felt by few
   2—Felt indoors; hanging objects swing
   3—Hanging objects shake; windows rattle
   4—Felt outdoors; doors swing; pendulum clocks affected
   5—Felt by all; difficult to stand; windows break
   6—Driving affected; chimneys fall; cracks in wet ground
   7—Frame structures shifted off foundation; conspicuous cracks in ground
   8—Frame houses destroyed; large-scale landslides; train rails slightly bent
   9—Train rails greatly bent; bridges and buildings destroyed
   10—Damage nearly total; objects thrown into air; large rock masses displaced

4. Mountain building—a combination of continental rifting, faulting, folding, volcanics, and geothermal heat result in the uplifting of the landscape into small hills (30 to 300 m, 400 to 4000 ft) and large mountain peaks that reach up to 9 km (29,000 ft). Five major types of mountains (photographs of major mountain ranges needed).
   a. Fault block
      (1) Created by movement along a fault plane
      (2) Movement is more rapid than the rate of erosion
      (3) The Grand Teton Range and the Sierra Nevada Mountains
   b. Folded
      (1) Created as a result of large-scale folding of the rock layers that make up the crustal surface
      (2) Folding can be the result of other tectonic activity, such as plate collisions
      (3) Colorado Rocky Mountains
   c. Volcanic
      (1) Direct result of volcanic activity
      (2) The continual eruption of one or many volcanoes
      (3) Highest peak usually being the most active volcano
      (4) Mount St. Helens (Washington state), Mount Fuji (Honshu, Japan), and Mount Kilimanjaro (Tanzania, Africa)
   d. Dome
      (1) Formed when molten rock attempts to force its way to the surface, pushing all of the rock layers above it upwards
      (2) Solid igneous rock core, under layers of sedimentary rocks
      (3) Sedimentary rock has been deformed both by the uplift and also the immense heat of the molten rock mass (temperatures in excess of 1000° F)
      (4) The Black Hills of South Dakota
   e. Orogenic
      (1) Formed as result of continental drift and plate collision

      (2) Individual mountains can be the result of any of the other mountain building mechanisms

      (3) The Appalachian Mountains and the Himalaya Mountains (Asia)

D. Geothermal heat and humanity

    1. Geothermal heat: heat produced from within the earth's crust

    2. This can have both negative and positive impacts on humanity

      a. Negative aspects

          (1) Destruction of life and property

          (2) Modern technology has attempted to reduce the amount of destruction, but has had few positive results

      b. Positive aspects

          (1) An alternative energy source

             (a) Heat from within the crust heats up the ground water

             (b) The hot water and steam produced can be used to heat buildings and generate electricity

             (c) Used as an alternative energy source for years in Italy and Australia

E. Erosional processes (natural forces continually acting on the earth's surface in an attempt to attain equilibrium, where everything is flat); three major types

    1. Wind—wind performs two kinds of erosional work

      a. Deflation—large scale removal of soil

          (1) Loose particles on the ground lifted into the air or rolled along the ground

          (2) Occurs wherever the ground is thoroughly dried out: dried river beds, beaches, and areas recently formed by glacial deposits

          (3) Transports loose particles in one of three ways depending upon their size

             (a) Suspension

                1. Very fine particles, such as clay and silt

                2. Particles are lifted and carried in the air

             (b) Saltation

                1. Fine particles, such as sand-size grains

                2. Wind cannot lift into air easily

                3. The sand grains are lifted when the wind is strongest and dropped once the wind speed decreases

             (c) Traction

                1. Gravel and rounded pebbles

                2. Cannot be lifted by the wind

                3. Moved when wind removes the sand and silt size particles that lay under and in front of these larger particles

                4. Gravel or pebbles, then, roll downwind

(When deflation occurs over a large area, it is called a blowout, or deflation hollow. This depression can be from a few meters to a kilometer or more in diameter, but is usually only a few meters deep. Blowouts form in plains regions where the grass cover is broken through.)

      b. Wind abrasion

    (1) Wind drives sand and dust particles across a flat area and drives them against an exposed rock or soil surface

    (2) Slow, continuous process

    (3) The obstruction is slowly worn away by the continual blasting by these particles

  c. Man-induced deflation (one example)

    (1) Big move to the Great Plains in the 1930s

    (2) Heavily cultivated by each new inhabitant

    (3) Major drought in the late 1930s

    (4) Resulted in a large-scale deflation of the area

    (5) Known as the Dust Bowl

    (6) Since this time, many improvements have been made to try to reduce the possibility of such large-scale blowouts occurring again

        (a) The use of listed furrows (deeply carved furrows), which act as traps to soil movement

        (b) The use of "no-till" planting, which keeps the plant remains from the previous crop in place to protect the soil through the winter months

        (c) Use of tree belts and wind fences to decrease the intensity of the wind at ground level

    (7) Causes of deflation, other than agricultural

        (a) Off-road vehicles, such as trail motorcycles

        (b) Four-wheel-drive recreation vehicles

2. Water

  a. Mechanical or fluvial processes

    (1) Dominates the continental land surfaces world wide

    (2) Almost every area of the earth has been affected by fluvial processes

    (3) Transports particles by the use of suspension, saltation, and traction

    (4) Water has a greater density than wind and can move objects and particles more easily

    (5) Fluvial processes can be separated into two major groups

        (a) Slope erosion

           1. Rain or melting ice provides the water

           2. Water carries particles down slope

           3. Combined with gravity, the water and particles increase speed and density down slope; the result is one of two possibilities

              a. Mass wasting—the whole side of the slope is washed down hill (landslide)

              b. Down-cutting, forming a stream

          (Show photograph of mass wasting.)

        (b) Stream erosion

           1. Streams erode differently depending on

              a. The slope of the stream bed

               b. The amount of discharge

               c. The amount of particles in suspension

           2. Fastest down-cutting occurs when

               a. Stream velocity is high

        b. Banks and stream bed are composed of un-consolidated or loosely consolidated rock material

        c. Stream load (amount of particles in suspension) is high

        d. Stream is at flood stage

(Show photographs of streams undercutting their banks. Photographs of the Colorado River and Grand Canyon will help illustrate stream load and down-cutting forces.)

  b. Chemical weathering

    (1) The alteration and breakdown of rock material

    (2) Water can come from

      (a) Rain

      (b) Lakes

      (c) Streams

    (3) Water contains two important gases from the atmosphere: oxygen and carbon dioxide

      (a) oxygen—causes oxidation of minerals

      (b) carbon dioxide—(CO_2) forms a weak acid (carbonic acid) that dissolves rock material

    (4) Acid rain is formed from the mixing of oxides of sulfur and nitrogen with rain to form solutions of sulfuric (H_2SO_4) and nitric (HNO_3) acids

      (a) Sulfur and nitrogen come from the burning of fossil fuels

      (b) Became a greater problem when smoke stacks were built higher to alleviate smog, putting the pollutants higher into the atmosphere

      (c) pH of 4 to 4.5 (slightly stronger than CO_2, pH of 5.6)

      (d) Change in pH affects the calcium in the water which the entire ecosystem relies on

      (e) This acid also dissolves rock more readily than carbonic acid (especially carbonate rock, such as limestone and marble)

(Show photographs of ancient buildings made of limestone and how they have been chemically eroded by sulfuric and nitric acids in rain.)

  c. Humanity's effect on water erosion

    (1) Grazing livestock

      (a) Tramples and compacts the top soil

      (b) Removes protective vegetation

    (2) Lumbering—deforestation

      (a) Exposes large amounts of land to erosional processes

      (b) Demand for timber resources and need for agricultural land

      (c) Tropical rain forests suffer worst destruction

        1. Forests protect tropical soils and water supplies

        2. Tropical rain forests have a sensitive balance that is compromised with heavy lumbering

    (3) Agriculture

      (a) Increases the amount of exposed soil

      (b) Decreases protective wind barriers

        (4)   Flood management and energy
            (a)   Damming of streams and rivers has altered the rate at which streams can achieve equilibrium
            (b)   Hydroelectric dams are created by flooding valleys, causing major changes in the down-cutting forces of the stream or river

   3.   Ice
      a.   Ice propagation
         (1)   Water leaks down into cracks of rock and soil
         (2)   Water expands as it freezes
         (3)   Ice forces the crack to become larger
         (4)   Pieces of the rock or soil begin to break off
         (5)   Rock or soil pieces are carried away by gravity or water
      b.   Glaciation
         (1)   Alpine (mountain)
            (a)   Snow accumulates in the higher elevations
            (b)   Snow is compacted into ice
            (c)   Ice becomes "plastic" under the increased weight
            (d)   The "plastic" ice sheet moves downhill as a result of increasing weight
            (e)   The ice scours the rock material and pushes unconsolidated material
         (2)   Continental
            (a)   Snow accumulates in higher latitudes
            (b)   Snow is compacted into ice
            (c)   Ice becomes "plastic" under the increased weight
            (d)   The "plastic" ice sheet moves out from the area of accumulation
            (e)   The ice scours rock material and pushes unconsolidated material
            (f)   As the ice melts (retreats), rock and debris are deposited
            (g)   This material is then subject to erosion

(Sketches showing a topography before and after glaciation will help illustrate the erosive power of a glacier.)

F.   How the earth's surface has been changed by humanity
   1.   Early travel was restricted to water
      a.   Major cities were built along trade routes of rivers
      b.   Alteration to stream erosion to keep cities out of the rivers
      c.   Damming of streams and rivers for both navigation and power supplies
      d.   Excavation of man-made canals to facilitate navigation
   2.   Invention of the railroads
      a.   Initially restricted to valleys
      b.   Development of major cities created need to excavate valleys
      c.   Development of more cities along railroad routes due to convenience
   3.   Usage of coal and other resources
      a.   Mining processes created mass wasting of many areas
      b.   Mining removed hills and created unnatural holes in the topography
      c.   Burning of coal affected the weather by placing more ash and dust particles into the atmosphere

    d. Burning of coal produced pollutants that killed large areas of forest

    e. Mining changed the amount of material being carried by the streams and rivers

  4. Development of cities (urbanization)

    a. Increase in larger and higher buildings have changed the wind patterns of many areas

    b. The need for superhighways has increased the amount of flat land across which wind can have a greater effect

    c. Industrialization has changed the chemical makeup of the air and rain

    d. Urbanization has resulted in the destruction of protective vegetation

G. Society's response to humanity's impact on the earth

  1. Reforestation

    a. Replanting of lumbered areas

    b. Development of special varieties of trees that grow back faster than original species

  2. Improved refinement of fossil fuels

    a. Unleaded gasoline

    b. Coal sulfur scrubbers

  3. Development of national parks and preserves

  4. Alternative energy sources

    a. Nuclear

    b. Solar

    c. Electric transportation

      (1) Electric automobiles

      (2) Electromagnetic railroads

  5. Rejuvenation of excavated areas

    a. Replanting of strip-mined areas

    b. Replacement of natural wind blocks in open areas

H. Celestial impact

  1. Formation of a crater

    a. Creates changes in topography instantaneously

    b. Can change the drainage patterns of the area

    c. Sunset Crater, Arizona

  2. Formation of a volcanic island

    a. Possible that a meteor large enough could puncture the earth's crust, resulting in a volcanic island

    b. Iceland—one theory is that it was created by a meteor impact

EARTH SCIENCE UNIT EXAM

FORMING OF THE EARTH'S SURFACE

Name:_____ Date:_____

Define the term and give an example for each.

  1. Fault

    Answer: A crack in the ground along which there is movement. San Andreas Fault, California.

2. Hot spot
   Answer: A place where molten rock is near the surface of the crust. It is not directly associated with plate tectonics. It stays in one spot as the plate moves over it. Hawaiian Islands.

3. Acid rain
   Answer: A solution of rain water and sulfuric or nitric acid kills plants and animals and erodes rock at a faster rate than carbonic acid. Upstate New York.

4. Mass wasting
   Answer: The downward movement of soil or rock material covering the slope of a hill or mountain. When heavy rains are the cause, this is considered a landslide.

5. Convection cell
   Answer: A body of molten rock in which the hotter material, heated from the center of the earth, rises to the top of the cell, and the material being cooled from its contact with earth's crust drops, creating circulation within the cell. Theorized to be below the Mid-Atlantic Ridge.

Multiple-Choice
Circle the response that best answers the question.

1. The term used to describe how wind carries very fine dust particles is:
   A. saltation.
   B. solution.
   C. secretion.
   <u>D.</u> suspension

2. What result between stress and shear factors must occur to cause slippage?
   A. Shear must overcome stress.
   B. Shear must be equal to stress.
   C. Stress and shear are not related to slippage.
   <u>D.</u> Stress must overcome shear.

3. Refer to Diagram 1.

a   Diagram 1

Fault "a" is a:
<u>A.</u> reverse fault because the hanging wall has moved down in relation to the foot wall.

    B.   normal fault because the hanging wall has moved up in relation to the foot wall.

    C.   normal fault because the hanging wall has moved down in relation to the foot wall.

    D.   strike slip fault because the hanging wall has moved down in relation to the foot wall.

4.   The cause of the Andes Mountains in South America is the result of:

    A.   a continental–continental plate collision.

    <u>B.</u>   a continental–oceanic plate collision.

    C.   a hot spot under the Pacific plate.

    D.   an oceanic–oceanic plate collision.

5.   Mountains that are the direct result of a continental–continental plate collision are considered to be:

    <u>A.</u>   orogenic.

    <u>B.</u>   volcanic.

    C.   Andean.

    D.   domal.

Short answer

1.   List and describe the three types of volcanic cones, and give an example of each.
Answer: Cinder cone—small, steep-sided cone comprised of cinder, ash, and bombs, which are expelled from the volcano and land on the slopes of the cone. The result of an explosive eruption. Paricutín in Mexico.
Shield cone—large, broad-based cone. The result of a nonexplosive eruption, made up of layers of lava. Hawaiian Islands.
Composite cone—the result of alternating explosive and nonexplosive eruptions. The cone is made up of layers of cinder and lava. Mount St. Helens.

2.   Defend your opinion on what society should do or should not do about acid rain. Use at least three logically sequential factual statements to support your opinion.

3.   Describe how it would be possible to have a mountain form in Illinois.
Answer: This could occur as a result of a hot spot locating under the part of the crust called Illinois. Or, as a result of continental drift, collision with another plate would form an orogenic mountain range.

4.   An earthquake with a magnitude of 6 on the Richter Scale has just occurred in your neighborhood. Describe the damage you see in your house and throughout the neighborhood that would verify the magnitude rating.
Answer: Everyone felt this earthquake. It was difficult to stand during the quake. The plaster on the walls has cracked and fallen. Windows and dishes are broken. The chimney has fallen, and the house has been moved off its foundation. Outside, tree branches have broken off, and cracks have appeared in the banks of a creek behind the house. A car has collided with a tree, because it was difficult to steer during the quake.

5. List at least three effects on the land the Army Corps of Engineers has caused by altering the course of the Mississippi River, and describe how these changes are different from what the river would naturally experience. Answers should include variations of these ideas:

   - A decrease in the discharge of the river because the natural down-cutting has been affected.

   - An increase in the depositing of sediments on the bottom of the channel because the river is still trying to reach equilibrium, even though the river is not down-cutting any more.

   - The channel position does not change because the banks of the river are kept constant.

   - The distribution of sediments on the river's delta has been skewed because the natural migration of the river channel has been controlled.

   - Larger cities can be built along the river because the threat of a large-scale flood has been reduced.

   - A more consistent development of the land along the river because the channel is controlled.

BIBLIOGRAPHY

Coble, Charles R., Murray, Elaine G., and Rice, Dale R. *Earth Science.* Englewood Cliffs, NJ: Prentice-Hall, 1981.

Namowitz, Samuel N., and Stone, Donald B. *Earth Science.* New York: American Book Company, 1981.

Ojakangas, Richard W., and Darby, David G. *The Earth Past and Present.* New York: McGraw-Hill, 1976.

Ritter, Dale F. *Process Geomorphology.* New York: Wm. C. Brown, 1978.

Seyfert, Carl K., and Sirkin, Leslie A. *Earth History and Plate Tectonics.* New York: Harper & Row, 1979.

Strahler, Arthur N., and Strahler, Alan H. *Modern Physical Geography.* New York: John Wiley, 1987.

Index

Note: Page numbers in italics indicate figures; page numbers followed by *t* indicate tabular material.

Ability, optional activities and, 122
Absence, extended, self-instructional packages for, 221
Abstract concepts, 65
Abstract relations, synthesis and, 40
Academic level, as source of instructional intent, 24–25
Academic status, preassessing, 60–61, 62
Achievement, as basis for grouping, 85–86
Achievement tests, 165–166
Administration
    approval of course objectives by, 61
    policies regarding field trips and, 84
    teacher evaluation by, 61, 183
Advisor, teacher as, 220
Affective domain, 41–44, 52
Age of Enlightenment, 6
Agility, in psychomotor domain, 47
Air, need for, 190
Alphabetical arrangement, for grouping, 85
American Youth Commission, 9
Amidon, Edmond J., 182
Amphetamines, to treat hyperactivity, 210
Analysis level
    in cognitive domain, 39–40
    multiple-choice items and, 153–154
Anecdotal records, 62
Application, of instruction, 118

Application level
    in cognitive domain, 39
    multiple-choice items and, 153
Application programs, 107
Appointments to clubs, sponsorship and, 244–245
Aptitude tests, 166–167
Assault, witnessed by teachers, 212
Assemblies, sponsorship of, 246
Assignments
    out-of-class, 86–88
    punitive, 200
Association, 118
Attitudes, affective plan and, 41–44
Audio aids, 95–97. *See also* Audiovisual aids
Audio recordings, in teacher evaluation, 182
Audiovisual aids, 102–104
    films and television as, 102–104
    multimedia kits as, 101
Auditory discrimination, in psychomotor domain, 45

Baker, Eva, 21, 22
Banishment, from classroom, 201, 212
Bank accounts, clubs and, 240–242
Baptiste de la Salle, Jean, 5
Barker, Larry L., 22
Basic-fundamental movements, in psychomotor domain, 45
Bathroom requests, 191

Battery, witnessed by teachers, 212
Behavioral Objectives and Instruction (Kibler, Barker, and Miles), 22
Behaviorism, 20
  field learning theory versus, 19–21
Behavior modification
  operant conditioning in, 201–205
  reality therapy for, 205–207
Bloom, Benjamin S., 37, 51–52
Bloom's taxonomy, 37
  use of, 37–38
Brainstorming, 81–82
Bridge-building, closure and, 64
Bruner, Jerome S., 112–113, 123
Bulletin boards, as visual aids, 98–99
Byngham, William, 4–5

CAI. *See* Computer-assisted instruction
California Achievement Tests, 165–166
Carnegie unit, 5
Cash box requisition, 240, *241*
Chalkboards, as visual aids, 100
Characterization, in affective domain, 44
Charts, as visual aids, 99–100
Check(s), issuance of, 242–243
Checklist, for evaluation procedures, 169
Chemotherapy, 210–211
China markers, for overhead projectors, 101
Clarity, of instructional objectives, 49–50
Class disruption, clubs and, 247
Classroom, banishment from, 201, 212
Classroom-associated organizations, sponsorship of, 238
Classroom management, 187–214
  guidelines for precluding discipline problems and, 198–201
  hyperactivity and, 210–211
  legal terms and issues in, 211–212
  needs hierarchy and, 189–198
  operant conditioning in, 201–205
  plan for dealing with problems in, 207–210
  potentially dangerous problems and, 210
  principles of, 188–189
  reality therapy in, 205–207
Closed-circuit television, 103–104
Closed container sales, sponsorship of, 240
Closure, 64–65, 130–131
Clubs. *See also* Co-curricular activities
  constitution of, 247
  sponsorship of, 235–237
Co-curricular activities, 233–249
  assemblies and, 246
  contracts and, 245
  disruption of classes by, 247
  elections and appointments and, 244–245
  extra pay for, 234–235
  objectives of, 247–248
  sales and money management and, 239–243
  school calendar and, 248–249

types of sponsorship and, 235–239
working with off-campus organizations and, 245–246
Cognitive domain, 38–41, 51–52
  analysis in, 39–40
  application in, 39
  comprehension in, 38–39
  evaluation in, 41
  knowledge in, 38
  synthesis in, 40–41
Cognitive level
  classifying objectives into, 54–55
  matching tests and, 157
  multiple-choice items and, 152–154
Commission on the Reorganization of Secondary Education (NEA), 8–9
Committee of Ten (NEA), 7–8
Committee on College Entrance Requirements (NEA), 8
Communication
  of instructional objectives, 50–51, 63–64
  nondiscursive, in psychomotor domain, 48–49
  unique, synthesis and, 40
  of utility of information, 114–115
Completion tests, 158, 159t
Comprehension level
  in cognitive domain, 38–39
  multiple-choice items and, 153
Computer(s)
  advantages of using, 105–107
  as instructional tools, 104–108
  problems in using, 105
  software programs for, 106–107
Computer-assisted instruction (CAI), 104–108
  developments in, 107–108
Concept(s)
  abstract, 65
  definition of, 65, 113
Concept lessons, 65
Condition(s), on instructional objectives, 26–28
Conditioning, operant, 201–205
Consequences, natural, self-control and, 189
Consistency, value of, 199
Constitutions, of clubs, 247
Construct validity, 147
Content
  organizing for instructional units, 112
  organizing instructional units by, 121–122
  in unit plan, 119–120
Content-area committees, in systems approach to individualized instruction, 218
Content validity, 146
  of teacher-made tests, 164
Contingency management, 201–205
Contracts
  grade, 171
  sponsorship and, 245

Convergent questions, 71
Coordinated abilities, in psychomotor domain, 46
Corporal punishment, 194
Crayons, for overhead projectors, 101
Creative writing club, 236
Credit–no credit grading, 179
Criterion-referenced evaluation, 148–149
Crowder, Norman, 94
Cuban, Larry, 1
Curriculum
    computer, integrated, 107–108
    effect of self-instructional packages on, 219–222
    safety and, 193–194
    student involvement in content of, 219

Dame schools, 7
Dances, sponsorship of, 239
Debating clubs, 236
Delivery rate, for lectures, 69
Demonstrations, as instructional procedure, 72–73
Deposit slip, 240, *242*
Detention, disadvantages of, 200
Dexedrine, to treat hyperactivity, 210
Dialectical method, 6
Differential Aptitude Test Battery, 166–167
Digression, in discussions, 76
Directed discussions, 76–77
Disabled students. See Mainstreaming
Disciplinary acts, teacher-initiated, 207–208
Discipline(s), structures of, 112–113
Discipline problems. See also Classroom management
    guidelines for precluding, 198–201
Discussions, 75–81
    digression in, 76
    evaluation of, 80–81
    exploratory, 80
    general, 76
    guided or directed, 76–77
    inquiry, 78–80
    panel, 82
    reflective, 77–78
Distractions, eliminating, 198
Divergent questions, 71–72
Do-not-disturb-others rule, 188–189
Drill-and-practice programs, 106

Educational dualism, 3, 7
Educational goals, 1–16. See also Instructional objectives
    broad, effects of, 13–15
    formal statements of, 6–13
    general, 2–6
    sample objectives and, 2
Educational Policies Commission, 10
Educational television (ETV), 103

Education for All Handicapped Children Act (Public Law 94–142), 62
Eight-Year Study, 5
Elections, sponsorship and, 244
Element(s), of problems, analysis of, 39
Elementary and Secondary Education Act, 11
Elimination, need for, 191
Endurance, in psychomotor domain, 46
Enrichment
    self-instructional packages for, 220–221
    tutorial programs for, 106
Essay tests, 160–162
Essentialism, 6
Esteem needs, 195–197
ETV. See Educational television
Evaluation, 144–185
    alternate procedures for, 167–169
    in cognitive domain, 41
    criterion-referenced, 148–149
    definition of, 145
    of discussions, 80–81
    frequency of, 145–146
    grade calculation and, 170–179
    grade reporting and, 179–180
    item analysis and, 169–170
    lesson plans and, 133
    of mediated instruction, 92
    norm-referenced, 149
    preassessment, 60–61, 62
    reliability in, 147–148
    standardized tests for, 164–167
    of student effort, 147
    subjectivity in grading and, 179
    in systems approach to individualized instruction, 218–219
    teacher-made tests for, 149–164
    of teachers. See Teacher evaluation
    validity in, 146–147
Events, sponsorship of, 238
Examples, use in lectures, 69
Exceptional students. See Mainstreaming
Exercise, disadvantages of using as punishment, 200–201
Expectations, reasonable, 198–199
Experimental experiences, optional, 122
Exploratory discussions, 80
Expressive movement, in psychomotor domain, 48
Expulsion, 212
Extended absence, self-instructional packages for, 221
Extortion, witnessed by teachers, 212
Extra-curricular activities. See Co-curricular activities
Extrapolation, comprehension and, 38
Extra schoolwork, disadvantages of, 200
Eyeballing, as a method of grading, 177–178

Face validity, 146
Fatigue, 191–192

Feedback. *See also* Evaluation
  frequency of, 145–146
  during practice, 73
  promptness of, 199
  from students, 182–183
Feedback loop, 22
Feelings, affective plan and, 41–44
Felt-tipped pens, use of, with overhead projectors, 101
Field learning theory, behaviorism learning theory versus, 19–21
Field psychology, 19–20
Field services club, 236
Field trips, 83–85
  sponsorship of, 238–239
Film(s), 96, 102–103
  information about, 121
Film libraries, 103
Filmstrips, 98
  information about, 121
Financing, of field trips, 84
First-order questions, 71
Flanders, Ned A., 182
Flanders' Interaction Analysis, 182
Flexibility, in psychomotor domain, 47
Follow-up
  for field trips, 85
  mediated instruction and, 92
Food, need for, 190–191
Food sales, sponsorship of, 239–240
Foreign-exchange student clubs, 236
Foreign-language clubs, 235
Forensics clubs, 236
Formal education, beginning of, 2–3
Formal lectures, 65
Format, for multiple-choice items, 156
Four-stage models of instruction, 21–22, *22*
Friendship, as basis for grouping, 85
Fundraising, 239–243
  for field trips, 84
  money management and, 240–243

General Aptitude Test Battery, 166–167
General discussions, 76
Generalization, 118
Gestalt psychology, 19, 20
Girls' athletic associations, 236
Glasser, William, 205
Glee club, 236
Globes, as visual aids, 99
Grade(s)
  assessment and, 146
  calculating, 170–179
  credit–no credit and, 179
  curve and, 171–177
  disadvantages of lowering for discipline, 201
  essay tests and, 160–162
  eyeballing and, 177–178

lowest, dropping, 146
preset levels for, 171
reporting, 179–180
subjectivity and, 179
valid and invalid, 147
Grade contracts, 171
Graphs, as visual aids, 100
Grease pencils, for overhead projectors, 101
Greeks, 4, 6
Group(s)
  activities for, 85–86
  disadvantages of computers for, 105
  makeup of, 85–86
Guest speakers, 73–74
Guided discussions, 76–77

Handicapped students. *See* Mainstreaming
Harrow, Anita J., 44, 52
Hebrews, 3, 4
Herbartian Unit, 118–119
Homework assignments, 86–88
  purposes of, 87
Hunger, 190–191
Hunter, Madelin, 64
Hyperactivity, chemotherapy to treat, 210–211

Illegal acts, witnessed by teachers, 212
Immediate practice, following demonstrations, 73
Individual differences, goal of providing for, 3–4
Individualized instruction, 216–231. *See also* Self-instructional packages systems approach to, 216–219
Industrial arts clubs, 236
Industrial Revolution, 7, 20
Informal lectures, 65–70
In loco parentis, 211
Inquiry discussions, 78–80
In-school suspension, 212
Instructional activities
  lesson plans and, 132–133
  organizing instructional units by, 121–122
  in unit plan, 120
  varying, 199
Instructional aids, for lectures, 67
Instructional intent, sources of, 23–25
Instructional media, 90–109
  audio aids as, 95–97
  audiovisual combinations as, 102–104
  computers as, 104–108
  general procedures for use of, 91–92
  reading materials as, 92–95
  in unit plan, 120–121
  visual aids as, 97–102
Instructional objectives, 18–57
  affective plan and, 41–44
  classification of, practice in, 53–56

Instructional objectives (*cont.*)
  cognitive domain and, 38–41
  cognitive levels and, 51–53
  communicating, 63–64
  complementary, 50
  field learning theory versus behaviorism
    learning theory and, 19–21
  four-stage models of instruction and, 21–
    22, *22*
  for impromptu lesson plans, 131–132
  in lesson plans, 130–132
  objective tests and, 150
  observable terminal behavior and, 25–30
  practice in working with, 30–34
  precise, 22–25, 50–51
  psychomotor domain and, 44–49
  selecting mediated instruction for, 91
  separate lesson plans for, 121
  taxonomy and, 37–38
  testing for clarity, 49–50
Instructional procedures, 59
  out-of-class assignments and, 86–88
  preassessment of academic status and, 60–
    61
  preassessment of mainstreamed students
    and, 62
  for small groups, 85–86
  Stanford skills and, 62–65
  student-directed, 59, 75–85
  student records and, 61–62
  teacher-directed, 59, 65–74
Instructional television (ITV), 103
Instructional units, 111–124
  abbreviated, 126–127
  Herbartian, 118–119
  optional activities in, 122
  organizing content for, 112–113
  organizing parts of, 121–122
  planning for evaluation and future use of,
    122–123
  rationales for, 116–117
  topical outlines for, 116
  unit planning and, 117–121
  Waimon knowledge structures and, 114–
    116
Integrated computer curriculum, 107–108
Intelligence tests, 165
Interaction analysis techniques, in teacher
  evaluation, 182
Interactive video, 108
Interest, as basis for grouping, 85
Interest inventories, 167
Interpretation, comprehension and, 38
Interpretative movements, in psychomotor
  domain, 49
Introduction, in unit plan, 119
Iowa Tests of Educational Development, 165–
  166
IQ scores, 165

Item analysis, 169–170
ITV. *See* Instructional television

Jenkins, W. L., 172
Jobs, preparation for, 9
Judgment. *See* Value judgments

Kibler, Robert J., 21–22
Kinesthetic discrimination, in psychomotor
  domain, 45
Knowledge, integration of, 4–6
Knowledge level
  in cognitive domain, 38
  multiple-choice items and, 152–153
Knowledge structures. *See* Waimon knowl-
  edge structures
Kounin, Jacob S., 207
Krathwohl, David R., 41, 52
Kuder Preference Records, 167

Land-Grant Act, 3, 7
Language
  in lecture delivery, 68
  objectives tests and, 150–151
Learning, learning how to, 6
Learning activities. *See* Instructional activities
Lectures
  delivering, 68–70
  disadvantages of, 69–70
  formal and informal, 65–70
  planning, 66–68
  uses of, 66
Legal issues
  in classrooom management, 211–212
  in food sales, 239
  punishment and, 194
  in student records, 62
  trips and, 239
Lesson(s)
  beginning of, 63
  closure of, 64–65, 130–131
  concept, 65
  disadvantages of carrying over, 130–131
Lesson plan(s), 128–142
  content in, 132
  disadvantages of computers and, 105
  evaluation in, 133
  impromptu, source for objectives for, 131–
    132
  instructional activities in, 132–133
  materials in, 133
  objectives in, 130–132
  pros and cons of, 129–130
  sample, 134–142
  separate, for each objective, 121
  time and, 131, 133–134
Lettermen clubs, 236
Libel, 212
Library club, 236

Linear programs, 94
Listening skills, 96
Lorge-Thorndike Intelligence Tests, 165
Love needs, 195

Mainstreaming
    optional activities and, 122
    preassessment and, 62
    self-instructional packages in, 219
Maps, as visual aids, 99
Maslow, Abraham H., 189
Maslow's hierarchy of needs, 189-198
Matching tests, 157-158
Materials, lesson plans and, 133
Math club, 236
Measurement. *See also* Evaluation
    definition of, 145
Mediated instruction. *See* Instructional media
Metropolitan Achievement Tests, 165-166
Microteaching, 63
Middle Ages, 4
Miles, David T., 22
Minimum acceptable standard
    adjustment of, mainstreaming and, 62
    grades and, 170, 171
    instructional objectives and, 28-30
    specifying, for evaluation, 167-168
Model, for evaluation procedures, 168
Money management, sales and, 240-243
Morrill Act, 7
Multimedia kits, as audiovisual aids, 102
Multiple-choice tests, 152-154
    levels of cognition and, 152-154
    principles for building, 154-156

National Assessment of Educational Programs, 11
National Association of Secondary School Principals, 10
National Commission on Excellence in Education, 11-13
National Defense Education Act, 10-11
National Education Association (NEA)
    Commission on the Reorganization of Secondary Education of, 8-9
    Committee of Ten of, 7-8
    Committee on College Entrance Requirements of, 8
Needs
    esteem, 195-197
    love, 195
    Maslow's hierarchy of, 189-198
    physiological, 190-192
    safety, 192-194
    self-actualization, 197-198
Negative reinforcement, 202
Neuromuscular development. *See* Psychomotor domain

Nondiscursive communication, in psychomotor domain, 48-49
Nonlinear programs, 94-95
Nonparticipation, in discussions, 81
Norm(s), for standardized tests, 164
Normal curve, grading and, 171-177, *172*
Norm-referenced evaluation, 149
Notes, for lectures, 67
Notetaking procedures, 67-68

Objectives. *See also* Instructional objectives
    in affective domain, 42
    of co-curricular activities, 247-248
Objective tests, 150-152
Observable terminal behavior, 25-30
Off-campus organizations, sponsorship and, 245-246
Opaque projectors, as visual aids, 97-98
Open-ended questions, 71
Operant conditioning, 201-205
    opposition to, 204
Optional activities, 122
Organization, in affective domain, 43-44
Organizational principles, analysis and, 39
Otis Quick-Scoring Mental Ability Test, 165
Out-of-class assignments, 86-88
    purposes of, 87
Out-of-school suspension, 212
Outline
    advantages of constructing, 120
    for knowledge structures, 114, 116
    of lecture, 66-67
    topical, 116
"Overhead" questioning technique, 70
Overhead projectors, as visual aids, 100-101

Panel discussions, 82
Parents, discipline and, 209
Parent-teacher conferences, grade reporting and, 180
Pay, for sponsoring co-curricular activities, 234-235
Peer acceptance, 197
    fostering, 199-200
Peer evaluations, of teachers, 183
Pencil-and-paper tests. *See* Standardized tests; Teacher-made tests
Pep groups, 236
    selecting members of, 244-245
    sponsorship of, 237-238
Perceptual abilities, in psychomotor domain, 45-46
Permission slips, for field trips, 84
Physical abilities, in psychomotor domain, 46-47
Physical distractions, eliminating, 198
Physical exercises, as punishment, 200-201
Physical movements, in lecture delivery, 69
Physiological needs, 190-192

Pictures, as visual aids, 97
Planning. *See also* Lesson plan(s); Unit plan
    for dealing with classroom problems, 207–210
    for evaluation and future use of instructional units, 122–123
    of field trips, 84
    of instructional units, 117–121
    of lectures, 66–68
    long-range, 120–121
    student participation in, 84, 198
    synthesis and, 40
Popham James, 21, 22
Positive reinforcement
    in operant conditioning, 202
    to preclude discipline problems, 199
Practice
    delayed, 73
    following demonstrations, 73
    feedback during, 73
    immediate, 73
Preassessment, 61–62
    of mainstreamed students, 62
Precision, of instructional objectives, 50–51
Predictive validity, 146–147
    of achievement tests, 166–167
Preparation
    content and, 119
    for instruction, 118
Prerequisite skills, preassessing, 60–61, 62
Presentation, 118
Preset levels, grading and, 171
Pressey, Sidney L., 95
Probing questions, 71
Process of Education, The (Bruner), 112–113, 123
Programmed instruction, 94–95
    linear programs and, 94
    nonlinear programs and, 94–95
Progressive Education Association, 5
Progressivism, 5, 6
Project Head Start, 11
Projectors
    opaque, 97–98
    overhead, 100–101
Psychomotor domain, 44–49, 52–53
    classifying objectives into, 55–56
Public Law 94-142 (Education for All Handicapped Children Act), 62
Punishment
    avoiding the use of, 200–201
    corporal, 194
    in operant conditioning, 202

Qualitative standards, instructional objectives and, 29–30
Quantitative standards, instructional objectives and, 28–29

Questions
    for beginning lessons, 63
    convergent, 71
    divergent, 71–72
    first-order, 71
    as instructional procedure, 70–72
    open-ended, 71
    probing, 71

Radio, as mediated instruction, 95
Random assignment, for grouping, 85
Rationales, for unit plans, 116–117
Reading materials, 92–95
    programmed textbooks as, 94–95
    traditional textbooks as, 92–94
Realia, as visual aids, 102
Reality therapy, 205–207
Receiving, in affective domain, 43
Recognition
    external, 196–197
    internal, 195–196
Reflective discussions, 77–78
Reflex movements, in psychomotor domain, 44–45
Reinforcement
    negative, 202
    positive, 199, 202
Relationships, analysis and, 39
Reliability, assessment and, 147–148
Reliability coefficient, 148
Remediation
    prerequisite skills and 60–61
    self-instructional packages for, 221
    tutorial programs for, 106
Repetitive sentences, disadvantages of, 200
Report cards, 180
Requisition form, 242, *243*
Resource units, 119
Respect, treating students with, 198
Responding, in affective domain, 43
Review session, for test, 159
Rhetorical questions, for beginning lessons, 63
"Ripple effects," of disciplinary actions, 207–208
Ritalin, to treat hyperactivity, 210
Romans, 4
Rules, minimizing number of, 188

Safety needs, 192–194
Sales, 239–243
    money management and, 240–243
Sarcasm, dangers of, 197
School board policies, field trips and, 84
School calendar, avoiding conflicts in, 248–249
School disciplinarian, referral to, 209
Science clubs, 235

"Science of Learning and the Art of Teaching, The" (Skinner), 94
Scientific method, 6
    inquiry discussions and, 78–80
Seating assignments, special, disadvantages of, 200
Secondary schools
    in 1700s, 7
    functions of, 7–8
    reorganization of, 8–9
Self-actualization needs, 197–198
Self-confidence, preparation and, 119
Self-control, as goal of classroom management, 188–189
Self-instructional packages
    creating, 225–231
    effect on curriculum, 219–222
    as enrichment activities, 220–221
    extended absences and, 221
    model of, 222–231
    modified systems programs and, 222
    for out-of-class assignments, 88
    partial programs using, 221–222
    purpose of, 219
    remedial use of, 221
    systems approach and, 218
    teacher as advisor and, 220
Self-pacing, 4. See also Self-instructional packages
Service organizations, sponsorship of, 238
Set induction, 63
Sexual interest, 192
Simulation programs, 106–107
Skilled movements, in psychomotor domain, 47–48
Skinner, B. F., 94
Slander, teachers as victims of, 212
Sleep, need for, 191–192
Slides, as visual aids, 98
Small-group activities, 85–86
Societal needs, as source of instructional intent, 23–24
Sociodramas, 82–83
Software packages, 106–107
Spencer, Herbert, 10
Sponsorship, of co-curricular activities, 235–239
Sputnik, National Defense Education Act and, 10
Standard, minimum acceptable. See Minimum acceptable standard
Standard deviation, calculation of, 172–174
Standard error, 165
Standardized tests, 164–167
    achievement, 165–167
    administration of, 167
    aptitude, 166–167
    intelligence, 165
    interest, 167

Stanford-Binet Intelligence Scale, 165
Stanford skills, 62–65
Stanines, 180
Stimulus variation, 64
Strength, in psychomotor domain, 46–47
Strong Vocational Interests Blanks, 167
Structure, of disciplines, 112–113
Student(s)
    facilitating successes for, 189
    grouping, 85–86
    mainstreaming. See Mainstreaming
    notetaking by, 67–68
    preparation for teleinterviews, 96
    preparing for mediated instruction, 91–92
    role in systems approach to individualized instruction, 218–219
    teacher evaluation by, 182–183
    treating with respect, 198
    violent, 193
Student ability. See also Mainstreaming
    rank-ordering according to, 149
Student assessment, frequency of, 145–146
Student cabinet, sponsorship of, 237
Student council, sponsorship of, 237
Student-directed instructional procedures, 59, 75–85
Student effort, assessment of, 147
Student government, sponsorship of, 237
Student needs, as source of instructional intent, 24–25
Student participation
    in discussions, 81
    in planning, 84, 198
    use in lectures, 69
Student records
    anecdotal, 62
    selecting instructional procedures and, 61–62
Subject-centered approach, 5
Subject-matter needs, as source of instructional intent, 24
Subjectivity, in grading, 179
Success, facilitating, 189
Suspension, in-school and out-of-school, 212
Syllogistic reasoning, 6
Synthesis, in cognitive domain, 40–41
Systematic Instruction (Popham and Baker), 21–22

Tactile discrimination, in psychomotor domain, 46
Tape recorders, as mediated instruction, 95–96
Taxonomy of Educational Objectives, Handbook I: Cognitive Domain (Bloom), 37, 41
Taxonomy of Educational Objectives, Handbook II: Affective Domain (Krathwohl), 41

Taxonomy of the Psychomotor Domain (Harrow), 37
Teacher(s)
  as advisor, 220
  computer training of, 105
  illegal acts witnessed by, 212
  role in systems approach to individualized instruction, 217–218
  as sponsor of co-curricular activities, 235–239
  student challenges and confrontations of, 197
  as victim of slander, 212
Teacher-directed instructional procedures, 59, 65–74
Teacher evaluation, 61, 180–183
  administrative, 183
  audio and video recordings in, 182
  interaction analysis techniques in, 182
  by peers, 183
  by students, 182–183
  teacher performance tests in, 181–182
Teacher-made tests, 149–164
  completion, 158, 159t
  essay, 160–162
  matching, 157–158
  multiple-choice, 152–156
  objective, 150–152
  preparing students for, 159–160
  true-false, 156–157
  validity and use of, 164
Teacher performance tests (TPT), 181–182
Teachers and Machines (Cuban), 1
Teaching-learning activities. *See* Instructional activities
Teleinterview, 96
Telephones, as mediated instruction, 96–97
Television
  as audiovisual aid, 103–104
  closed-circuit, 103–104
  educational, 103
  instructional, 103
  as mediated instruction, 96
  video cassette recorders and, 104
Test(s)
  alternatives to, 167–169
  answering students' questions during, 152
  interrupting students during, 152
  length of, reliability and, 148
  pencil-and-paper. *See* Standardized tests; Teacher-made tests.
  preassessment, 60
  review sessions for, 159
  teacher-made. *See* Teacher-made tests
  of teacher performance, 181–182
  time required for, 148
Test items
  analysis of, 169–170
  completion, 158, 159t

difficulty of, 148–149, 170
  independence of, 151–152
  matching, 157–158
  mixing types of, 162
  multiple-choice, building, 154–156
  pattern for correct responses to, 152
  sequence of, 159
  trick or trivial, 152
  true-false, 157–158
Test norms, 164
Textbooks
  programmed, 94–95
  traditional, 92–94
Thespians club, 236
Thirst, 191
Thurstone Interest Schedule, 167
Time
  for essay tests, 161–162
  lesson plans and, 131, 133–134
  required for tests, 148
Time-frames, Waimon knowledge structures and, 113
Title page, for instructional units, 123
Topical outlines, 116
TPT. *See* Teacher performance tests
Translation, comprehension and, 38
Transparencies, for overhead projectors, 101
Transportation, for field trips, 84
Trick questions, on tests, 152
Trips, 83–85
  sponsorship of, 238–239
True-false items, 156–157
Tutorial programs, 106
Tyler, Ralph, 22, 23

Unique communications, synthesis and, 40
Unit plan, 118. *See also* Instructional units
  components of, 119–121
Universal education, as goal, 2–3
Upward Bound, 11

Validity, 146–147
  construct, 147
  content, 146, 164
  definition of, 146
  face, 146, 164
  predictive, 146–147, 166–167
  of teacher-made tests, 164
Value(s), affective plan and, 41–44
Value judgments
  in cognitive domain, 41
  objective tests and, 150
Valuing, in affective domain, 43
Variable Speech Control (VSC), 96–97
Verbal behaviors, of teachers, evaluation of, 182
Video, interactive, 108

Video recordings
  as audiovisual aid, 104
  in teacher evaluation, 182
Violence, by students, 193, 210
Visual aids, 97–102. *See also* Audiovisual aids
  bulletin boards as, 98–99
  chalkboards as, 100
  charts and graphs as, 99–100
  maps and globes as, 99–100
  opaque projectors as, 97–98
  overhead projectors as, 100–101
  pictures as, 97
  realia as, 102
  slides and filmstrips as, 98
Visual discrimination, in psychomotor domain, 45

Visual reinforcement, in lectures, 68, 69
Vocational preparation, American Youth
  Commission and, 9
Voice, use in lectures, 68–69
VSC. *See* Variable Speech Control

Waimon, Morton D., 113–116
Waimon knowledge structures, 113–116
  communicating utility of information with,
    114–115
  outline format for, 114
  rationales for, 116–117
  structure, sample, 125
Water, need for, 191
Wechsler Intelligence Scales, 165
World friendship club, 236